TIMEBOMB

'The demographic timebomb is one of the most pressing challenges facing Europe today. Giles Merritt provides a compelling and necessary wake-up call. As the generational imbalance deepens, public policies on pensions, healthcare and the labour market will face unprecedented strain. Merritt lays out these challenges with clarity and urges policy makers to act before it's too late.'

Enrico Letta, former Prime Minister of Italy and author of the EU's Letta Report on Europe's future

'Giles Merritt takes a deep dive into one of the most significant challenges Europe faces, posing hard-hitting questions for decision-makers. His thoughtful work outlines the problems and puts forward brave and far-reaching measures to address the slow-burning crisis. It would be folly not to heed his call for action.'

Layla Moran MP, Liberal Democrat Chair of the UK Parliament Select Committee on Health and Social Care

'Giles Merritt is right: Europeans must think hard about demographic reality and assess ageing's economic, social and political risks. Ageing may seem a slow-burning crisis, but this book tells us how massive and imminent its consequences are. Merritt underlines growing imbalances of population growth within the EU, and stresses the need for more policy coordination.'

László Andor, Secretary-General of the Foundation for European Progressive Studies and former EU Commissioner

'Demography really matters. If you want to understand why you simply have to read Giles Merritt's superb account.'

Sergio Arzeni, former Director at OECD and President of the International Network of SMEs

'Sheds light on the crucial yet overlooked challenge of ageing to nearly every aspect of social, economic, financial and personal life. Giles Merritt applies his analytical expertise to bring new insights in a book that is essential reading for anyone concerned about the future.'

Sir Michael Leigh, former Director-General in the EU Commission and Adjunct Professor at SAIS Europe

'Demographics doesn't always have to be destiny, but the ageing and eventual shrinkage of Europe's population is as threatening to our way of life as climate change. Giles Merritt boldly sets out the challenging path we must follow to avoid a disastrous fate. His book is essential reading for those who care about younger generations.'

Erik Jones, Director of the Robert Schuman Centre at the European University Institute

'Giles Merritt's book is an extraordinary wake-up call to Europe's dramatic demographic problem. Merritt offers insights, a great deal of data and a slew of policy recommendations. He believes it's time to tackle ageing with measures that confront social pressures and that also encourage the integration of migrants into our societies.'

Ferdinando Nelli Feroce, former Ambassador and Permanent Representative of Italy to the EU and former President of the Istituto Affari Internazionali, Rome

'An impressive warning to Europeans of demographic decline's clear and present danger. Giles Merritt's urgent wake-up call sets out the range of policy responses needed to defuse this timebomb. Ageing is becoming a massively destructive force that has to be heeded by politicians.'

Paul Révay, former European Director of the Trilateral Commission

'There's no growth without children! But Europe's population is in long-term decline and must come up with answers to its worrying demographic situation. Giles Merritt tackles an issue too long neglected by European leaders.'

Jean Dominique Giulian, President of the Fondation Robert Schuman, Paris

'Giles Merritt does what he does best: shaking Europeans' complacency. He applies Gramsci's 'pessimism of the intellect' to the ten detonators of ageing's ticking timebomb, and happily he also believes in the 'optimism of the will' with advice on how to defuse the detonators.'

Jim Cloos, Secretary-General of the Trans-European Policy Studies Association

'Giles Merritt identifies the fundamental issue lying behind those being given far greater attention such as defence, climate change, competitiveness and immigration. Unless Europe follows Merritt's excellent recommendations and faces up to ageing's impact, none of these challenges will be solvable.'

Bill Emmott, author and former Editor-in-Chief of *The Economist*

'Greater longevity is a blessing and a threat. Giles Merritt's 'Ten Commandments' are sound and helpful proposals for adapting our societies to ageing's existential challenge.'

Enrique Baron Crespo, former President of the European Parliament

TIMEBOMB

When Ageing Explodes

Giles Merritt

P

First published in Great Britain in 2025 by

Policy Press, an imprint of
Bristol University Press
University of Bristol
1–9 Old Park Hill
Bristol
BS2 8BB
UK
+44 (0)117 374 6645
bup-info@bristol.ac.uk

Details of international sales and distribution partners are available at
policy.bristoluniversitypress.co.uk

British Library Cataloguing in Publication Data
A catalogue record for this book is available from the British Library

ISBN 978-1-4473-7594-4 paperback
ISBN 978-1-4473-7595-1 ePub
ISBN 978-1-4473-7596-8 ePdf

Cover design: Keenan Design
Cover image: Shutterstock

Bristol University Press' authorised representative in the European
Union is: Easy Access System Europe, Mustamäe tee 50,
10621 Tallinn, Estonia, Email: gpsr.requests@easproject.com

In memory of my
greatly loved daughter
Olivia (Widge) Merritt
(1976–2024)

Contents

About the author

Giles Merritt has written on European politics and economics for more than half a century. He was a *Financial Times* foreign correspondent (Paris, Dublin-Belfast, Brussels) for 15 years, and then an EU affairs columnist on the Op-Ed pages of the *International Herald Tribune* for 20. In 1999, he founded Friends of Europe, the prominent Brussels think tank for which he continues to write his fortnightly 'Frankly Speaking' commentaries. Named in 2010 by the *Financial Times* as one of 30 'Eurostars' who influence the policy debate on Europe's future, Giles became in 2023 a Senior Associate Fellow of Belgium's prestigious Egmont Institute for International Relations.

About this book
(and why it's all about you, the reader)

This book is about the future, and it's a future in which demographic shifts seriously threaten our standards of living. Barely noticeable though it is, ageing is beginning to exert hugely disruptive pressures on our economic and political stability.

Europe is ageing much faster than we realise, and faster than society can adapt to. We Europeans face decline and division unless we wake to the scale of demographic change and tackle it.

Ageing is a ticking timebomb that sooner or later must explode. What form that detonation will take is hard to predict. It's impossible to forecast precisely how Europe's rapidly increasing elderly population will trigger trouble, but it is certain that it will do so.

My view of these unfolding crises reflects the ringside seat I've had on European politics for over half a century. I've reported from continental Europe since 1972, and became a Brussels-based think tanker in the early 1990s. As a journalist, commentator and policy analyst, I've met political leaders, top officials and authoritative experts from across Europe and around the world. My focus has been the uniting of Europe's disparate nations into a more cohesive and prosperous force.

It has been an erratic path, often consisting of two steps forward and one step back. My first 25 years as an EU watcher saw remarkable progress as it expanded its members and its powers. Europe was on the up, and looked set to wield greater influence and economic clout in a globalising world.

After the turn of the century, however, the outlook turned gloomier. Europeans haven't embraced new technologies as effectively as Asians and Americans, and have shown a navel-gazing preoccupation with intra-European questions. And they have neglected the reforms needed to streamline Europe's industrial base and to confront the consequences of ageing.

These have been confusing years for Europe. In 1980 it accounted for almost a third of the global economy, but now just 15 per cent. On the other hand, Europe was mostly a geographical description then; the EU numbered nine countries, whereas today it has three times as many, its own currency and an embryo political structure. The bloc is potentially a super-power.

Europeans' ability to overcome centuries of cultural separation and armed conflict is essential to their future prosperity, but the ageing of its population risks wrecking the drive for closer integration.

Ageing is a largely invisible problem. To use a nautical metaphor, Europe's ship of state may appear to be sailing serenely onwards, but it is holed below the waterline by its demography. Britain is no less vulnerable for having left the EU, and perhaps more so.

This book presents a Europe-wide picture of the problems that ageing is creating, and also draws substantially on developments and research in the UK. Its overall message is that ageing is hitting almost all developed nations to a greater or lesser degree, and risks undoing much that the EU's economic and political integration has achieved.

Greater longevity in richer countries and runaway fertility in many poorer ones are game-changers. They are also a reality that only some other natural or man-made catastrophe could alter. But it's not too late to address these problems, because although we can't divert the demographic tsunami rolling towards us, we can surf it rather than sink and drown.

Ageing's impact could be softened by an array of policy measures that would adapt our 20th-century structures to the exigencies of the 21st. The snag is that doing so would impose an immediately heavier tax burden to alleviate the crushing costs awaiting the taxpayers of tomorrow. The other option of borrowing to add to European countries' teetering debt mountains would cynically aggravate the financial troubles we are imposing on today's youth.

When asked about the future, most young people see climate change as their toxic legacy. There's no disputing that mankind is failing to tackle global warming with the necessary speed and determination, but that doesn't lessen ageing's threats. Both are massively disruptive forces. My modest hope is that this book will help to draw more attention to ageing's consequences and will stimulate efforts to counter them.

Giles Merritt
Brussels, 2025

1

The timebomb's ten detonators

Ageing is the 21st century's imperceptible crisis. It risks being devastating because it will disrupt the social and economic structures that hold our societies together. Longevity and infertility are upsetting the age-old generational balance. Longer lives are a blessing and a curse, and an explosive force whose ten 'detonators' must urgently be defused.

In the league table of threats to the future, ageing scarcely gets a mention. Climate change, global conflict in a nuclear age, famine, killer pandemics and 'rogue' artificial intelligence (AI) are all listed, but demographic change is nowhere to be found. It's a strange oversight because unprecedented social shifts are starting to overturn previously immutable aspects of our lives.

The ageing crisis is upon us, and will get a lot worse unless we wake up and confront its consequences. The last 40 or so years have seen the break-up of a pattern as old as time – generational continuity. The 14th century's Black Death profoundly altered medieval Europe's social and economic structures, but bubonic plague killed young and old alike. Now, largely unnoticed except by demographers, the balance between generations is being irremediably upset.

Baby busts in rich countries that include China, Japan and much of East Asia contrast starkly with population explosions in poorer ones, notably in Africa. Both are deeply disruptive, and the imbalance will seriously perturb the global political economy. In what ways is hard to predict, but it's clear that the way ageing and its problems are handled will determine the course of the 21st century as much as the threats in the global crisis league table.

This book is about ageing, primarily in Europe and therefore in Britain, but also takes a more global look at demographic shifts. Its focus isn't the human condition of ageing but rather the wider impact of longer lives and fewer births. For the first time in human history, younger generations in Europe and other wealthier regions are smaller in number than older ones. The upshot is far more dramatic than it sounds.

Ageing reaches into almost every facet of society. Paradoxically, it's because it touches so many aspects of people's lives that it's less noticed and its dangers unappreciated. Ten 'detonators' are primed to explode the timebomb of ageing, and there's a range of steps that need to be taken if they are to be defused.

Detonator 1: The economic impact – most people will be poorer

Every now and then a political leader will acknowledge that ageing is the new reality across Europe, and that by mid-century the population will also be shrinking. The same politicians usually go on to say reassuringly that fewer people will mean there's more wealth to go around. It's a 'Lump of Money' fallacy akin to the 'Lump of Labour' one, which misleadingly holds that the number of available jobs is finite, so immigrants 'steal' work.

In fact, smaller workforces are very bad news. Fewer people produce less, and that shrinks the economy and therefore diminishes the tax revenues that fund healthcare, pensions and so on. Some politicians say fewer workers can be compensated for by boosting productivity, but output per person has been flatlining for several decades, and few experts are staking their reputations on miraculous improvements in the foreseeable future.

Automation in the shape of ever-smarter robots and AI might eventually boost productivity enough to substantially raise the output of fewer workers. Even so, there will be fewer consumers and taxpayers, and that's a big economic drag. Bill Gates, Microsoft's billionaire founder, is among those calling for robots to be taxed as much as the workers they've replaced, but there seems little immediate likelihood of that.[1]

At the same time, most analysts agree that digitalisation is accelerating, and that a huge shakeout of labour markets is therefore inevitable. As employers resort to more and more automation, tens of millions of office, factory and retail jobs across Europe and America are forecast to vanish. Lower wage costs and big savings on payroll taxes are irresistible incentives for companies to sack staff. It's an old story, but this time it isn't about outdated rust-bowl industries but service sectors ranging from the law to accountancy, and even to medicine and scientific research.

Now that so many European countries are suffering, like Britain, from serious labour shortages, there's a temptation to say the redundancies created by the digital revolution will release much-needed workers onto the jobs market. But this would require a parallel revolution in the reskilling of those workers, along with a further revolution to make Europeans as geographically mobile as, say, Americans.

The uncomfortable truth is that so far automation has pushed real wages down and reduced people's spending power, making it harder than ever for Europeans to adapt to robotisation's turmoil and uncertainty.

It's not just factory workers and clerical employees whose jobs are being affected. Hitherto protected professions and executive functions are also threatened. Ageing can't be blamed for the impact of labour-saving technologies, but the dwindling number of young people joining Europe's labour markets is seriously aggravating the economic fallout.

To address these unsettling trends, we're going to need a drastic rethink of the way our market economies are structured. If we don't, and rely instead on muddling through, we must expect to see domino-style collapses of our familiar social and business models.

The first pillar of market economies to have crumbled is the ratio of wage-earners to pensioners, which will make it increasingly difficult to fund people's retirement. In the 1950s and 1960s, when Britain and the rest of Europe were clawing their way out of the post-war economic doldrums, there were as many as five workers for each pensioner. Right up to the end of the last century, that ratio between Europe's active taxpayers and inactive welfare recipients stabilised at an average of 4:1.

Those happy days are long gone. The ratio in most parts of Europe has fallen to 2.9:1, and EU forecasters warn that it's likely to settle at 1.7:1 unless there's a big change in many of the factors that determine who works and who doesn't. Needless to say, ageing is the reason for this destructive threat to Europeans' prized 'social contract'.

That people are able to enjoy much longer lifespans is a welcome development. But it comes at a cost that risks proving socially explosive. Too few young people will be coming onto Europe's labour markets to pay for the upkeep of the elderly population. And although there are ways to defuse this timebomb, they involve long-term thinking and substantial investment at a time when political 'short-termism' predominates.

Detonator 2: Democracy – ageing will disrupt Left–Right politics

The stability of Europe's parliamentary democracies depends on how voters perceive fairness. The new element being added to the age-old tension between capital and labour is the increasingly sharp divergence between the interests of older and younger generations.

The political parties of the Left and Right will have to contend with an unfamiliar wild card – Europe's ageing is creating unfairnesses that pit young people against their elders. Long-standing Left-Right politics will have to adjust to a third dimension of ageing. Younger people will contest the heavy handicaps being imposed on them by the needs of their elders. Older voters' response will be to defy them and wield their in-built electoral majorities.

The over-sixties account for around a quarter of the European population, and by mid-century that will be a third. When it comes to protecting pensions and healthcare, the elderly are well-equipped politically to resist pleas for lighter taxation of the young and much-needed help with housing. Yet older people's likely refusal to concede to such demands will be in no one's longer-term interest. Europeans' core problem is low fertility compounded by reduced spending power and inadequate housing.

Unless couples can get back to averaging at least two children – the replacement rate – Europe will continue to age and shrink. In the wake of the Second World War, its population grew by a very healthy quarter, peaking in 2015 at around half a billion. This will remain stable up to 2040, although getting older, and thereafter is forecast to start dropping rapidly. As this century draws to a close, Europe will have shrunk by some 80 million people, roughly the population of Germany.[2]

The problem is twofold. First, fewer people means less consumption, thus reducing demand for goods and services. Reduced wealth means greater political volatility. Second, there's the increasingly fraught relationship between asset-rich older people and underprivileged younger ones.

Assessing 'well-being' rather than fixating on per capita gross domestic product (GDP) is much debated nowadays, but whichever way the statistics are compiled, younger Europeans trail far behind. This was ever the way, of course, but much longer lifespans mean that property, savings and investments are no longer passed on to inheriting generations at the same steady rhythm as before.

In addition to housing woes and living standards that are significantly lower than those their parents enjoyed at the same age, Europe's younger generations are being saddled with their seniors' soaring social benefit and pensions costs. In theory, this burden could be lightened by overhauling tax arrangements in favour of the young, but to do so would first entail overcoming older voters' resistance.

The pressures of demographic change have already done much to slow Europe's innovation and growth, even if commentators have been slow to recognise this. A fair share of the blame also belongs to capitalism's shortcomings and the failure of Europe's market economies to adjust to changed global conditions. The price to be paid is populism, chiefly on the far right. Populist parties' electoral successes reflect voters' discontent rather than support for any clear proposals, but that's of little comfort to vote-losing mainstream politicians.

In their attempts to defend themselves against populism, centre-right parties in a growing number of European countries are shifting towards more authoritarian and less enlightened policies. This is a form of political suicide because the populists will always be more extreme, and the 'solutions' they are embracing will exacerbate ageing's challenges.

The answer, electorally unattractive though it may well be, would be for embattled mainstream parties to campaign on platforms that focus public attention on generational imbalances and their dangers. Doing so might cost votes in the short term, but could also spark a Europe-wide debate on the painful measures needed to defuse ageing's explosive impact. Unlike populists, responsible politicians would advocate strategic answers to these deep-seated challenges.

Detonator 3: Employment – jobs aplenty, but too few good ones

'Mismatch' is the jargon term used by labour market analysts to describe jobseekers whose skills don't match employers' needs. It's often a geographical problem, posing the key question of whether governments should try to take more jobs to the people – meaning depressed regions – or help people to move to jobs in more prosperous cities.

Until quite recently, mismatch wasn't a major element in the smooth running of labour markets. Now it is, because ageing is turning familiar employment policies on their heads, with digitalisation an added ingredient.

There aren't enough young people coming onto European countries' jobs markets, and those there are have to face mounting difficulties. Young jobseekers often don't have adequate technical qualifications, and even when they do they are frequently prevented by housing difficulties or poor public transport from commuting to work or moving house.

Labour shortages have become a serious headache throughout Europe, not just in retailing and fast food but also in research laboratories and high-tech industries. This is aggravated by older people leaving the workforce, in some cases prematurely or involuntarily, to draw a state pension that's largely funded by younger workers whose wages are lower than those that were earned at a comparable period by their parents.

Mismatch has become a crisis rather than a footnote in economic reports. The impact of labour-saving technologies has been sudden and brutal, dividing the labour market between highly paid and tech-savvy elites and the growing body of the less educated whose working conditions and modest pay packets are being further sapped by digitalisation. Low-wage economies in Europe are in no one's interest, but the signs are that even worsening labour scarcities won't lift the pay levels of the unskilled.

Demographers are finding it harder than ever to make long-term projections because of changing social attitudes and wildcard factors such as the COVID-19 pandemic. They nevertheless feel able to point to deteriorating overall conditions in the years ahead.

Counting the UK in with the 27 EU countries, Europe's labour force of roughly 220 million men and women must expect to lose about 50 million workers over the quarter-century to 2050. They will move from the tax-paying side of the balance sheet to the benefit-receiving column. Because lengthening lifespans will bring in a further 10 million old people who in years past would have died, in all there will by mid-century be 60 million more European pensioners.

The picture is made darker still by the shrinking number of working age people. At present there are something like 80 million under 30 year olds in the EU and the UK, not counting children up to 15, and by 2080 this age cohort may number 50 million or less. How well educated and computer literate they will be remains to be seen, but it's already evident everywhere that huge strides must be made to improve training.

Of today's 220 million European workers, it's reckoned that 90 million need reskilling because of radical changes to the nature of their jobs. It's not just a factory floor problem, as almost three-quarters of recent scientific and engineering graduates reportedly struggle to find suitable employment as they haven't been trained appropriately.

Higher wages are clearly needed for many, along with an enlightened rethink about how to adjust labour markets for today's fast-changing digitalised economies. Employment is central to how Europeans will address ageing, but there are many daunting barriers still to be overcome.

Detonator 4: The social fabric – now tattered, soon to be ripped apart

Just as Britons pride themselves on their National Health Service (NHS) of the late 1940s being the forerunner of so many other universal healthcare systems, continental Europeans proudly compare their 'social safety nets' with America's rough and tumble social security.

But ageing is making Europeans' prized healthcare and social benefit systems more and more unaffordable. Forecast to double by mid-century, healthcare costs are being driven relentlessly upwards by Europe's booming over-65s population, and most of all by the over-eighties, whose numbers will go from today's 14 million or so to 40 million.

In most European countries, beleaguered public healthcare services have coped with the pressures of ageing populations, but in the knowledge that far greater difficulties lie ahead. Older people's healthcare costs can be eight to ten times higher than those of the under-forties. The shifting generational balance looks set to bankrupt many countries' health services. It's not just hospitals and medical staff that need more money: day care for invalids and in retirement homes is crying out for adequate funding.[3]

The shortage of professional carers is already acute and is being severely aggravated by low wages. If demand for carers were to be satisfied, their share of the European workforce would more than double. It will in any case go from around 2 per cent today to nearer 5 per cent by 2050. Semi-skilled carers will be as sought-after as highly qualified doctors and nurses, who themselves are in increasingly short supply.

Why aren't these uncomfortable forecasts a more prominent feature of political debates? Perhaps because the initial impact of ageing in the UK and the rest of Europe has so far been softened by innovation and ingenuity. An important buffer has also been the 'fiscal elasticity' available to governments of comparatively rich countries through modest tax hikes and budget cutbacks. It's doubtful that these can suffice for much longer.

France offers a good example of what's to come. Few analysts believe it can sustain its generous social benefits, so there's a risk that sooner or later cutbacks will spark political unrest. Along with the state pensions that are already a politically volatile issue, combined spending on health and social welfare has been snowballing. These 'social fabric' sectors absorbed a quarter of the country's GDP in the 1990s, have since risen to over 31 per cent and are heading fast to a third.

The outlook for taxpayers, not just in France but everywhere in Europe, is that governments must levy more and more to fund these runaway social costs and ease the burden on younger people. Threats to their future pension rights, unaffordable housing and the reduced spending power of the 'working poor' are a volatile mix. How European democracies will handle these seemingly unreconcilable pressures is a crucial question that few politicians want to address.

The need for carers, and indeed for more taxpaying workers throughout Europe, could be met by more open immigration policies that would train, house and integrate newcomers. But that runs contrary to the public mood that has been fuelling support for populist parties. It's clear that a massive effort to inform and educate public opinion would have to be among the first steps in handling the looming ageing crisis.

Detonator 5: Wealth – widening gaps risk becoming unbridgeable chasms

Arguments about the 'wealth gap' between people and nations have absorbed rivers of ink, but without much result. Now these debates have become increasingly bitter and politically explosive. The ways in which the rich get richer while the 'working poor' are more poverty-stricken than ever makes an eventual flashpoint inevitable. The wealth gap has widened faster than ever since the global financial crisis of 2008, and the austerity policies introduced in its wake have made it dangerously toxic.

The disparities between haves and have nots have accelerated so much that even the super-rich seem to agree widening wealth gaps are undesirable. A growing intellectual consensus on this has sadly done nothing to slow the widening process. The salaries and bonuses of millionaire corporate bosses compared with employees' slender pay packets make embarrassing headlines, but have yet to bring about a narrowing of the gap.

Arguably, though, the wealth gap that matters even more is between young and old. After a lifetime of working and saving, older people are of course wealthier than the young. How much richer, and whether their assets can be redistributed more fairly after their deaths, are becoming key questions. It's a very confused picture because runaway property values reflecting housing shortages distort matters, but the bottom line is that the post-war 'baby boomer' generation now owns a hugely disproportionate share of Europe's wealth, and how that will be handed down in inheritances is key to resolving many of the wider problems of ageing.

The International Monetary Fund (IMF) reported in the aftermath of the 2008 financial crisis that younger rather than older Europeans were suffering the chief financial handicaps. The under-35s today own less than 5 per cent of total net wealth in Europe. That's not the only yardstick measuring their disadvantages; other reports have focused on housing and found the outlook for younger people has deteriorated dramatically. A third of 'millennials' born around the end of the last century have become reconciled to never owning their own home.[4]

Public sympathy is often outraged when older homeowners have to sell up to pay for their healthcare and retirement costs. These cases can involve tough moral choices, but it's inevitable that the years ahead will see the practice becoming more widespread. Other arrangements that seem increasingly likely and desirable would increase taxes on wealthier old people and on inheritances. The overall aim would be to release more housing to the homeless young.

More generally, a substantial effort is needed by European governments to redress the seemingly inexorable widening of the wealth gap. The last century's post-war ethos was to flatten wealth disparities and equalise opportunity. This produced a revolution in higher education across Europe – not least in Britain – and a rapid expansion of the so-called middle classes with secure jobs. In comparison to the challenges that lie ahead, it was a golden era.

That virtuous circle will turn vicious unless ageing's pressures can be substantially reduced. However, 'soaking the rich' isn't quite as straightforward as is often claimed. Calculations that show only a tiny number of the fabulously rich 'owning' huge proportions of the world's wealth are something of a red herring. Their money isn't kept under the bed, but contributes to the trade and investment flows that are essential to economic activity.

That said, there's no disputing the fact that the 21st century has seen a strong shift in favour of capital at the expense of labour. 'Stakeholder capitalism' has been a rallying call for those who believe corporate profits should be redistributed more to employees and society at large, but these proponents have yet to deliver results. Big business and under-regulated financial markets have not yet been significantly reined back, either in Europe or America.

Detonator 6: Housing – key to jobs and increased fertility

Europeans unquestionably need radical new strategies to attack pernicious housing shortages, yet affordable homes remain low on many governments' priority lists. Ageing will be a game-changer here because it's turning housing from a slow-burning issue into a potentially explosive crisis.

For 50 years, new homes construction has lagged far behind demand. Europe's population increased at breakneck speed between the mid-1960s and 2015, yet home building remained stuck in the doldrums. The 15 years of urgent reconstruction immediately after the Second World War still account for the majority of dwellings built in Europe in eight decades.

The problems created by housing shortages are legion. Labour markets don't work well when there are too few affordable homes in high-growth regions. Birthrates are depressed when young couples don't have enough space for larger families, and see their spending power greatly reduced by soaring rent or mortgage costs. And in wider economic terms, growth is hamstrung when investment in new companies and business sectors is discouraged by labour shortages that stem from housing shortages.

The challenge of finding a suitable home, both as accommodation and as a secure investment, has turned in recent years from being an irritant into a severe limitation on many Europeans' standard of living. Longer lifespans are slowing the transfer of properties from older to younger people, and the steep increase in demand for single person accommodation, especially for the elderly, is also imposing new pressures.

One European in three either complains of being impoverished by sky-high housing costs or has given up hope of home ownership. The worst hit are inevitably the young. In the UK, only 8 per cent of 25–34 year olds – the generation looked to for a badly needed 'baby boom' – are homeowners, down from 20 per cent in the 1990s.[5]

Of all ageing's threats to the future, housing is the easiest to fix, requiring measures that although tough are doable. A multi-pronged strategy of tax incentives and bonfires of red tape could transform home construction and open the way to more dynamic economic growth and greater social harmony.

But doing so would require almost unheard-of levels of political courage and consensus between fractious interests. The prize would be to head off rising discontent over housing that so far has strengthened only the populists.

Most housing policies are national, if not regional or municipal, yet there's a good case for introducing a European dimension. Governments' housing measures can easily be disruptive and uncomfortable in the short term, so the collective responsibility of a Europe-wide housing initiative would offer valuable 'political cover' as well as a sense of greater solidarity. More broadly, because ageing's impact is greater in the poorer nations of southern and eastern Europe, financial mechanisms that will help them address it are going to be crucial to the EU's cohesion and popularity.

Detonator 7: Taxation – the nightmare fiscal pressures of ageing

Far fewer taxpaying workers and many more recipients of welfare and healthcare are a politically explosive mixture. That's the reality, even if politicians try to woo voters with talk of lower taxes and cutbacks to some aspects of government spending.

Taxation doesn't have to be a blunt instrument that bludgeons citizens and businesses. It can be a sophisticated tool for gently resolving conflicts and guiding people towards a brighter future. Ageing is an unprecedented challenge to tax systems that are anyway long overdue for reform. If handled with courage and imagination, updated taxes could do much to tackle intergenerational unfairnesses.

It's impossible to calculate with any precision the past, present and future costs of Europe's ageing. Shrinking workforces and growing numbers of pensioners are already braking economic growth, but by how much varies from country to country and depends on how governments choose to present the figures.

Official statistics rarely point to demographic pressures as a major factor responsible for the slowdown in growth that has been such an unwelcome feature of the 21st century. What they can't hide, though, is that Europe's spluttering economies have been growing by little more than a single percentage point a year, creating a legacy of social tensions for the future.

Most European nations, including Brexit-battered Britain, have proved remarkably resilient to the double whammy of the COVID-19 pandemic and Russia's war against Ukraine. But their underlying problems are still there, with economic growth trapped in the same sluggish rhythm as in the doldrum years that followed the 2008 global financial crisis. There are several explanations for Europeans' weakened international competitiveness, but a major factor is ageing.

Older workers' productivity reduces with age, say researchers, but that's not the chief culprit. Above all, the shrinking numbers of workers is depressing growth. Well before the 2008 financial crisis, top officials in the European Commission were warning that fewer workers in even the richest EU countries would reduce both output and consumption. Growth in Europe was at that time averaging 2.3 per cent yearly, but they were forecasting that this would fall to 1.8 per cent at most for 2010–30, and 1.3 per cent for 2030–50.[6]

The years ahead will see furious debates over how to increase tax revenues and redistribute tax burdens. Soaking the rich will be the Left's slogan, and cutting 'overly generous' social security that of the Right. Neither can resolve Europeans' fiscal problems. These will continue to grow until governments bite the bullet and foreswear competitive tax loopholes to attract investment. If they introduce new wealth taxes, they will trigger capital outflows to tax havens elsewhere. Sad to say, governments around the world are the architects of their own fiscal misfortunes.

Nevertheless, ageing Europe will have no option but to rethink tax arrangements that have long defied genuine reform and have instead been complicated by layers of new and sometimes contradictory legislation. The intellectual case for an EU-wide model overriding member states' beggar-thy-neighbour tax breaks is clear, even if its political prospects are close to zero.

Quite apart from ageing's future costs, sharp increases are needed in tax revenues to fund spending already incurred in most parts of Europe. These are in large part being paid for by increased debt, and no one can say how long the international financial markets will continue to lend on this scale to cash-strapped governments. With low interest rates now a fading memory, governments are increasingly hard put to service their teetering debt mountains.

Still more fundamental to the tax conundrum is its unfairness on younger people. The solution certainly can't be to kick the can down the road through heavier debt burdens on already much-disadvantaged younger generations. It's impossible to say how long Europe's younger taxpayers will remain passive, but the threat of tax revolts and civil disobedience is beginning to loom larger.

Detonator 8: Debt – borrowing today taxes the young of tomorrow

Because many governments have already been on borrowing sprees that impose unfairly heavy future costs on today's young, debt is a toxic topic. There's little agreement on how sustainable it is. 'Generational accounting' is the jargon term used by economists who want to see more responsible borrowing policies. They argue that rising levels of public borrowing are not only handicapping economic growth but also guarantee impossibly high taxes in the years ahead.

Not everyone accepts this. There are those who say debt is more a notional than a practical problem. They argue that governments that are able to borrow in their own currency, notably the US, can more or less ignore constraints. In theory, that should also be the case for the eurozone with its single currency. But memories of the sovereign debt crises in the eurozone's poorer southern members are still fresh, so it's unlikely Europeans would take the risk, not least because the poorer EU countries are the most vulnerable to ageing.

The surge in public debt after the 2008–10 global financial and economic crises, and then the costs of COVID-19, are liable to be the precursors of yet more government borrowing to finance ageing. The outlook is bleak: in the eurozone, the ratio of debt to GDP has long overrun its targeted 60 per cent, reaching at one point 95 per cent, and in the UK it's over 100 per cent.

Reduction and even repayment of these debts may sound distant and somewhat abstract, but paying interest on them is immediate and costly. When the UK's public debt edged past its total GDP, the cost of servicing government borrowings rose to a tenth of its spending.

Nobody can say how elastic the global debt market will be in the years ahead. The 2010–20 period saw the number of countries around the world whose debt exceeds 300 per cent of GDP rise fourfold from a half-dozen to two dozen. It's likely that higher interest rates will choke off some governments' appetite for borrowing, but ageing's pressure for more public spending will make it hard for many European governments to kick the habit.

Advocates of 'fiscal fairness' for Britain's younger generations say an immediate 10 per cent hike in income tax is needed. This would weigh more heavily on richer, older taxpayers, so it would help to ease the future burden on millennials now in their thirties and on their Gen-Z juniors.

But the likelihood seems remote that politicians of any hue will call for such a massive tax increase. To do so has yet to feature in any of Europe's national political debates. More borrowing rather than higher direct taxes remains governments' preferred option. The longer-term economic and political consequences of this are potentially disastrous. It's possible, though, that a catastrophic global debt crisis may eventually intervene; at that point, we'll discover whether borrowing really is one of those gifts that keep on giving.

Detonator 9: The Europe dimension – ageing's threat to EU solidarity

The 'march of history' since the Second World War has seen progress towards a unified Europe that few had thought possible. Now Europe's ageing is an unexpected barrier in the way of further progress.

The speed and costs of ageing are to be hugely divisive. The EU's newcomers will suffer disproportionately, and this threatens to undo Europe's drive towards political unity through economic cohesion. Most of these countries are not only ageing but also shrinking fast in size because of very low birth rates and the emigration of their young people to more prosperous parts of Europe.

Successive EU enlargements since 2004 have brought the free movement of people, goods and capital to countries that were in many cases Soviet satellites, unleashing a host of unintended consequences. Western Europe's higher wages are tempting tens of millions of people away from central and Eastern Europe, from the Baltic republics and, increasingly, from the Balkans. The prospect of Ukraine joining long-standing Balkan candidates for EU membership is raising the spectre of an unmanageable exodus of people to the west.

Romania's population is by 2050 likely to have shrunk by a quarter, and Bulgaria's by as much as four-tenths. This pattern will be repeated to greater or lesser degrees in all the newcomer or would-be member states, depressing their economies and raising their need for generous economic assistance from richer EU countries.

The EU has notoriously daunting problems of its own, but it nevertheless prides itself on being a magnet for aspiring members. That openness will be severely tested by the financial demands of candidates who stand to be overwhelmed by ageing. It won't be the first time the EU has faced this dilemma: after the Berlin Wall fell and the Soviet bloc disintegrated, Western Europe pondered the cost of bringing in Russia's bankrupted former satellites, and concluded that it dare not leave so politically volatile a region on the outside.

A similar calculation is being made now, but the EU is economically much less robust and is itself beset by ageing. If further enlargement proves unavoidable, there's a danger the strains will weaken popular support for the EU, and perhaps fatally erode its solidarity from within.

Detonator 10: Global dimension – the weakening of 'Old Europe'

It was always to be expected that the rise of emerging giants such as China, India, Brazil and Indonesia would loosen Europeans' centuries-old grip on the world economy and challenge America's primacy. For Europe, ageing is accelerating this trend and compounding its weaknesses.

Tough global competition is exacerbating Europe's demographic vulnerability. The three decades since Soviet-led communism collapsed have seen remarkable strides in Europe's integration, yet at the same time it has been sleepwalking economically and losing international competitiveness.

European public opinion has seemed indifferent to falling birth rates and complacent about weak technological innovation and shrinking global market share. Asia's rise has also forced a reduction in America's share of the world economy – to a quarter from over a third 30 years ago – but Europe's has plummeted further and faster. Its third of the global economic cake in the 1970s shrunk to a quarter by 1990, and has today shrivelled to 15 per cent. It's hard to identify the precise reasons for this and allocate blame, not least because it reflects healthy development elsewhere in the world, but the suspicion is that Europe's ageing has already played a part.

Shrinking workforces, sluggish productivity growth, mounting social tensions and stagnant public and private investment have all been sapping Europe's strength. Political leaders try to reassure voters by comparing Europeans' living standards and general well-being with those of developing nations, but the more telltale comparison is with the US. Thanks in large part to its positive demography, the US has been running rings around ageing Europe.

It's a fairly recent development: for most of the post-Second World War period Europe was level-pegging with America economically, although not militarily or as a global hegemon. Before the 2008 financial crisis, the EU's economy outstripped in size that of the US, standing at over $16 trillion a year when America's was $14.7 trillion. Fifteen years later, the US turned the tables with an economic output that has grown to be a third larger than that of the EU and UK combined.

There are many excuses for this humiliating reversal of fortunes. In the key technologies that are shaping the future, Europe's shortcomings can be ascribed to overly timid investment and under-resourced research. Whatever the reasons, the slide has been dizzying. In 1990, Europeans manufactured almost half of the semiconductor chips that fuel the digital revolution. Today its share is down to 9 per cent. Of the world's top 20 high-tech companies, seven are American and only two European.

How important is this global dimension, and what can be done about it? The more fatalistic policy analysts apparently accept the inevitability of Europe's ageing, saying in effect that we must learn to grow old gracefully. It's an alarmingly complacent view when the world is in the throes of rapid and unpredictable change.

There are no quick fixes that could deliver a geopolitical rebalancing to restore Europe's past leadership. Europeans, including the UK, need to focus more than ever on collaborative research and innovation. That has been the European Commission's rallying cry for decades, but it has been stymied by member states' rivalries and by penny-pinching.

If Europeans do not address the challenges of ageing, they will see their international influence fading, and with that a weakening of their stability and well-being. To get back on its feet, Europe not only needs a world-beating high-tech strategy but also an EU-wide educational and training drive to ensure that more of its young jobseekers are adequately trained in digital skills. Europe has more or less been holding its own internationally in pure research, but failing abysmally in applying the innovations that are essential to a future productivity bonanza. More wealth generated by fewer people will, after all, be the only way out of the ageing crisis.

It's time for a 'bomb squad' to defuse ageing's dangers

Unless defused, these ten detonators will sooner or later explode the demographic timebomb. They won't necessarily go off all at once, but any one of them is capable of sparking a chain reaction that would spread across Europe.

The European dimension is often derided, but it's crucially important. For governments to raise their revenues by enough to pay for ageing requires the political cover that only a collective strategy can offer. Without this, few if any EU member governments will risk the electoral defeats that anti-ageing measures are sure to provoke.

What might a pan-European approach look like? Certainly not a rigid EU-based agreement, but rather a broad consensus on the threats created by ageing and the measures needed to address them.

Ageing's costs need concerted fiscal policies to avoid intra-European tax competition, but fiscal harmonisation is anathema to the EU's national governments. Politicians hate to surrender the power and influence of taxation, and even the most pro-EU ones are suspicious that Brussels might somehow use new taxes to create a 'super-state'. There are nevertheless acceptable degrees of tax cooperation. European governments could, say experts, easily raise €200 billion a year through a fairly modest coordinated levy on the super-wealthy, although EU members have shown little interest in the idea.

Although tax is vital to any Europe-wide strategy for softening ageing's impact, it isn't the most important element. The key to tackling demographic decline is simply to admit that it's taking place. The two opening decades of the 21st century saw political parties across the EU, whether in government or not, twisting and turning to avoid acknowledging that ageing is a long-term threat to living standards.

Politicians know that elections can only be lost, never won, by asking today's voters to make sacrifices for those of tomorrow. Europe's Green parties can attest to the difficulties of persuading people that climate change is already here, and to people's resistance to any measures that impinge on their lifestyles.

It's only recently that voters in industrialised Europe have begun to accept the need for environmentally responsible policies. Applying them is a struggle, and 2024 election results in some countries showed a weakening of support for the Greens. By the same token, if Europeans are not to rue the day when they ignored warnings of demographic decline, an electoral awakening of ageing's consequences is essential.

As well as an EU consensus on ageing – which despite Brexit the UK could be part of – there should also be a new framework for intergovernmental cooperation and best practice, not necessarily run by the EU but possibly by an ad hoc agency. The Brussels institutions have, contrary to popular myth, limited resources and manpower, and are tied by treaty obligations.

The European Commission would at first seem the natural choice for a leading role on ageing, but it has yet to seize this. When Germany's Ursula von der Leyen took over as commission president in 2019, she created a new mandate for demographic issues, but didn't back the portfolio with a significant budget or a directorate of full-time officials. It's possible she may do so in her second term, but rather than trying to overcome political and bureaucratic hurdles it could make more sense to go outside the EU and establish an independent body. Open to all of Europe, this could focus on the coordination of ageing-related policies.

Every country has its particular way of doing things – its own democratic and political systems and its welfare and healthcare structures. What they have in common is that all are prey to the pressures of ageing. An information exchange offering advice and examples of policy solutions would be useful and cheap. It could also arm national policy makers with persuasive arguments for change in areas ruled by ingrained conservatism.

Overhauling schools and hospitals for a new era of fewer students but many more elderly patients will be complex and fraught with imponderables. Exchanges of best practice and advice on introducing technologies such as AI could save time and prevent useless duplications of effort. They would also underline the message that ageing is going to be Europe's 'Great Disruptor'.

Messaging will be crucial. Young people need reassurance that their future won't be bleak, and that their unfairly low wages and high housing costs will be tackled within years, not decades. Less skilled and undervalued younger Europeans who have been swelling the ranks of the 'working poor' need bold action to improve their lot, and that means a similarly determined European strategy to impart skills and education, including to migrants and asylum seekers.

Policies to confront workforce shortages have eluded European governments for far too long. From training to housing, and job mobility to immigration and the integration of newcomers, Europe needs to be far more forward-looking. The message responsible political leaders should convey is straightforward: scarcely visible though it is, the ageing crisis is already upon us, and unless confronted and defused will within a few short years devastate our well-being.

2

This timebomb is ticking fast

Ageing's pressures are tightening their grip, even though their speed and disruptiveness have yet to come into plain sight. A third of Europeans will be over 65 by the mid-2030s, up from a fifth today. Fewer taxpayers and many more pensioners risks bankrupting welfare safety nets, creating thorny political divisions. Politicians may wish to ignore these dangers, but cannot escape their consequences.

For good or ill, Europeans' political choices over the coming half-century are to be imposed on them by older voters. The snowballing 'silver vote' could either prove dangerously selfish or perhaps admirably level-headed.

Conventional wisdom has it that the fast-growing constituency of pensioners will defend its own interests at the expense of younger people, and so compound intergenerational unfairness. That may not turn out to be the case; there's an opposing view − counter-intuitive though it may sound − which is that instead of backing conservative values, elderly voters will opt for revolutionary change.

This encouraging thesis argues that although populism is now such a prominent feature of European politics, the populists are doomed to fail. The right-wing extremists who hope to sweep to power across Europe have yet to devise, let alone implement, sustainable policies that will improve living standards. When this failure to deliver becomes plain, runs the argument, the political focus will shift to the issues surrounding ageing.

The impact of ageing − its dislocation of the balance between generations − is certain to disrupt long-standing political patterns. Although ageing is still largely invisible in political terms, policies to soften its impact demand a new consensus. What these measures should be are key to defusing Europe's demographic timebomb.

Grey power flexes its muscles in rural England

The ancient county town of Winchester in southern England may seem an unlikely barometer for testing the UK's political climate. Yet it points towards the profoundly disruptive nature of demographic change.

Historically, Winchester has been no stranger to politics and political upsets. It was the stronghold of Alfred the Great, the 9th-century Anglo-Saxon king, and was England's capital long before London. Its democratic roots are deep: it returned two members to England's first real parliament in 1295, 80 years after Magna Carta – a version of which is displayed in Winchester Cathedral.

Winchester is old nowadays in a very different sense. Its rapidly ageing population has triggered political turmoil that contrasts sharply with its sleepy medieval image. The town's High Street has been pedestrianised, but is also crammed with mobility scooters and motorised wheelchairs that enable the elderly to do their shopping … and voting.

Winchester was long a safe 'true blue' parliamentary seat for the Conservative Party, but the 2024 general election delivered a humiliating wipe-out for the incumbent Tories. The Liberal Democrats seized the seat with 30,000 votes, twice as many as the defeated Conservative candidate.

This should have come as no surprise; the town's old folks have been on the march for some time. In 2010, Winchester awarded the Tories a whopping 13,000 majority, but this shrivelled to less than 1,000 in 2019. Boundary changes since 1997 saw the seat oscillate between the Liberal Democrats and the Tories, but the clear message has been that older voters who in bygone days would have been staunchly conservative nowadays reject any policies that fail to meet their needs.

The details of the Tory debacle in this once traditionally conservative seat are debated, but the inescapable factor is ageing. Almost a third of Winchester's inhabitants draw a pension or are close to retirement. They have to contend with a lengthening list of problems connected to housing, pensions and healthcare, and these have sapped their long-standing loyalties.

Winchester's population grew by almost a tenth from 2011 to 2021, the most recent census period, while the over-65s there rose by a quarter. This is just the start of the projected surge in its elderly population. Local estate agents point to cut-throat demand for single-person housing in the town and nearby villages. This is by no means a phenomenon peculiar to rural Hampshire, because by the late 2030s four in ten British households will consist of an older person living alone.

It would be a stretch to present Winchester as an unerring guide to the future direction of British politics, let alone those of continental Europe. But the growth in its older voters – the over-fifties make up 40 per cent of the town's population, and well over half its registered voters – is a trend that can be found right across Europe, and promises a new style of politics. Younger people, whose opportunities and lifestyles are equally threatened by demographic change, should take heed of this 'silver stranglehold' of older electorates.

About 250 miles to the east, another town with an equally famous name mirrors Winchester's demographic pattern. Waterloo, on the outskirts of Brussels, is ageing just as fast. Its battlefield museum and the carefully restored building that was the Duke of Wellington's headquarters when he defeated Napoleon in 1815 attracts lively summertime crowds of tourists, but the town itself is coming to resemble a sprawling retirement community. Like Winchester, it's a microcosm of the nation. Belgium has seen its proportion of over-65s rise to 20 per cent from 13 per cent in the 1970s, and by 2030 or so a quarter of the Belgian population will be pensioners.

Throughout Europe, demographic decline is starting to sap long-established social structures and local economies, especially in vulnerable rural areas. The small town of Riez in the deeply rural *département* of the Alpes de Haute Provence is a prime example of the way France's 'desertification' trend is being exacerbated by ageing, with serious political and economic consequences already visible.

In the summer months, when tourists crowd the picturesque streets of Riez, the preponderance of older inhabitants isn't so striking. Outside the tourist season, however, the town's twice-weekly market of local produce reveals at a glance how the elderly account for an overwhelming share of its permanent residents. Their children and grandchildren have left, drawn by the nearby magnets of Marseille and Aix-en-Provence.

Riez is a microcosm not just of France but of Europe. Low fertility and acute shortages of jobs and such amenities as shops, hospitals and schools is draining the lifeblood of rural Europe. Small surprise, therefore, that the drift towards populism and extremist 'solutions' to these ills is gathering momentum there and in so many regions of Europe.

Successive crises – the financial near-meltdown of 2008, COVID-19, Ukraine, Gaza and the worsening Israel–Palestine conflict – have meant demographic change remains little more than a cloud on Europe's horizon. But it's quietly brewing up into a destructive maelstrom. An eerie political calm still surrounds ageing, but when the storm breaks, social cohesion will be threatened. It's impossible to say how people will react when they wake to the unfairnesses of ageing, but Europe seems likely to see some dramatic reappraisals of the creation and distribution of wealth.

The calm before ageing's storm

How much longer young Europeans will remain supine and apolitical on issues other than climate change is an open question. What *is* clear is that European society – and throughout this book that includes the UK – is on borrowed time. The intergenerational bargains that have supported us from infancy to senility are crumbling, and threaten to unleash political volatility of a kind we haven't experienced before. History will not be a helpful guide to the future.

Open a newspaper or click on a current affairs TV show and the chances are that some pundit or other will observe that the whole world shares Europe's ageing problem. 'The Chinese will get old before they get rich' has been the mantra of Western opinion-formers, who try to reassure us that, whatever happens, the West will keep its wealth.

China's future as a world leader may be uncertain, but there seems little doubt that the global population will peak at around

10 billion and that humankind as a whole is getting older. So if all the world is ageing, why should Europe's demographics be particularly damaging? And are Europeans right to view their demographic decline so complacently? The general public's view seems to be that although there are more elderly people than before, that's nothing to be overly concerned about.

The reality is that the coming decades will see ageing trigger social and political turmoil in European society, even if few politicians, business chiefs or civil leaders choose to talk about it.

A variety of reasons explain this *omertà*. Some are socio-cultural – a feeling that it's crass to discuss the rising numbers of very old people needing care. When they reach their eighties or nineties the elderly may have earned their juniors' respect, but they may also be seen as a drain on limited resources. 'Bed blockers' is the term used in Britain to describe older patients who have to remain hospitalised because the care homes sector can't cope.

Other reasons for this silence are political. The threatened upset to the balance between governments' tax revenues and spending portends political trouble on an almost unimaginable scale. The Left–Right tussle between haves and have-nots will be accentuated, and compounded by newer and more volatile Old–Young tensions.

The demographic changes taking place across Europe result from longer lifespans and greatly reduced birthrates. Instead of the three or four children per couple once common in most countries – and six to eight in the more devoutly Catholic ones – Europe's average fertility rate is down to less than one and a half children per couple. The downward drift began in the 1960s, and since the 1980s has accelerated.

Two generations – the millennials and Generation Z – are slated to finance Europe's growing population of pensioners. Just as the equilibrium between the young, middle-aged and elderly is being skewed, so too is the trade-off between tax revenues and state spending. Fewer young people coming on to Europe's labour markets, and therefore contributing tax money to their government's coffers, means there will be less cash to pay for soaring pension and healthcare costs.

Younger people are far less privileged than were their parents at the same age, yet they face a future of being clobbered by the state for a much larger chunk of their earnings. It's already harder to get onto the home-owning ladder, and many earn less than their forebears although their jobs are far less secure. They also stand to be outvoted by their elders whenever reforms are mooted that might correct, or at least soften, these injustices.

Although the cards are stacked against them, the young won't be the only losers. The growing imbalance between young wage-earners and older asset-owners is in no one's interest. Without progressive new policies, there simply won't be enough money in most of Europe's national economies to finance the retirements of people now in their fifties.

'Demographic Doomsday' scenarios

It isn't uncommon to hear arguments that caution against panic responses. These suggest that judicious adjustments to economic and social policies will be enough to cope with the combination of smaller families and longer lives. Productivity is said to be the solution to shrinking workforces, with new technologies revolutionising the manufacturing and service sectors and thus creating much more wealth.

Another argument along similar lines is that once the baby boomer generation born in the wake of the Second World War has disappeared, more housing will become available and there will be more inherited wealth for millennials and Gen-Zers. The idea is that while longer lifespans will delay younger people's access to their elders' assets, once they inherit they will be able to fund the costs of ageing. The glaring flaw here is that lower fertility rates will already have shrunk economic growth.

Other optimists – perhaps more aptly called 'demographics deniers' – advance the idea that the tailing-off of student populations will create spare educational capacity, enabling underprivileged communities, especially migrants, to benefit. Similar reasoning is applied to housing and jobs, although experts in these fields are sceptical and warn that social deprivation is so deep-seated a problem that it's not open to retro-solutions. In other words, scrimping on primary education cannot be compensated for later by more university places.

The reality is that the shifts taking place in society today are nothing short of tectonic. Whatever the future may bring, living standards are going to come under sustained pressure. How much so will depend on the speed and far-sightedness of policy solutions that have yet even to be proposed, let alone publicly debated. Politicians around Europe have undoubtedly noted the fate of the UK's 'Remainers', whose campaign against Brexit rightly warned of the economic cost of leaving the EU but was branded as 'Project Fear'. The lesson many have drawn is that voters don't necessarily respond rationally to facts they find unwelcome.

Messaging will thus be key to pricking the complacency bubble over ageing's consequences. A glance at the demographic projections collated by European governments makes the point: most are highly technical, poorly presented and muddled in their focus. None of them highlight 'killer facts' such as the collapsing size of the tax-paying workforce and the burgeoning ranks of the retired and inactive who must be supported by taxpayers.

Health and social policies are a litmus test for governments' determination and inventiveness. Of all the policy challenges piling up in ministerial in-trays, healthcare is among the thorniest. The economic and social pressures are irresistible, yet across Europe the mounting costs of healthcare already make it so expensive that it risks bankrupting many countries' public finances.

Because medical advances help us to live longer, there's a temptation to assume we're a healthier society. That's far from the case. In Britain and elsewhere in continental Europe, absenteeism owing to health problems is aggravating labour shortages and applying a brake to economic growth. The answer is to increase funding to improve physical and mental health, and so return as many people as possible to productive jobs. Economic historians point to the way improved public health in late Victorian times created a more productive workforce and transformed Britain's 'dark satanic mills' into wealth-producing modern industries.

A former chief economist at the Bank of England, Andy Haldane, observes that health standards in Britain are going backwards. From having been a tailwind boosting the UK's economic growth, public health has instead become a headwind. He has warned that something like a third of people on low incomes living in underprivileged regions suffer from chronically poor health and that the incidence of ill-health is rising fast; in 2010, 5 million people were registered as long-term sick in the UK, and a decade later (before COVID-19) that had risen to 7 million.[1]

As well as weighing heavily on healthcare costs, poor health is sapping the active workforce. Better health and greater longevity boosted productivity and doubled Britain's workforce during the 20th century. But that virtuous circle is turning vicious, and is raising doubts about the UK's long-term healthcare strategy. How is it that runaway healthcare budgets are being paralleled by lengthening disability lists? And are dazzling breakthroughs in medical science distracting attention from sounder public health policies?

The costs of caring for Europe's elderly are snowballing. Economists at the IMF warned against this almost 20 years ago. In 2006, they expected European healthcare costs to double by 2050, reaching an average 15 per cent of GDPs. The Organisation for Economic Co-operation and Development (OECD) also reckons the costs of social security benefits and state pensions are likely to reach 12 per cent of GDP by then, so around a quarter of the European economy will be devoted to activities associated with ageing. We can't be sure mid-century will be the high point, because after 2050 the average lifespan of male babies born today will be 86, and for girls 90.

How should European governments handle this trade-off between healthcare spending and the economic burden of ill-health? And what will the political debate look like? The UK seems headed for the most dramatic tensions of all, when the irresistible demands of healthcare meet the immovable bulk of ageing. Britain's healthcare costs have been rising the fastest in Europe against a background of runaway ageing that will take the over-sixties to almost a third of the population by 2050.

Dissatisfaction with medical services had been simmering before COVID-19, and the pandemic brought it near to boiling point. Although the lockdowns highlighted the shortcomings of hospital care and the diminishing availability of general practitioners, the underlying pressures are those created by ageing. Across Europe, two-thirds of all health spending now goes on the over-65s.

Ageing's 'unaffordable' costs

The coming quarter-century features two starkly contrasting graphs. The line showing Europe's elderly population points sharply upwards, while that of the working-age population points down, shrinking from almost 60 per cent of adults at present to only half. Today's 265 million working-age Europeans will be down to 230 million by mid-century and 220 million by 2070.

If businesses were booming across Europe, this divergence between the producers and consumers of wealth could be viewed with equanimity. Policy makers' proposed recipes would be to stir in the greater productivity that new technologies are said to promise, and season the whole with modest additions of older workers, women and migrants to Europe's labour force. The resulting concoction might be only sustaining rather than nourishing, but governments would at least be able to make ends meet.

But business isn't booming and capitalism is no longer delivering adequate returns. Some blame 'short-termism' and criticise major corporations' preoccupation with quarterly profits for their shareholders rather than giving priority to long-term strategies. Others point to the decline of heavy industries such as steel or shipbuilding and European boardrooms' failure to replace these by investing adventurously in the high-tech sectors that have transformed many Asian economies.

While Europe pioneered the highly profitable industrial revolutions of the 19th century, it has since been caught up with and even overtaken by emerging global competitors. America's post-Second World War pre-eminence is another factor, along with the globalisation of trade and investment that has eroded Europeans' comparative advantages.

The important question isn't how Europe, including the UK, lost its mojo but how it might recover it. The first step is arguably for Europeans to abandon illusions about simple choices between labour and capital or between financial profit and social equity. The fact that pension funds' investments are no longer producing enough money to fund private retirement schemes is a significant warning that a wide-ranging overhaul of our market economies is overdue.

This means taking the challenge of ageing seriously, and going back to the drawing board to devise new policies. The ageing phenomenon is on such a large scale that tweaking ideas suited to a century ago isn't the answer. Nor is muddling through at a purely national level when Europe has been redefined by the EU's single market rulebook. To address demographic change, Europeans need a common framework that can ensure national measures won't become beggar-thy-neighbour protectionist devices.

The EU 'project' of ever-closer political and economic union has done much to reshape and revitalise Europe. Its achievements have been hard fought and at times erratic – two steps forward, one step back – but the EU has unquestionably forged its member states into a powerful bloc commanding global respect of a sort that few would merit individually. But it's a work in progress, and ageing could undo much that's been achieved.

Demographic change will hit the poorer member states of eastern and southern Europe the hardest, presenting a very real danger of disintegration. The sustained pressures exerted by the economic consequences of ageing are likely to be even more disruptive than the effects of the sovereign debt crisis that hit Greece and other southern 'Club Med' EU members after the 2008–09 global financial crisis.

To be effective, Europe's responses to these new vulnerabilities would have to be coordinated in a common approach. The 'sovereign' social and industrial policies of individual countries need to be grouped into a shared framework. If governments insist on separate and perhaps competing policies, then the pressures of demographic change risk tearing the EU apart. Far from sparing the UK from any fallout from a disintegrating Europe, Brexit is making the British economy more vulnerable to volatility on the continent.

It's impossible to tell when external debt burdens will 'go critical', but governments obviously can't continue to borrow at the present rate indefinitely. The speed with which international bond markets demolished UK premier Liz Truss's promised borrowing spree in October 2022 was a foretaste of the future. Within weeks of that debacle and Truss's resignation, the UK Treasury was reportedly planning what market analysts called a 'cataclysmic flood of debt sales' amounting to £1.25 trillion over five years, with the unanswered question 'who'll buy, and at what price?'[2]

Tax is the elephant in the room

The internet age is producing many surprises, one of the most heart-warming being the victory of a youthful Dutch academic over Fox News, Rupert Murdoch's mighty US-based TV channel. It's an episode that may also point to a future tax revolution big enough to whittle the costs of ageing down to manageable proportions.

Rutger Bregman is a youthful-looking Amsterdam-based economic historian who shot to modest fame in 2019 when, like Daniel in the lions' den, he went to the World Economic Forum in the Swiss ski resort of Davos and told an audience of billionaires and corporate bosses that the solution to many of the world's problems is 'taxation, taxation, taxation'.

Stony silence greeted his presentation, and it received little press coverage. However, the Fox News ultra-conservative 'anchor' Tucker Carlson threw down the gauntlet and invited Bregman to defend his views on air. Bregman roundly defeated his blustering opponent with quietly spoken arguments for greater fairness and an end to tax evasion by the rich.

Fox News decided not to broadcast the interview – perhaps because as well as being bested Carlson had angrily ended it with an outburst of profanities. But the power of the internet is such that once the Bregman interview was posted on YouTube it quickly chalked up 11 million hits, and is still viewed many more times than if it had been a run-of-the-mill news item.

The point of this anecdote is that tax is a vital key to unlocking the straitjacket of ageing. Tax reform always sounds desirable and fairly straightforward, yet is anything but. It isn't about dipping into the pockets of plutocrat billionaires and transferring their wealth to the needy. That governments will require far greater tax revenues to fund neglected sectors such as housing, healthcare and pensions is indisputable, but how to go about boosting them is complex and highly controversial.

Clamping down on tax evasion seems an obvious first step. The US and the EU each reckon their illegally unpaid taxes at a trillion dollars, or euros, a year. If it were easy to recover these illicit debts, both would have done so long since. The snag is the tax havens that the governments of richer countries either can't or won't prevent each other from operating. Whether constrained by the lobbying of the influential rich or by concerns that international investment flows might be destabilised, governments complain loudly about tax dodging while also being quietly responsible for much of it.

The foremost attempt to achieve an international consensus on tax is that of the Paris-based OECD. Originally set up as a hybrid think tank-cum-diplomatic mechanism to further Europe's post-Second World War reconstruction, it has since morphed into a 38-member grouping of the world's richer countries. Its latest achievement is an agreement by its members to each charge a minimum 15 per cent corporation tax, most notably on the big multinational companies that elude national taxes.

This is an encouraging development providing no one breaks ranks. Even EU member states, although bound together in so many other ways, refuse to get real on tax. The member governments resist surrendering or even diluting their national tax-raising powers. European countries are also divided internally by fierce ideological disagreements over how heavy or light taxes should be. Some politicians believe that state revenues are better able to fund public services if the taxable economy is encouraged to grow faster by light-touch taxation. They argue that heavier taxes stifle growth.

Ranged against them are countries that have prospered in spite of being highly taxed. Scandinavians present a convincing case in favour of taxes that allow for generous spending on the childcare, education, training, housing and social benefits that form the basis of their high-wage economies.

Right-of-centre politicians, whose stars have been rising in much of Europe, continue to reject this approach. It wasn't just Tory hardliners in the UK with their dreams of 'Singapore on Thames' who have advocated low tax models; a good many EU governments believe that to a greater or lesser degree, tax increases discourage inward flows of investment that would fuel faster economic growth.

The view that low taxes can boost prosperity isn't shared by the IMF. To make the point that rich countries levy higher taxes, it cites Germany's tax rates as opposed to the UK's far lower ones. From 1991 to 2019, tax revenues in Germany averaged 45 per cent of GDP and those of the UK only 35 per cent, yet by the end of that period Germans' per capita GDP was 16 per cent higher.[3]

The two opposing camps find common ground, however, in resisting moves to award the EU a greater say on tax issues. In 2022, the EU was reluctantly granted by member governments its first-ever borrowing powers for a COVID-19 recovery fund to bail out the hardest-hit member states. But Brussels remains a long way from getting permanent powers to finance the burdens of ageing that will hit the southern and eastern EU member states hardest.

Because demographic change is a creeping phenomenon, nobody can calculate with any precision the eventual costs of ageing. There's also so little research into the measures needed to soften their impact that there are few figures on the fiscal gaps to be covered. British researchers have made a stab at it, though, and their findings should be ringing alarm bells in high and low tax countries alike.

A House of Commons report in 2017 calculated the debt burden being handed down to Britain's younger generations at £7.6 trillion, equivalent to five times the then annual GDP. To pay this off, it suggested a rise in tax revenues equal to 6 per cent of GDP. Long before that, Oxford University's Institute of Population Ageing had said in 2004 that a 10 per cent hike in income tax was needed to plug the gap.

These figures underline the case for a far-reaching rethink of tax policies across Europe, and even then they understate the scale of the challenge. Although they put a price tag on kicking the debt can down the road and sparing today's taxpayers by over-burdening tomorrow's, they focus on debt that has already piled up rather than looking forward to ageing's future costs.

More housing, better education, digital retraining and higher spending on healthcare and pensions would all impose huge extra costs. Yet ambitious investment strategies in house construction, regional development, transport links, reskilling, targeted education and more home care for infants and the elderly are precisely what is needed. Investment in these sectors would pay off handsomely and strengthen European society before ageing's devastating costs hit in the 2040s.

These are hard times, so it is difficult to convince governments of the need for extensive public investments. Tackling structural weaknesses sooner rather than later would cushion the effects of ageing in the years ahead, but the economic conditions of the 2020s are far from propitious. The COVID-19 pandemic's lockdowns followed by the Ukraine conflict have aggravated underlying weaknesses in the economies of many European countries, making it harder than ever to argue for spending drives. The EU's stimulus efforts − its €800 billion post-COVID-19 recovery plan NextGenerationEU and its €1 trillion Green Deal strategy − sound impressive, but spread over a decade they are relatively modest when set against Europeans' needs.

The days of easy money and low interest rates are a fading memory. Governments' ability to fund investment strategies by borrowing have been greatly constrained. Even if they were to heed arguments that these investments trigger sound growth, the only reliable source of money to fund them is taxation, with its political consequences.

Ageing's early warnings were ignored

Well before ageing's costs will begin to bite in earnest, Europe found itself engulfed in the cost of living crisis triggered by Russia's invasion of Ukraine and by the debilitating aftershocks of the COVID-19 pandemic. Governments can't be blamed for unforeseeable events, but it's also true to say the crisis of the mid-2020s cloaks a deeper malaise they had been repeatedly warned of since the start of this century.

A host of international bodies and authoritative experts had queued up to issue reports that left no room for doubt about trouble ahead. The IMF, the World Bank, the OECD and the European Commission all warned in great detail of the impoverishment that will result from demographic decline.

One of the acknowledged leaders in the field, professor Wolfgang Lutz at the Vienna Institute of Demography, set out the stark message that Europe's workforce would shrink by more than a quarter between 2015 and 2060. Lutz's work with the

Oxford Institute of Population Ageing was paralleled by a report from the university's Oxford Martin School. This assembled a Commission for Future Generations to look at the implications for younger people. Although its 20 distinguished politicians and academics published hard-hitting proposals in 2013, these created scarcely a ripple.

That spate of worrying predictions came at an awkward time. Not only Europe but also the global economy was recovering from the severe financial crisis triggered in 2008–09 by the sub-prime mortgage collapse in the US. Governments wrestling with controversial austerity policies they had introduced to balance the books had little bandwidth for economic problems that lay in the future.

An obvious long-term solution to ageing's shrinkage of active workforces across Europe is immigration, but this issue has been poisoning European politics more than any other. The political price to be paid for opening up to many more economic migrants continues to be the chief reason politicians ignore demographic decline.

Increased immigration is among the policy responses to ageing that are proposed in the closing chapter of this book. But it's so toxic an issue that it risks eclipsing a more strategic approach to ageing and its consequences. The ramifications of demographic change go far beyond the need for more workers and larger families; the politics of inequality will dominate debate in the coming years, as will the political power of older people.

After retirement, pensioners no longer contribute much tax. Yet their built-in electoral majorities mean they can promote their interests at the expense of those of the taxpaying young. Demographic imbalances condemn Europe's under-fifties to being an electoral minority for at least the next 40 years. Devices that might correct this – for instance, lower voting ages and quotas for younger parliamentarians – have yet to catch the public imagination anywhere in Europe.

European politics are becoming more unpredictable than ever. Far from moving towards consensus on major challenges, politicians are polarising divisive issues and exploiting envy and despair. The prospect of national politics across Europe becoming semi-paralysed by Young–Old electoral imbalances bodes ill for common policies on ageing. Yet it's clearly vital that Europeans, including the UK, should agree on a shared agenda. Ageing is exacerbating socio-economic inequalities, and European nations need to adopt similar policies to combat these.

Another common factor is the widely held view that older people are worse off than the young. The less privileged elderly are often the focus of social concern, but in general terms they often fare better than younger ones. As the Resolution Foundation in the UK put it, 'A better starting point is to recognise that Britain's booming stock of wealth is increasingly concentrated in older generations and that it is also increasingly lightly taxed.'[4]

This imbalance has been aggravated by shocks such as the COVID-19 pandemic. The economic damage caused by lockdowns that emptied shops, offices and factories around the world was immediate, but the longer-term effects are equally worrying. While more flexi-time jobs, more people working from home and for some a shorter working week look like positive developments, the wider picture is reduced job security for younger people and a further shrinking of Europe's active labour force.

Ageing is starting to aggravate a number of very sensitive spots in the world of work. Not only employees but also the unemployed are suffering from income erosion. The Resolution Foundation has calculated that unemployment benefit in the UK, when compared with employed people's average earnings, buys someone on the dole half as much as 50 years ago.

The situation of employed people, not only in Britain but also in other 'rich' countries, has also deteriorated. When the dust of the COVID-19 pandemic began to settle, the UN's Geneva-based International Labour Organization (ILO) came up with research that shines some light on the 'Great Resignation', when millions of people – most notably in the UK – didn't return to work. They quite simply weren't earning enough to find paid employment worthwhile.

The ILO study found that employees in relatively high-income countries have worked harder than ever in the first two decades of this century, yet in real terms they've seen their incomes fall. The average worker's purchasing power, said the ILO, has fallen faster than wages have risen.[5]

Research findings like these suggest that some fundamental questions now hang over the 'social contract' between capital and labour that has changed only marginally since the Second World War. Other than near-monopolies and some noted high-tech innovators, many companies no longer enjoy enough profits to pay higher wages.

Surely the answer is greater productivity?

Productivity is the magic wand that politicians wish they could wave over ailing economies and struggling welfare states. Getting more economic output year on year per worker in both manufacturing and service sectors worked well in the 1950s and 1960s, but is no longer the easy answer it once was.

It's always possible that Europe's drooping and uneven productivity growth will be magically transformed as the digital revolution accelerates, but realists are cautious. 'Europe's ageing population is going to cause a sharp productivity slowdown, and cause serious economic problems,' says the World Economic Forum, the organisers of the annual Davos meetings in Switzerland.[6]

Their warning has been amplified by a flood of studies. The UK's productivity position was succinctly summed-up in a study by the Resolution Foundation and the Centre for Economic Performance at the London School of Economics (LSE): 'The decade to 2019 saw the lowest productivity growth in 120 years,' its authors reported. Germany and France are about 15 per cent more productive than the UK, so just a halving of that gap could boost household incomes across Britain by an average £2,500 a year.

The main culprits are weak investment in businesses and a reluctance to install efficient new high-tech equipment. Moreover, because the British workforce has been ageing fast – its average age has risen since 1999 by four years, from 39 to 43 – it features more older workers who are less inclined to change occupation and move to a more productive new job. A robotisation study in 2017 revealed that manufacturers in South Korea had 630 robots per 10,000 workers, Germany less than half that at 310 robots and the UK a miserable 70 robots.[7]

That abysmally low level of robotisation in Britain may well reflect the dwindling of the manufacturing base. In any case, there's clearly some way to go before British industry starts to enjoy the fruits of digital technologies. It's the only option open to Europe as a whole. The European Commission has emphasised, in a paper it entitled 'Policy challenges for ageing societies', that 'labour productivity growth is projected to be the sole source of potential output growth in the EU'.[8]

The case is sometimes made that older workers' experience can make them more efficient, so on that basis Europe's ageing workforces will be more productive in years to come. The IMF is unconvinced, and has argued that Europe's ageing instead condemns it to a sharp productivity slowdown. Commenting that 'European productivity is already poor by historical standards', the IMF analysts said 'ageing will take a considerable toll on productivity growth over the medium- to long-term. Total factor productivity growth in the euro area is forecast to be around 0.8 per cent.' It added that perhaps that could rise to 1 per cent yearly 'if we shut down the effect of workforce ageing'.[9]

The Resolution Foundation and LSE study's aim is to discourage UK policy makers' tendency to muddle through rather than set out a structured, strategic approach to Britain's economic woes. Its publication in May 2021 launched a research project into the policies needed up to 2030, which it calls 'the UK's decisive decade' because it will determine the country's trajectory to mid-century.

Boosting productivity will therefore be crucial. Because there will be fewer people at work, raising their output will be the only way Britain and its European neighbours can pay for the rising costs of ageing. But a blanket approach to productivity is liable to be misleading; the benefits are not evenly distributed and in recent years have gone to older and richer parts of society rather than to poorer young people. 'Top earners have captured most of the proceeds of productivity growth over the last three years', the authors of a Sheffield-based research project reported in 2018.[10]

A study by The Equality Trust in London underlined the point when it reported that not only is income inequality in the UK very great when compared to other developed countries, but also that income statistics tend to hide the true facts. Over a five-year period it found that while average incomes had risen by 2.2 per cent yearly to £34,200, this was chiefly because the country's top 20 per cent enjoyed a 4.7 per cent increase, while the disposable incomes of the bottom fifth shrank by 1.6 per cent.[11]

No one doubts that inequalities are compounded in an economic downturn, but the wider point in all this is that hopes of a productivity spurt are dim. Unless, that is, new technologies really *can* come to the rescue and transform the efficiency of a sizeable number of businesses. What are the chances, then, of Europe's catching up with the digital revolution?

Could AI boost flagging productivity?

The advent of AI is hailed as a vitally important game-changer and economic asset, even though so far it's a largely American-owned sector. So how real is the prospect of AI and ever-smarter computer systems streamlining European workplaces and magically creating greater wealth?

To date, the miraculous benefits of digital technology have been a pipe dream for Europe. New technologies have paid off handsomely for Asian countries that have been industrialising almost from scratch, but have delivered only mixed results in Europe and in America too.

Introducing efficient new technologies into existing manufacturing or service businesses sounds like a perfect solution. Sadly, it has instead been widening the gaps between the haves and have nots – between the better educated and the less skilled. Despite all the fanfare surrounding the 'Fourth Industrial Revolution', more jobs are reportedly being lost than created.

It wasn't always like this; the post-war years until the late 1980s saw new jobs triggered by automation easily outstripping those that were lost to it. A survey by Daron Acemoglu at the Massachusetts Institute of Technology (MIT) has found that some 17 per cent of jobs had been lost to automation between 1947 and 1977, but 19 per cent new ones were created. For 1987–2016, he found the reverse – 16 per cent jobs lost and only 10 per cent created. This, he observed, was a 'double whammy' because the less skilled people who were being made redundant by automation lacked the know-how to compete for one of the newer jobs.[12]

Acemoglu is among the leading experts on the disruptive effects of new technologies, and the author of an influential 2012 book called *Why Nations Fail*. In November 2021, he testified to a US House of Representatives committee on the reasons why automation, although far more sophisticated than before, is failing to deliver. He explained that in the post-1945 years 'it increased worker productivity in a diverse set of industries and created myriad opportunities'. But now that automation targets a more limited number of tasks, he went on, 'it is highly detrimental to workers, and especially low-education workers'.

His assessment was echoed by Janet Yellen, US Treasury Secretary in the Biden administration, when she told delegates at the Davos conference that technologically driven productivity gains were liable to increase social and economic inequalities. Speaking while the COVID-19 pandemic was still raging, she noted that lockdowns were inducing a surge in telework that would ultimately increase America's productivity by a healthy 2.7 per cent. She then added, though, that the gains would mainly go to upper income white collar workers, in the same way that online learning has been used most of all by wealthier, white students.

A snapshot of automation's likely impact in Europe has forecast that an extra 4 million jobs may be created, but shares the view that lower-skilled workers will be the losers. Researchers for the McKinsey Global Institute predict that although only 5 per cent of occupations can be wholly automated, the jobs of 30 million office workers in continental Europe and Britain along with 25 million production jobs are susceptible to change 'by adapting currently demonstrated technologies'.

Retail sales assistants, secretaries, stock clerks and cashiers will probably make up a fifth of the people whose relatively low-wage jobs will disappear. On the other hand, the study identified 15 professional, executive, scientific and cultural occupations that will account for almost a third of the promised new jobs. 'What lies ahead is not a sudden robot takeover,' say its authors, 'but ongoing, and perhaps accelerated, change in the mix of jobs and work activities in the economy'.[13]

Most of these forecasts focus on digital technologies rather than breakthroughs in biosciences. As with AI, the implications of biochemical innovations are far from clear. Scientists are contemplating what some say is a 'new era' being ushered in by the use of AI to predict the shape of a protein, thus revolutionising the speed with which new drugs can be developed. What this may portend for humankind is anyone's guess.

It's much the same story for digital advances and AI itself. While COVID-19 and its lockdowns was so dominating the news that little else was discussed, a new supercomputing milestone was quietly reached. Researchers in the US hailed the arrival of the 'exaflop' – computing power that within a single second can deliver a quintillion calculations, which is a billion times a billion. That announcement coincided with a survey of 1,500 corporate leaders by the Washington DC-based Brookings Institution, doyen of America's left-leaning think tanks. It found only 17 per cent of them had even a hazy idea of what AI might involve for their business.

Such developments can seem so conceptual and abstruse that it's hard to escape a sense of science fiction when pondering their possible impact. What we can conclude so far is that it's easier to install new technologies in 'virgin' conditions – a developing country or a new industry – than to patch them onto existing ones.

The disruptive effects of automation are presenting governments with awkward consequences rather than immediate answers to society's problems. Instead of productivity improvements, governments have had to handle the fallout from industrial lay-offs and bear the economic costs of redundancies in already depressed regions. Digitalisation and bioengineering may eventually deliver a new dynamism, but in the short term these risk aggravating ageing's challenges instead of offering solutions.

The growing proportion of less skilled people in workforces that are being shrunk by ageing means a minority of educated wage earners will be asked to shoulder a growing tax burden. Increased productivity thanks to game-changing scientific advances can't be ruled out, but the more immediate policy choice is increased immigration, despite all the turmoil that would undoubtedly trigger.

The economic case for bringing more economic migrants to Europe is clear-cut, but the politics are murky. Politicians who understand the ill-effects of labour shortages and low birthrates also know the price to be exacted at the polls by populist rivals if they openly encourage more immigration. Europe's political landscape has been transformed by anti-migrant voters, with the UK's Brexit referendum the most high-profile example.

Wanted: a level-headed (and courageous) debate on immigration

How many new workers are needed as Europe's active population shrinks, from where should they come and what criteria should they meet? These are the questions that policy makers in the UK and throughout Europe should be asking themselves.

Labour shortages have been increasing for some time, which is in large part why governments have been able to boast of reducing unemployment. Yet it's plain to all but the wilfully blind that manpower is in short supply; walk down any high street in Britain or continental Europe and 'Now Hiring' and 'Help Wanted' signs are displayed everywhere.

The obvious solution is more migrant labour, even though that isn't a prospect welcomed by large swathes of public opinion. Rather than be accused of xenophobia or racism, opponents of immigration say their country is overcrowded and also that lower-waged newcomers 'steal' jobs by undercutting local labour. A host of research has shown that neither charge stands up to scrutiny.

In some EU states – notably Germany and Sweden – in-depth questions about immigration have been addressed realistically even when that meant braving the wrath of far-right politicians and their supporters. In most European countries, though, immigration hasn't been openly debated with the voters. As to Britain, Conservative governments from 2010 to 2024 refused to ask or answer serious questions on the issue. The controversy stirred over the 'small boats crisis' of asylum seekers who brave the English Channel in rubber dinghies was used to distract attention from the post-Brexit labour shortages wreaking havoc in the UK's agriculture and hospitality sectors.

Rather than dissect the labour needs of individual countries, it's worth looking at the overall European position. In 2010, a 'wise men' report led by former Spanish premier Felipe González warned that Europe would need 100 million immigrants by mid-century to compensate for ageing and the shrinkage of its working population. This bombshell was quietly buried by the EU governments that had commissioned it.

Migrant labour is widely acknowledged to be hugely beneficial for both host countries and the immigrants themselves. The McKinsey Global Institute says migrants produce about 40 per cent more in economic output than if they were working in their home country. Migrant workers account for a bit more than 3 per cent of the world's population, and nearly 10 per cent of the global economy.

The drawbacks of increased immigration are far better known than its advantages. Language, religion and race are all formidable barriers to integration, and they have been compounded by host countries' short-sighted, penny-pinching failure to invest adequately in the housing and education of newcomers. Squalid tenements and sub-standard schools have too often been the grudging welcome extended to Europe's immigrants.

It's hardly surprising that these poor conditions produce poor results. The less skilled a worker is, the less is added to a country's wealth. Underprivileged second or third generation children of migrants are also more likely to become antisocial and unemployable. When contemplating their need for more manpower, governments must learn from past mistakes. As well as being a source of labour, migrants' often have larger families, and these are an important counterweight to Europe's falling birthrates.

Future generations of 'new Europeans' from Africa, the Middle East, Central Asia and Latin America promise a brighter future for an ageing continent. But that presupposes a radical rethink of their welcomes. They must be seen as an invaluable resource that if properly invested in will yield social and economic dividends. Seeing immigration in cost terms is dangerously misleading, as Germany discovered in the wake of the 2015–16 'migrant crisis' that saw an influx of over a million largely Syrian refugees. The immediate €10 billion cost to German taxpayers is expected to turn into a yearly economic gain of €26 billion.[14]

The migration picture has been blurred by the arrival of so many Ukrainian refugees fleeing Russia's invading forces. Some

5 million people, mostly women and children, have sought refuge, mainly in EU countries. The UK has accepted about 180,000, roughly the same as the US or Canada but fewer than Spain. It is impossible to tell what effect this surge will have on Europe in general because much will depend on the duration and outcome of the conflict. What is plain, however, is that the arrival of Ukrainian refugees has obscured the wider question of how European countries could fashion a truly coherent immigration strategy.

Most of the policy shifts that ageing demands are purely national, even if concerting them at a European level would greatly enhance their effectiveness. Migration policies are an area where an EU-wide approach has been much discussed but without concrete results. A quarter-century has passed since the leaders of the EU's then 15 member states met in the Finnish industrial town of Tampere to fashion a common asylum and migration policy. Back in 1999 it was hailed as a political milestone, but has since looked more like a tombstone.

Spurred by a surge of 300,000 Balkan refugees from the civil wars in former Yugoslavia, the Tampere summit issued a stirring declaration on immigration. 'Our aim is to develop a European Union that is open to those led justifiably to seek access in our territory, and which is able to respond to humanitarian needs on the basis of solidarity.'

Fine words, but a common policy still eludes the EU in all but name. Its members' national policies are fragmented and at times downright competitive in the lengths they'll go to reject asylum seekers and economic migrants. In 2020, the European Commission announced a New Migration Pact, which was at once dismissed as unconvincing by the non-governmental organisations (NGOs) that handle irregular migration problems. It certainly came nowhere near the strategic approach required by Europe's manpower needs. In early 2023, the EU's member states aggravated their labour shortages by announcing tougher measures for returning failed asylum seekers to their country of origin.

This refusal to fashion immigration policies that are humanitarian and economically sound is matched by European governments' inability to confront their common problem of ageing. The symptoms of demographic decline – shortages of workers, housing, healthcare workers and taxpayers – are all national problems, but would obviously be better dealt with through consensus.

The most striking feature of the way governments turn a blind eye to ageing is their reluctance to see it in its global context. By mid-century, Europeans will represent only 4 per cent of the world's population and no more than a tenth of global GDP. The EU's role on the world stage will be much diminished unless it can revive its economic fortunes. China, India and Indonesia will be dominant economies, along with the United States, which, at 390 million people, will have drawn level with Europe in population size and greatly consolidated its economic lead. The UK will probably drop to tenth place in the global ranking of GDPs.[15]

This is the world that awaits a shrunken and fractured Europe refusing to face the realities of demographic change. In spite of a long history of industrial leadership, worldwide investment and scientific and cultural trail-blazing, Europe appears condemned to relentless decline unless it can shake itself awake. The EU is at risk of having flared as a brave adventure that then flickered and died. Its death certificate may well read 'Succumbed to old age.'

3

Wealth gaps will soon be chasms

Some say the world is getting fairer, and that billions of people have been raised out of poverty. Others say 'peak fairness' is behind us, replaced by the selfishness of a privileged few. Ageing is the new catalyst now widening the inequality gap in Europe, and its chief victims will be the young.

Turn on the TV or glance at your smartphone and the young are everywhere. They dominate social media and the airwaves, determine fashion, music and even what is or isn't morally acceptable. The world seems to belong to the young. Dig deeper, though, and these are merely surface signs that hide profound unfairnesses.

The under-forties are being dealt a poor hand, not only in Europe but also in America, China and Japan. Compared with previous generations, young Europeans are underpaid, poorly housed and saddled with the rising cost of pensioners, who themselves have enjoyed more privileged lives and still own the bulk of financial assets like property, shares or cash in the bank.

This growing generational imbalance is down to ageing. In Britain and across Europe people are living longer than at any time in human history, and of late they also have far fewer children. Everyone knows this, yet we tend to see Europe's ageing as a common problem that affects us all equally.

The ageing of European society is compounding old inequalities and creating new ones. In the years ahead, today's young together with the underprivileged 'working poor' are going to suffer disproportionately. The only equality is that society as a whole will have to bear the brunt of political turmoil if discontent over ageing's consequences turns into more open forms of conflict.

The extent to which these unfairnesses can be tackled will decide the future of Europe. This raises a host of difficult and politically divisive questions, and the best chance of finding consensus solutions will be through a wider appreciation of the intergenerational pressures created by ageing and diminished fertility. We Europeans must rediscover our sense of social equity.

It is drilled into us as children to be fair and to share what we have. On reaching adulthood, it dawns on us that life isn't fair and that equal opportunity is a myth. We nevertheless cling to the moral imperative of fairness, elusive though we know it to be. At the same time, we are conscious of winners and losers in the market economy, and it's obvious that slower growth in recent decades has widened the gaps.

Human society is based on interdependence, so fairness is in everyone's interest. Unless the common good is served, the resentments of the underprivileged will sooner or later boil over and erupt. It behoves those who enjoy privilege to reduce unfairness, even if that involves making sacrifices.

There's a strong case for a 'back to the future' rethink of Europeans' political realities. The Europe of the 1950s had been so ravaged by war that most people's lives could only improve. Both victors and vanquished had suffered terribly and could only look forward to better times.

The hard slog of rebuilding shattered economies generated a spirit of cautious optimism and generosity. In this collective post-war 'Euro-mood', politicians understood that the protectionism and beggar-thy-neighbour rivalries of the 1930s were only recipes for renewed conflict. They knew economic growth must be shared to be durable, and the fruit of this was the EU.

The EU's own future is much discussed nowadays, but the point here is that its framework offers national governments the practical mechanisms as well as the 'political cover' needed to take the difficult decisions on reintroducing social fairness for the disadvantaged young.

Younger people across Europe have been the principal victims of rising inequality. Media attention tends to highlight older people's struggles to make ends meet when facing health and housing problems, but the reality is that longer lifespans mean assets pass to younger generations much more slowly than before.

This slowdown in inheritances of property and financial assets is being compounded by factors that affect younger people but that their parents were spared. Their career prospects are far more uncertain, while the 'Digital Age' that was supposed to usher in a golden future of productivity growth and rising wages hasn't delivered, and instead seems darkly threatening.

Digital technologies, the experts promised, were going to deliver productivity improvements that would swell people's pay packets. They have so far chiefly spawned new businesses in the 'gig economy' that on average pay less. Cash-strapped students, economic migrants and the unskilled at first welcomed the flexibility of zero-hours contracts, but the honeymoon has since soured and weakened job security is raising uncomfortable questions about the future of 'Social Europe'.

It's the young who suffer most from glaring inequalities

The handicaps that millennials and Gen-Zers have to contend with don't earn them the sympathy that they deserve. Deeply rooted inequalities are being heaped on younger people. They are the first generations to have poorer lifetime prospects than their parents, and if that's not tackled it's hard to see how they will be able to fund the costs of ageing.

When the IMF and the OECD looked at inequality in Europe they didn't mince their words on how unfair life has become for the young. 'They are more likely to fall into poverty in the event of an income shock' (i.e., losing their job) 'because they typically lack asset wealth that acts as a buffer,' said the IMF's report 'Inequality and Poverty across Generations'.

The IMF researchers found that Europe's 16–34 year olds own less than 5 per cent of the net wealth, and usually have only a tenth of the wealth of the average 65 year old. In Europe, they are slightly better off than their American contemporaries, who have only 3 per cent of net wealth. The post-Second World War baby boomers, by contrast, had at the same age owned a healthy 21 per cent.[1]

The IMF analysis foresaw a daunting future for young Europeans. It warned that they are 'adversely affected by economic stagnation and labour market developments, as well as gaps in the social safety net', and are therefore at greater risk than previous generations of falling into poverty.

Its most significant warning was that widening inequality isn't a temporary phenomenon. 'Higher poverty and joblessness among the young have adverse and long-lasting consequences for today's youth as well as for tomorrow's economic prospects,' it concluded.

A broadly similar OECD analysis made special mention of Britain in its league table of generational unfairness. 'The United Kingdom is one of the most unequal countries in terms of income distribution,' it said in its study of wealth disparities. It also found that the 10 per cent of richest households in the OECD countries own half of the net wealth.[2]

In Britain, wealth ownership – assets as distinct from incomes – is about average for OECD countries thanks to inheritances from parents and grandparents. But these have the disadvantage of aggravating socio-economic divisions, and so are a growing problem. In the UK, the value of inheritances more than doubled to nearly £90 billion a year over the first two decades of this century, and are forecast to double again by 2035.[3]

Elsewhere in Europe, it's a mixed picture. In Germany, where many people rent rather than buy their homes, property inheritances are a lesser feature. In overwhelmingly house-owning Belgium, inherited properties are so common that their divisive effects are less obvious. In France they are dwindling: 50 years ago, a third of all privately held wealth was inherited, and that has since slipped to a quarter.[4]

Whether through an inheritance or help from the 'bank of Mum and Dad', only a small minority of young people in Britain are sheltered from the greatest inequality of all – the difficulty of getting a foot on the property ladder. Housing difficulties translate into smaller families and lower birthrates, and in the UK a young couple's chances of owning their home are slim, and getting slimmer. Runaway property prices have far outpaced sluggish salary levels, lifting house buying far beyond the means of most young people. Nowadays the average home costs 12 to 15 times more than the average annual salary, whereas back in 1980 it had been an affordable four times earnings.

The inequalities that dominate housing, wages and job opportunities are discussed in later chapters. In the meantime, it's worth pointing out that although less privileged older people are often the focus of social concern, in overall terms earlier generations have fared better than today's young. The Resolution Foundation in the UK observes that 'A better starting point is to recognise that Britain's booming stock of wealth is increasingly concentrated in older generations, and that it is also increasingly lightly taxed.'

Assessing the outlook for Europe's youth is inevitably a huge generalisation, depending as it must on a range of very variable factors. In any case, commentators and analysts don't necessarily share the same concerns about the fate of younger people. Some see Gen-Z's 'zoomers' as work-shy if not antisocial. Critics point to younger people's preoccupation with digital media and to their embrace of a more relaxed work–life balance, notably in the wake of the COVID-19 lockdowns.

The same critics say that although the young may complain it's harder to find work appropriate to their education and skills, they were very much to the fore of the 'Great Resignation' after COVID-19 had subsided when people opted to stay home or work only part-time. This perhaps reflected younger people's more relaxed attitude to the traditional work–life balance, but it's equally possible that it's a telling comment on the shrinking rewards of being a full-time employee.

How instructive are all these statistics? It's clear that younger people aren't as well off as their parents and grandparents were at the same age. But European economies aren't performing nowadays as buoyantly as in the 1970s and 1990s. Some millennials and Gen-Zers will eventually inherit from family members, but as their forebears are living so much longer than earlier generations, when is increasingly hard to tell. These considerations don't, in any event, alter the fact that most younger people across Europe are unfairly handicapped by low wages and high rents, and that the political consequences of this are uncomfortable and may be disastrous.

Global unfairness is also on the rise

It would be easier to identify policy solutions to address unfairness if unequal opportunity and unfair handicaps were uniquely

European problems. But they are a global challenge, despite the comforting mantra heard in richer countries that the 21st century has already seen 'over a billion people pulled out of poverty'. A substantial proportion of them have been Chinese, whose livelihoods improved when their huge country was riding the crest of the demographic wave that is now subsiding.

The world is getting more unfair, not less. Recent years have seen the global wealth gap widen faster than at any time since the Second World War. The trend towards increasingly concerted international development policies has also gone sharply into reverse. Hunger – exacerbated by the COVID-19 pandemic and its aftermaths – is growing. Five UN agencies jointly reported in mid-2023 that 9.2 per cent of humanity, some three-quarters of a billion people, are chronically undernourished. Africans are the chief victims, but food insecurity is also rampant in Latin America. In Brazil, for example, half the population suffers from poor diets and irregular nourishment.[5]

The plight of the world's hungry is a familiar topic of TV reporting, and it's even possible that these reports may have blunted rather than sharpened the impact on public opinion. Global television has arguably contributed a more reassuring image of skyscrapers and prosperous cityscapes in what were formerly labelled 'Third World' countries, hiding the reality of the widening gap between the very rich and the poor. A top tenth of humankind owns well over half the world's wealth, while a tiny 8.5 per cent of that wealth is spread among the 4.5 billion people who make up the bottom half of the global population.[6]

Only a fifth of the UN's 200 or so member states can claim to genuinely share prosperity between their citizens, according to a new way to measure inequalities. This was devised in 2011 by a Chilean economist working in the UK at Cambridge University. José Gabriel Palma's index reflects the ratio between the income shared between a country's wealthiest top 10 per cent and that to be shared out to the bottom 40 per cent. Unlike the long-established Gini coefficient, the Palma Index doesn't focus solely on shifting wealth patterns within the global middle-class, and therefore underlines the way the rich have been getting richer.

The rise around the world of a new global middle-class is nevertheless an important counterweight to the polarisation of wealth. In the 1980s, four-tenths of mankind still lived in conditions of extreme poverty. Since then, urbanisation and education have seen a huge shift away from subsistence farming into more added-value jobs, so today only 8 per cent are classified as living in extreme poverty.

Perceptions are shaped, though, by visibility. In a world of almost instant communications, people in rich countries may know a bit more about the poor, but the world's underprivileged who had previously been unaware of the extent of their plight are now bombarded by media images of wealth elsewhere. Add to this the pressures of climate change on agrarian communities, and the ingredients for geopolitical disruption are hard to ignore. The world's richer countries may fret over their slow growth since the financial and economic crises of 2008–10, exacerbated by the COVID-19 pandemic, but it's the so-called Global South that suffers the most.

Today's unfairnesses may not be those of tomorrow

It's tempting to see socio-economic trends in straight lines, but the disruptive potential of digital and biological technologies is liable to throw some very large spanners in the works. It's therefore too soon to say whether technological revolutions such as AI or genetically modified organisms (GMO) will, in the context of Europe's ageing, be forces for good or bad.

The positive view of robotisation and AI is that it will spawn products and services that compensate for our shrinking workforces, and thus resolve many of the problems of ageing. But not everyone accepts the idea that the problems of ageing can be resolved by digital technologies. The counter-view is that these will benefit only a small elite and greatly disadvantage the bulk of European citizens who lack know-how and resources to invest.

If AI does indeed polarise societies, then it seems fair to assume that it will aggravate the tensions already being created by ageing. The OECD has warned that the mass adoption of generative AI in the workplace is likely to trigger a wave of job losses, along with a host of difficult and highly divisive ethical issues.

These ethical questions are becoming worryingly familiar and widespread. AI will pose serious challenges to transparency, accountability and privacy. Legislators in different countries and with opposing political sympathies are trying hard, but so far unsuccessfully, to agree new rules that will protect humanity from misuses of invasive new software.

It is plain that the digital revolution will challenge professions and processes that have long been sheltered from change, or have resisted it. Many jobs in medicine, finance and the law are at risk from the greater efficiencies of AI and robotics. The OECD reckons that along with managerial jobs and those in financial services, more than a quarter of all employment in developed countries will be vulnerable to AI.

It's not just skilled factory workers and engineers who could be replaced by smart machines, but also 'creative' occupations that rely on experience, judgement and even pure talent. Finding new work opportunities for displaced professionals, executives and senior civil servants won't be easy, and promises years of turmoil in the labour markets. Goldman Sachs estimates that 300 million jobs could be lost worldwide.

These would in the main be well-paid positions, so mass redundancies in private sector corporations and public administrations could easily turn the insecurities of ageing in Europe into a more chaotic upheaval of its market economies. The highly privileged elites of wealthy Western nations might themselves become the victims of unfairness.

That's the gloomier side of the AI/robotics coin. The sunnier side holds promise for technically proficient younger people. The Goldman Sachs analysts who forecast massive job losses also predict surging productivity improvements that might in the long run help compensate for so many redundancies.

If generative AI can be harnessed to hundreds of less efficient jobs, they say, a 7 per cent increase in global output could be achieved by around 2035. Another study reckons that generative AI could eventually add $4 trillion a year – as much as Germany's GDP – to the global economy, adding that non-generative AI and automation could boost it over the coming decades by a further $11 trillion.[7]

But sceptics point out that digitalisation has yet to deliver the productivity bonanza first promised back in the 1990s. With labour shortages now braking economic growth in most European countries, the need for a productivity fillip is greater than ever. Optimists hope that AI's new era of 'thinking' super-computers will at last make up for the declining numbers of workers, and therefore taxpayers.

That would still leave the problem of the millions of computer innumerate people who make up the bulk of European society. Just as in the late 19th century, Arthur Balfour in Britain and Jules Ferry in France championed hugely ambitious education drives to create more literate workforces, so too should computer literacy be the basis of sweeping education reforms across Europe. The aim should be to ensure there won't be a resentful new *lumpenproletariat* condemned to unskilled low-wage jobs.

Could Europe's ageing trigger a 'fairness' revolution?

Ancient Athens struggled with wealth distribution problems that were remarkably similar to those we face today. Solon, the 6th-century BC city-state's ruler and lawgiver, was so concerned that the gap between rich and poor threatened stability that he introduced rules limiting aristocrats' political power and influence. It was a very early form of democracy, even though he's seldom credited for this.

Despite being a privileged aristocrat himself, Solon's solution to the excessive wealth of the Athenian high-born was to abolish their hereditary rights to public office and encourage the emerging middle-class to enter politics. He also promoted the spread of schooling among the lower orders, thus preceding by almost three millennia Labour prime minister Tony Blair's call in the mid-1990s for 'education, education, education' as the solution to Britain's problems.

Solon's worry was that the widening gap between the rich and poor would eventually tear society apart. Much the same fears can today be heard across Europe, and in America too, with falling living standards among the underprivileged fuelling right-wing extremism more visibly than they stimulate electoral support for the left. Solon's solution was to increase the involvement of the citizenry in the political process, and to limit the powers of the super-wealthy. A comparable exercise might conceivably emerge in European countries if the tensions of ageing continue to grow so great that they make radical reform the less daunting option.

Measures that might narrow the wealth gaps in Europe are suggested throughout this book in the relevant chapters, and are broadly summed up in a 'ten-point strategy' in the final chapter. It's worth emphasising that in addition to practical steps such as overhauling property taxes and pensions, a clear distinction should be drawn between the two very separate areas of wealth – income and assets.

Britain is a case in point. The OECD's observation that the UK has the dubious distinction of being one of the most unequal countries anywhere in terms of income distribution is borne out by its wages profile. A majority of British households take home less than the average pay packet – which in 2022 meant a disposable annual income of £32,000. The top fifth of UK households averaged incomes of almost £84,000 and the bottom fifth only £13,000.

Asset inequalities are even more startling, and here the UK is only averagely unfair. The top tenth of the populations of the OECD's rich countries own half the wealth as expressed in property and financial assets, while the bottom four-tenths own only 3 per cent of the national wealth.

These yawning and politically dangerous disparities are hardly a secret. More than a dozen carefully researched books on wealth inequalities have been published in Britain in less than a decade. But more worrying than the statistics and case histories these authors have assembled is the way they've been unable to ignite the sort of fiery debate they had clearly hoped for. The UK's indolent and irresponsible media has much to answer for.[8]

How to level the playing field

Expropriating the assets of the wealthy isn't the answer, whereas creating a strong wind at the backs of those playing uphill clearly is. It's here that the likely consequences of Europe's demographic change can be turned around to play a positive role.

Rather than repeat the same socially desirable urgings for a fairer society, the predictable impact of the ageing crisis as it evolves offers a practical timeline for reform. The same was said of climate change, and the slowness and reluctance with which environmental goals are being met stands as a warning. Unless society suffers warning pains, its usual response to looming disaster is inertia.

As it happens, ageing is beginning to exert discomfort that will before long deteriorate into pain. Youth unemployment at a time when labour shortages are starting to bite hard is a good example, as are the strains on public healthcare imposed by ageing. More than a tenth of under-thirties in the UK and continental Europe are now stuck in the limbo of being neither in education nor in a job. Many of them are in a household without a breadwinner, and so are entirely dependent on social security benefits.

These underprivileged and usually undereducated young people could yet make a huge contribution to European society and to the economy. The number of young unemployed had begun to shrink as EU countries emerged from the austerity conditions that followed the 2008–10 financial crisis. Now, with employers crying out more desperately than ever for workers, the conditions are ripe for much more ambitious training and education programmes.

The same goes for immigrants, both second-generation and more recent arrivals. They represent a strand of European society that has too often been denied the privileges of indigenous young people, and as a result are either in low-skilled work or are unemployed. They, too, should be given greater training and educational advantages. Their manpower is crucially important to European countries suffering waves of retirements, and that before long will see their populations shrinking.

Younger people classified as 'inactive' make up a valuable reservoir of potential workers. Some could help tackle the problems of public healthcare where projected needs not just of hospitals and general practice surgeries are a growing headache, as is the unsatisfied demand for home carers. A revolutionary approach to carers' wages, back-up and training is essential, and inactive young people and underprivileged immigrants could help fill multiplying vacancies.

These and other ideas for engaging with the millions of Europeans listed as 'discouraged' from the active labour force may be derided as pie in the sky, but the sheer scale of European countries' demographic shifts says otherwise. These countries, whether in the EU or out, face unprecedented problems that will not be resolved by the timid fine-tuning of outdated policies.

Shrinking workforces will mean a reduced output of goods and services unless there's a huge productivity boost. With the digital era's robotics having so far failed to deliver hoped-for improvements in productivity, it's down to AI to streamline the European economies. As the hoary old Irish joke has it, 'If I wanted to get there, I wouldn't have started from here.'

As matters stand, ageing Europe has little option but to harness more manpower to its economy – more workers and therefore more taxpayers – while waiting for the so-called fourth industrial revolution to pay greater dividends. This isn't a message that Europeans' political leaderships are keen to broadcast. As well as offending many voters, it would involve sacrifices by the 'haves' as part of a concerted effort to restore a better socio-economic equilibrium with the 'have nots'.

We don't need to go back to Solon of Athens to see what happens when warnings of social imbalance are ignored. The 18th-century *philosophes* like Voltaire who presaged the French Revolution and the fall of the Bourbon monarchy's *ancien régime* were followed by Karl Marx and other 19th-century thinkers who paved the way to the Bolshevik revolution in Russia and the chaos of the 20th century. There's much ominous talk these days of the patterns of 1930s Europe being repeated a century later.

It's always possible that Europeans' vaunted social guarantees will save their countries from bloody upheavals, but that might not spare their economies from dying from a thousand cuts. Unless Europeans wake fully to the scale of ageing and its debilitating effects, they may find themselves echoing the words of T.S. Eliot in his poem 'The Hollow Men': 'This is the way the world ends; not with a bang but a whimper.'

4

Europe's grim demographics

Europe's demographics are a rollercoaster. At first its population exploded, and then its birthrate imploded. From 1970 to 2015, Europeans increased in number by 25 per cent to about half a billion, but fertility plummeted. The population is stable until 2040, but will be ageing fast, and then it will shrink rapidly, with 50 million fewer people. The average birthrate of 1.5 children per couple means dwindling workforces and thus stagnating economies. Africa and the Arab world share the dynamism and the dangers of population explosions.

'Demography is destiny' say those who believe a country's population size and generational balance define its horizons and limitations. Others disagree, warning that these projections are revised often enough to dangerously mislead policy makers.

Demographers are sometimes dismissed as wonks who battle fruitlessly over statistical nuances. Until fairly recently, demographics seemed the preserve of nerds who pore over census figures and social surveys but fail to produce 'useful' policy guidance.

That's no longer true, if it ever was; politicians and business leaders are waking to the tectonic shifts that demographers track. Although only a small subgroup of the 'Dismal Science' of economics, and few in number compared with the legions of economists in banks and big corporations, demographers' projections are winning more and more respect.

The big picture that demographers paint is of a world turned upside down. Regions long vulnerable to overpopulation are being reassessed as possessing human resources vital to sustained economic growth. By mid-century, the world's ten largest countries by population will include Nigeria, Pakistan, Bangladesh and Ethiopia. Richer countries, meanwhile, must brace for the ill-effects of ageing and population shrinkage.

Straight-line projections are inherently unreliable; the COVID-19 pandemic and the war in Ukraine trashed some futurologists' most confident scenarios. Demographers fare better, even if their projections sometimes vary because they aren't always based on the same premises. These disagreements can blunt the impact of their warnings, but that shouldn't deafen policy makers to their messages; on major trends such as lifespans, health and social attitudes there's solid consensus.

Demographers emphasise that they deal in hard facts, which isn't always the case with economists. Their raw material is registered births and deaths and the resulting long-term trends that either stimulate or depress economic activity. They can't tell us how social attitudes will evolve or how politics will respond, but they are able to warn of the pressures reshaping many aspects of society in Europe and elsewhere.

It's not only demographers who have been sounding alarm bells. Before being sidelined by China's president Xi Jinping, Jack Ma, the billionaire founder of the online giant Alibaba, joined with Tesla's Elon Musk to warn why population collapse will be a major global problem in the years ahead. When the two business leaders shared a platform at a Shanghai conference on AI, they pinpointed the worldwide 'baby bust' as the greatest challenge to economic growth and living standards.

That was back in 2019, the same year that saw a similar message from Vladimir Putin. The Russian leader confided to journalists that of all his country's problems, population decline 'haunts' him the most. Some Kremlin-watchers speculate that his invasion of Ukraine in 2022 was not so much a land grab but a people grab: 'recovering' Ukraine's population of 44 million would help compensate for the Russian Federation's drastic demographic shrinkage.

Not everyone shares the view that demography is a signpost to the future. 'Don't place too much faith in demographic forecasts,' warns a journalist friend. As a globe-trotting Reuters correspondent, he reckons that more than a few 'black swan' surprises from a maverick politician or an external economic shock have upended policies based on seemingly incontrovertible forecasts. Black swans are certain to abound in the years ahead, and they'll be breeding enough troublesome cygnets to show how relatively stable the world economy was in the latter part of the 20th century.

Population shifts, migrations and changing patterns of births and deaths have been hotly debated since Thomas Malthus, who warned in early 19th-century England against overpopulation, to John Maynard Keynes. In Britain's post-Depression doldrums of the latter 1930s, Keynes theorised that demographic decline brings falling demand and rising unemployment. Before long, though, the baby boom that followed the Second World War quelled fears of depopulation.

Keynes was following in the footsteps of fellow Englishman John Graunt, generally acknowledged as the founder of demographic research. After his prosperous drapery business burned down in the Great Fire of London in 1666, Graunt turned to what was then dubbed 'political arithmetic' and trashed claims that London's population was 2 million strong. He used parish records of births and deaths to prove it was less than 400,000. The Crown's revenue officials would at least have concrete facts to go on.

To return to 21st-century demographics, even outsized black swans such as COVID-19 and the war in Ukraine cannot alter the overall pattern of a shrinking, ageing Europe. This shrinkage is inevitable. Although its speed and scale are debated, both will certainly come as a surprise to all those policy makers whose thinking is based on years of constant population increases.

Until quite recently, Europe's population had been growing very healthily. Improved healthcare and living conditions were leading to longer lifespans, and that compensated for falling birthrates and the smaller families that had become the norm. Suddenly in 2015, this long-standing trend came to an abrupt end, freezing 55 years of uninterrupted growth in the number of Europeans. Until then Europe's population had been expanding year on year, rising by 25 per cent to peak at just over half a billion souls.[1]

Europe's population figures won't be making any headlines for a while as they are expected to stabilise, or some would say stagnate, until the 2040s. But massive changes are taking shape beneath this placid surface, so the 2040s will trigger a vertiginous downward spiral. Experts at the UN expect the population of the EU – excluding that of the UK and other non-EU countries – to have dropped by the end of this century from its present 446 million to 365 million.

There's a wild card that could slow this trend, and needless to say it's immigration. About 40 million people currently living in Europe were born elsewhere, and over the last half-century they have contributed a sizeable demographic boost. Europe's pool of manpower is reducing at a fast pace, and whether immigration can top it up is an open question. Over 5 million legal migrants arrived in the EU in 2022, many of them Ukrainians, but before then an average year saw about 2 million legal newcomers.

It's impossible to say where Europe's increasingly frenzied political debates over immigration are going, but it's unlikely to counterbalance ageing. If legal immigration stays at today's levels, the EU's working age population will probably shrink from its present 240 million to just 207 million by mid-century. And if public opinion increasingly opposes immigration, so that the flow of newcomers is substantially reduced, the economic impact would be disastrous.[2]

The UN figures, and its scenario for Europe's overall population shrinkage, may in any case turn out to be optimistic. Researchers at the Institute for Health Metrics and Evaluation in the US West Coast city of Seattle created a stir among demographers in mid-2020 when they published an article in the authoritative British medical journal *The Lancet* predicting an even greater fall in the EU's population.

Their alarming estimate is that the population of the 27-nation EU is going to shrink to 308 million rather than the UN-estimated 365 million. They base this on Europe's stubbornly low birthrates. Instead of accepting the UN's premise of an average 1.75 children for each woman in Europe, they reckon on a fertility rate of only 1.41. It's uncertain how abrupt the shift would be from a flourishing population to one that's evaporating before our eyes, but what we can say is that the implications of these two different scenarios range from the troublesome to the catastrophic.[3]

Few people will be aware that up to 2015 Europe's population grew by about 120 million people, because we are far more conscious of our history of emigration. From the 1850s to the outbreak of the First World War, more than 40 million people left for the New World. Some fled anti-semitic pogroms in Russia, Poland and central Europe; others were driven out by famine, as in Ireland, or quite simply by unemployment and wretched living conditions.[4]

That 19th-century exodus didn't check Europe's 20th-century development. This partly explains why opinion is nowadays so divided over the likely impact of demographic change in the 21st century. Optimists cite the environmental benefits of there being fewer people, and even suggest 'less crowding' may be socially advantageous. Pessimists, or realists as they would insist, point to the hard economic facts of life: smaller workforces mean less demand and reduced tax revenues to fund progressive social policies.

Whatever the future holds, some tough adjustments to Europeans' lifestyles and political arrangements lie ahead. There's room for argument over the pros and cons of fewer people, especially in countries where public opinion complains of overcrowding. But that's not true of ageing. The unavoidable fact is that Europeans, whether in the EU or not, are getting older as well as fewer. That's the result of not enough babies at one end of the generational spectrum and substantially longer lives at the other.

The different statistics produced by demographers in universities and research outfits across Europe can be confusing. As well as national statistics, there are averaged figures for EU member states, for all European countries and, because Brexit is comparatively recent, there are still figures for an EU28 that include UK statistics. These gradations, however, can't disguise the broad picture of Europe's future shape and size.

Mid-21st-century scenarios

The demographic projections outlined so far have tended to focus on Europe as it enters the 22nd century. But looking eight decades ahead is too far for most policy scenarios, so it makes more sense to concentrate on mid-century forecasts. These show Europe's ageing acting as a drag on economic growth. It may be that retraining schemes and tax incentives will prompt more enlightened hiring practices that favour older workers, but right now scheduled retirements are set to dramatically shrink the size of workforces.

By 2050, Europeans' median age will be approaching 50 years old, with declining birthrates and longer lifespans having brought about revolutionary changes in our social structures. To put that mid-century average age in perspective, it stood at 36 in 1975 and 25 years later had risen to 38. The first two decades of this century saw it reach 43 in 2020, and by mid-century it will have got to 48.2 and still be rising.[5]

This skewing of the proportion of older folk in relation to younger ones is turning Europe into a gerontocracy. It's far from being just a European problem, but for a number of reasons it's particularly problematic in Europe. The share of 15–29 year olds in the EU population will by mid-century be only 14.9 per cent, down from 16.3 per cent in 2021. It may not sound at first like a dramatic reduction, but this Eurostat projection underscores the speed and scale with which the active workforce is going to shrink.

These numbers haven't yet had much, if any, impact on public consciousness, even though their implications are so serious. Our attitudes to the roles of younger and older people in society and in the workplace are likely to undergo a radical rethink. Young people who have suffered many disadvantages in recent years will most probably win much greater respect when they become middle-aged breadwinners. Older people who have complained of being 'thrown on the scrapheap' when they reach their sixties may also find a new lease of life when employers have to compete for scarce labour.

Until a turnaround occurs in our attitudes to different generations, the manpower shortages caused by ageing and reduced birthrates will bite harder than ever. They will also combine with other maverick factors to create a perfect storm. Russia's invasion of Ukraine, the mounting costs of climate change and rising geopolitical tensions in Asia and across the Pacific Ocean all threaten economic consequences that will be greatly exacerbated by demographic problems.

For Europe, these ill-effects will be most serious in Eastern and Central Europe, where the formerly communist countries that are now EU members already suffer from the exodus of young job-seekers attracted by Western Europe's higher wages. The newer member states' dissatisfaction with the EU's rules and procedures has in recent years become a prominent feature of the EU policy debate, and is likely to deteriorate further.

These are difficulties that demand prompt attention. But they risk eclipsing the more fundamental handicaps that ageing is imposing on Europe. Relatively short-term policy considerations are distracting governments' attention away from long-term trends that also need to be tackled urgently.

It's a short-sightedness that can partly be ascribed to demographers' and economic forecasters' reliance on numbers at the expense of images, so however gloomy their reports may be they don't seize the public imagination. Quality newspapers occasionally publish features and special sections on the different facets of ageing, but these are rarely taken up by the popular press or by ratings-driven TV programmes.

The mass media's appetite for long-term trends could arguably be stimulated by a more imaginative approach from officialdom. It might help, too, if Europe's demographic decline were to be presented as a snowball instead of the near-incomprehensible 'Christmas tree' graphs demographers habitually favour. The growth of the snowball would dramatically illustrate the speed with which society is being transformed. In 1950, only one European in 13 was over 65 years old; today it's approaching one in four.

The easiest 'ready reckoner' way of looking at how its snowballing older population will affect Europe's economy is to trace the shrinkage of the working age population relative to people of pensionable age. In post-Second World War Britain, the ratio of workers to pensioners was 5:1. From the 1960s onwards, that level was sustained for many years by the arrival on labour markets of baby boomers born after the war.

Until fairly recently, the European average had stabilised at around 4:1, so that there were four working age taxpayers to pay for the retirement and healthcare costs of each pensioner. But this 'dependency ratio' is slipping fast, with potentially devastating consequences. It's by no means a new discussion: in the early years of this century, the IMF in Washington, DC predicted that by 2050 the average dependency ratio in Europe will have halved to 2:1. How national governments could fund this widening fiscal chasm became the subject of anxious, but fruitless, discussion among policy makers and their political masters.

Their concerns (and no doubt their sense of helplessness) must have deepened when it was suggested that the IMF's figures erred on the side of optimism. In Brussels, the European Commission revealed that the ratio had by 2019 already reached 2.9:1 and by 2070 is forecast to shrink to 1.7:1. The implications of fewer than two tax paying wage earners to support each pensioner are almost too grim to contemplate.[6]

EU-level statistics hide widening internal chasms

EU officials in Brussels strive to present a coherent overall picture of the European economy. In doing so, they risk disguising stark demographic differences between EU members. These are more than statistical quirks because they point to tensions that could one day tear the EU apart.

Germany is a prime example. Famously seen as the 'locomotive' of the EU economy, it has for many years been uneasily aware of its own demographic vulnerability. The German dependency ratio is forecast to shrink to as little as 1.4:1 by 2050, which conjures visions of a society so desperately short of manpower that the question of whether it can still be Europe's economic locomotive is now seldom heard.[7]

As well as raising doubts over the future health of the European economy, the demographic profiles of EU countries and those outside it are significant for a number of other reasons. The right to free movement between EU countries is one of the cornerstones of the 'European project', but an unintended consequence is that it's sapping solidarity between member governments. The flow of younger people from poorer EU countries to richer ones is compounding the less wealthy member states' demographic difficulties.

Germany

The federal government in Berlin has been deeply concerned for some time by Germany's demographic vulnerability. It has been putting in place strategies to counter the effects of ageing and population shrinkage. Forewarned is forearmed, so Germany's position may eventually turn out to be brighter than those of European countries where politicians have surrendered to ostrich tactics, and have buried their heads in the sand in the hope that labour-saving technologies will come miraculously to the rescue.

Germany's situation is nevertheless serious and urgent, and Berlin's chief response has been to greatly increase immigration. Between 2010 and 2020 average net immigration of around a million people more or less compensated for the low birthrate. But that won't be enough now the growing weight of ageing is beginning to tip the country's problem into free-fall.

As well as ageing, there's a parallel problem on the wealth-creating side of the balance sheet. The industries that made many German companies the envy of their competitors around the world risk becoming obsolescent. Germany's prosperity stems in large part from the post-war *wirtschaftswunder* years, when its highly competitive industrial base carved out lucrative export markets around the world.

Germans fear that their diminished labour force will exacerbate the problems of an increasingly outdated manufacturing base, most notably in the engineering and automotive sectors. The spectre that haunts Germany's boardrooms is of ever-tougher competition from Asia now that microelectronics are supplanting mechanical engineering. A third of Germany's population will be over 60 years old by 2050, up from around a quarter in 2020, so some leading German policy makers are beginning to advocate a more aggressive immigration strategy. The overall population peaked not long ago at just over 83 million, having edged up from 82.5 million in 2005, but by 2050 it is forecast to drop vertiginously to below 69 million.[8]

It's not just the shortage of workers that worries Germany but also the squeeze on consumption and tax revenues. Unless something can be done to attract more migrants, the under-twenties who represent tomorrow's pool of labour will within a few years have shrunk to 15 per cent of the population from 30 per cent in the post-war years.

The political significance of waves of newcomers coming to Germany isn't lost on the planners. If they succeed in enticing the 20 million immigrants who many of them believe are needed, the country's non-native migrant community will by mid-century have surged from around 13 per cent of the present population to a quarter or more.

Germany is already embroiled in an increasingly bitter political tussle between those who urge more immigration and populist politicians who are capitalising on negative public opinion. The German people who at first accepted the 1.5 million or so Syrians and Afghans who arrived during the 2015–16 'migrant crisis' – just as they later accommodated streams of Ukrainian refugees – are becoming less welcoming. There are growing doubts over public tolerance of immigration in the long term.

France

In common with other European nations, France faces demographic disruption. But so far its long-standing policy of subsidising larger families is cushioning it from the worst effects. French anxieties about fertility can perhaps be traced back to the First World War of 1914–18 and the slaughter of the flower of the nation's youth. It was after the Second World War, however, that President Charles de Gaulle's ministers introduced measures to reward higher birthrates.

As well as the French government's financial inducements, employers are required to grant generous maternity leave and guarantee post-natal job security. The result has been a stable population when the rest of Europe has been struggling with reductions in overall numbers and in the size of their active workforce. A fertility rate of around 1.9 children per woman has, with a modest topping up through net immigration, maintained metropolitan France's population at 65 million. The figures are confused by the further 2.25 million people in France's overseas *départements* in the Caribbean and elsewhere, but the key population number that French demographers foresee is 70 million by 2050. At that point, France overtakes Germany's predicted 69 million inhabitants to become the EU's most populous member state.

That doesn't mean France escapes the problems of ageing suffered by other European nations, although they will be less intense. Years of buoyant birthrates have done much to help France sustain the size of its workforce. In 2010, the French fertility rate had climbed back to 2.02 from its mid-1990s slump of around 1.7. That was still only a shade above the replacement rate of 2.01 children per couple, and far from the 3.0 rate France chalked up during the 1960s.

The growth of the elderly population is France's chief concern. By mid-century, the present cohort of 13 million over-sixties will have almost doubled to 22 million, half of whom will be over 75 years old. Looked at in healthcare terms, the most worrying increase of all is the way France's 1 million over-85s will by mid-century have snowballed to 4 million.

United Kingdom

The crown for total population size in Europe at one point looked set to go outside the EU. The UK could yet become the most populous European country if it were to accept EU countries' average levels of immigration, both from continental Europe and elsewhere.

The UK birthrate was until recently 1.9 children per couple, almost the same as France's, but the post-Brexit slowdown in youthful economic migrants from other European countries, coupled with the retirement of Britain's large baby boomer cohort, is substantially eroding that advantage. The birthrate has slumped close to the European average of 1.5, with cutbacks to financial supports for low-income families thought to be the chief reason.

Before Brexit, the Office for National Statistics projected a population of 73 million by 2045. The expected increase from 67 million in 2020 reflected a combination of the factors that had made the UK a powerful magnet for young people from continental Europe. Their arrival had been swelling the British labour force at a speed envied by the rest of Europe. Since Brexit, that inflow has been slowed by restrictive measures that pandered to voters' supposed anti-immigrant prejudices.

The combination of factors that brought millions of young workers to Britain cannot easily be replicated. Flexible employment conditions, the familiarity of many younger Europeans with the English language and a booming services sector, especially in bars and restaurants, had attracted comparatively well-educated migrant labour to add value to the British economy.

Pre-Brexit Britain was a textbook example of the benefits of immigration as a counterbalance to long-standing labour shortages in farms and factories. This advantage was discarded almost overnight after the UK's mid-2016 referendum decision to leave the EU, and when anti-immigration sentiment was cited by the then Conservative government as a reason to choke off younger migrant workers.

As Britain adapts to life outside the EU, there are hopes that common sense will prevail over the nationalism and even outright xenophobia that brought the Brexiteers their increasingly regretted referendum victory. In the meantime, 'Global Britain' must shape its economic policy making to a future in which a quarter of the population will be of pensionable age by as soon as 2040. The strains on the country's public finances may in the intervening years become so serious that the 'taking back control' mantra will give way to more concrete needs.

Italy, Spain and Poland

Italy, Spain and Poland have all seen their birthrates tumble. The three most traditionally Catholic of the EU's bigger countries, where large families had been the norm, are nowadays among Europe's least fertile nations.

Their demographic profiles have become major sources of political friction. Anti-migrant sentiment fuelled controversial populist policies in Poland (in contrast with many Poles' humanitarian sympathy for Ukrainian refugees) and has been a political catalyst in Italy and Spain.

The rejection of increased immigration by many voters has seriously negative implications. All three countries combine depressed birthrates with low levels of female participation in the active workforce. If public opinion continues to oppose African and Arab immigration that could stabilise their shrinking workforces, these countries will have to reconcile themselves to mounting economic woes.

In Spain the fertility rate is 1.23 children per woman, in Italy 1.27 and in Poland 1.3, so the demographic outlook for all three is grim. There have been predictions in Italy of native Italians 'becoming a minority in their own country' by 2080 if the current yearly shrinkage of the indigenous population continues.

That may be anti-migrant rhetoric, but the reduction of the country's already slender tax base is real enough. Unless immigration is allowed to pick up substantially, predictions that Italy's population will shrink disastrously from some 60 million to only 28 million by this century's end might turn out to be correct.

Spain has in the past been able to call on Latin America for migrant labour. The severe recession after the 2008 global financial crisis saw several million workers in the construction industry return home, but they are still seen as a useful Spanish-speaking resource that Madrid can rely upon. Spain's major difficulty once the demographic crisis fully takes hold will be rural depopulation. Almost two-thirds of its territory is classed as severely underpopulated, and that trend is accelerating.

Eastern and Central Europe

The newest members of the EU will be the hardest hit by population ageing and shrinking. Two decades after achieving their post-communist ambitions of admission to the EU, they find themselves paying a heavy price for membership. Their young people have been leaving in droves for the higher salaries and more attractive lifestyles of western Europe.

The years since the 1989 fall of the Berlin Wall have seen more and more people from former Soviet satellite countries moving to Western Europe. The exodus gathered pace after 2004, once EU membership opened the way to the free movement of people, goods and capital within the EU. More than 8 million have left over 15 years, most of them younger men and women whose departure significantly lowered the birthrates of the countries they were quitting.[9]

The countries of mainland Europe that joined the EU as part of the 'Big Bang' enlargement of 2004 – not counting, therefore,

Malta and Cyprus – are extremely vulnerable to demographic change. Their very low fertility is combining with emigration to create an alarmingly vicious circle. Bulgaria is perhaps the worst hit, as it expects its population to decrease by 40 per cent over the six decades to mid-century. Comparatively prosperous Croatia is almost as badly affected, and is bracing to cope with a likely 25 per cent shrinkage.

Outside the EU, the impact will be equally bad in the Balkans because of intractable development problems there. The countries that suffered most in the fighting of the 1990s must steel themselves for dizzying falls in their populations. By 2050, Kosovo will be 11 per cent smaller in population, Serbia 24 per cent and Bosnia 37 per cent.[10]

This haemorrhaging of poorer countries' young people to richer ones threatens profound geopolitical consequences. Enlargement of the EU was designed to accelerate economic convergence within a Europe that had been divided by the Iron Curtain. But demographic decline and the lure of Western Europe's better jobs risks cancelling out the benefits that EU membership promised to the poorer newcomers. The wealth gap between Western and Eastern Europe is set to widen rather than narrow, imposing strains on Europe's cohesion and even the future integrity of the EU.

Baltic Republics

Emigration and low fertility are major problems, too, for the Baltic republics. The difference is that Estonia, Latvia and Lithuania also enjoy much higher standards of living and excellent educational levels that have placed them in the vanguard of the Digital Age. The speed with which all three adapted their economies to digital technologies has, though, proved to be a double-edged sword. Many of their multilingual, highly educated youngsters have seized on better-paid job opportunities elsewhere in the EU, and most of all in the UK.

In the quarter-century after their independence from the defunct USSR, the Baltic republics collectively suffered the world's steepest proportional drop in population. By 2015, one person in five had emigrated, and this has set a pattern of demographic decline that continues apace.

In the wider scheme of things, a steady flow of bright young Balts heading west isn't earth-shaking. But the Baltic republics' very difficult relationship with neighbouring Russia introduces a sensitive geopolitical and security element. In Latvia, one person emigrates every half-hour. 'Latvia may cease to be a nation' warns a prominent journalist in Riga, the capital. He was echoing forecasts that its population will be almost halved by the end of this century to 1.25 million from over 2.4 million in 2000.

Much the same population drain prevails in its neighbours. Lithuania's 1990 population of 3.7 million is due to fall to 2.5 million by 2060, while Estonians may number only 1.1 million by 2030. All three Baltic republics have successfully embraced Europe and the rigours of transition to a market economy, but the lure of greater personal opportunities is enticing away a worryingly high proportion of their younger people.

Russian Federation

Three-quarters of Russia's population lives west of the Urals, and the contrast between 'European Russia' and the sparsely inhabited steppes and wildernesses of Siberia underlines the fact that Russia not only shares Europe's demographic destiny but is also much harder hit by it. The slowdown in births that has gripped Russia with increasing severity since the end of the Second World War looks set to be compounded by the consequences of President Vladimir Putin's invasion of Ukraine.

Within weeks of Putin's 'special military operation' against the Kyiv government, an astounding 300,000 young Russians, many with advanced technical qualifications, left for neighbouring countries. As well as Turkey, others headed for Scandinavian and Baltic states. A similar number reportedly left in a second wave when conscription was announced. Over the 20 years of Putin's presidency, estimates the nation's Rosstat statistical service, upwards of 5 million people have emigrated to make a new life elsewhere.[11]

Russia's demographic decline began long before that of Western Europe. The deaths of 23 million or more people in the 'Great Patriotic War', as Russians call the Second World War, were not only the highest toll in the struggle against Nazi Germany but also a demographic body blow from which the nation has never recovered. Because most of those deaths were among the young men and women of the Red Army, the progeny of future generations has progressively shrunk.

The most radical and pessimistic projections for Russia predict a fall in the population of almost a third over the first half of the 21st century. Its 145 million people in 2000 could be reduced to 104 million by 2050, according to a UN forecast. Less dramatically, the World Bank sees mid-century Russia numbering 132 million people, while in Moscow, RANEPA, the National Economy and Public Administration, reckons 128 million.

The US Census Bureau reported in 2003 that it expects the Russian population to dip to 118 million. In 1999, the late Murray Feshbach, a prominent American expert on Russia's demography, had predicted its mid-21st-century population would slump to an astounding 80 million, calling the country a 'sick and shrinking nation'.

The gaps between these projections are chiefly explained by the variable factors that determine population shifts – in other words, births and deaths. Russia records more abortions proportionately than any other nation on earth, and is making major efforts to reduce this. In rural areas, abortion was seen in Soviet days as a form of contraception: in 1965, there were 5.5 million abortions nationwide; in 2000, that had shrunk to just over 2 million, and Moscow aims to halve the present yearly total of 0.5 million within the coming years.

Russian abortion rates reflect economic as well as cultural influences. The mounting hardships imposed on many Russians in the wake of the Ukraine war is expected to further discourage larger families. Russia's fertility rate is already very low, having dropped from 1.5 children per childbearing woman at the turn of the century to 1.4 today, and is slated to drop lower still.

The other factor is, of course, deaths. Russia's combination of high rates of smoking and drinking with relatively modest healthcare has produced one of the highest mortality levels among developed countries. It has been getting worse over the past half-century: in 1970, there were nine deaths annually per 1,000 people, and by 2020, partially boosted by the COVID-19 pandemic, that had risen to almost 13 deaths.

Russia's population shrinkage is at odds with Vladimir Putin's vision of a full return to the superpower status of the Soviet Union, or of the Tsarist Russian empire before 1917. However ambitious its military designs may be, Russia's diminishing workforce condemns it to economic stagnation and falling living standards. By 2030, there are due to be a quarter fewer 20–40-year-old workers than 20 years earlier, presaging a dramatic fall-off in Russia's productivity and well-being.[12]

It's not just Europe that's ageing and shrinking

China, Japan and South-East Asia

There's broad agreement among demographers that over the next 50 years China is doomed to follow many of its Asian neighbours along the road to an ageing, shrinking society. It is hard to imagine this when China's massive and increasingly sophisticated workforce is making inroads into global markets, but the evidence is irrefutable.

The ruthless 'one-child policy' introduced in 1973 is at the root of China's declining population. Chinese society's strong cultural preference for boy children also led to the widespread abortion of girl babies during the policy's 30-year span. The precise speed and scale of China's looming demographic change is much debated. The factors that will determine the details are variables, but the fundamental facts are clear – the Chinese are getting older and fewer in number at an accelerating pace.

By the end of this century, China's population of 1.4 billion may have halved to 730 million. That's the forecast of researchers at the University of Washington in Seattle – often called '*The Lancet* team' because their arresting projections are published in this highly regarded British medical science journal. The core of the Seattle-based team's findings on China and elsewhere is their questioning of long-standing fertility assumptions. They posit even lower birthrates. China's fertility rate of 1.6 children per woman is already lower than America's 1.73, and for political and cultural reasons China seems certain to refuse large-scale immigration to stem the shrinkage of its population and of its productive labour force.

The one-child policy was formally scrapped in 2015 and abortions are now actively discouraged. But the damage has been done. Also, expensive housing and the rising cost of living have dampened many people's desire for a large family, so coupled with the irreversible impact of the one-child years, the shape of Chinese society is changing astonishingly fast.

As recently as 2000, nine people in China's active workforce supported each pensioner, but by mid-century that dependency ratio will have shrunk to 2:1. The 9:1 figure was the legacy of China's previous fertility rate of 4.6 children per couple, and its abrupt reduction is responsible for the dramatic shrinkage of the workforce that's now under way.

The corollary to infertility is the pace at which China is ageing. By 2045, the proportion of over-65s in the Chinese population will have climbed from today's 12 per cent to 25 per cent, and by some calculations may even reach 33 per cent. This huge nation that transformed itself from a peasant society into the workshop of the world is changing once again, this time into a vast retirement home.

In China as elsewhere, no one can know whether new technologies will revolutionise long-standing industrial and agricultural practices, but a radical change in the balance between producers and consumers seems unlikely. The reduction in available manpower coupled with the ballooning of unproductive older people suggests a different nation to today's assertive China with its superpower ambitions.

What of China's Asian neighbours? The unyielding pressures of demographic change that 'Rising China' will encounter are vividly illustrated by Japan and South Korea. Within living memory, Japan has gone from being a fearsome industrial powerhouse wreaking havoc among its international competitors to an increasingly geriatric and inward-looking society. As to South Korea, its economic dynamism is threatened by ageing trends that will see almost half of the population over 65 by mid-century. This is already transforming the country's age-old social structures.

Although Japan skilfully adapted to pronounced ageing with an array of social measures, it now has to face the long-term consequences of a diminishing population. It offers a case study of demographic change's impact on a sophisticated and wealthy economy. 'Japanisation' has become shorthand to describe the choking off of growth once the active labour force begins to shrink and rural areas lose their young people.

Japan's population peaked in 2008 at 128 million, but according to some forecasts it could plunge to 100 million by the late 2040s and drift lower still to 86 million by 2060. The IMF has warned that the combination of an ageing and shrinking population is severely affecting the Japanese economy, knocking a percentage point off its GDP growth rate for the foreseeable future.

South Korea's situation is no less alarming. It holds the world record for infertility, having seen births per woman of child-bearing age drop precipitously from 0.98 in 2018 to 0.84 in 2020. That same year also saw the country's population reach almost 52 million, the beginning of a long slide toward a projected 30 million or so by 2090. The impact on the extraordinarily dynamic South Korean high-tech industries remains to be seen. The overall economic effect is unlikely to be positive as a fifth of the population is already over 65 years old, and by the late 2060s the country's elderly retirees are projected to outnumber the active workforce.

The outlook for the industrial giants of East Asia is very different to those of the ten generally poorer countries that make up the Association of Southeast Asian Nations (ASEAN). Although they are an extremely mixed bag, ranging in size from tiny Singapore and Brunei up to the Philippines and Indonesia, their overall demographic picture is comparatively stable and positive. The decade up to 2030 sees ASEAN's combined populations rising from some 650 million to 725 million with a fast-growing youthful labour force. Indonesia accounts for around half of the bloc's weight and clout, but as a group they will represent significant economic competition in the years ahead.

In the Asian numbers game, India and Pakistan will unsurprisingly be the major players as the 21st century unfolds. Although India's fertility rate has dropped to 2.0, just below the replacement rate of 2.1 children per couple, its already youthful population is set to push its total numbers to 1.6 billion by 2050. Pakistan's fertility rate of around 3.5, meanwhile, will by 2050 have boosted its population to 300 million from 220 million in the mid-2020s.

Both of these slowly developing giants of the Indian subcontinent have a long way to go in their efforts to catch up industrially with other Asian nations, but the economic advantages of youthful and increasingly educated workforces make them likely winners in an international economy now being turned upside down by demographic shifts.

Africa and the Arab world

A quarter of all the people on earth will by mid-century be Africans, and by 2100 that could be a third. The African population's 2.5 per cent yearly growth rate means it's increasing at twice the rate of the global population. By 2050, the African continent's population will have risen from 1.2 billion to 2.5 billion, and possibly 2.7 billion.

Of late, there appears to be a slowdown in Africa's fertility rate, with a UN survey showing that Nigeria's projected population by 2100 rising from its present 220 million or so to 550 million rather than the almost 900 million once forecast. That's based on a fertility rate in Nigeria that was almost six children per couple in 2015 and by 2021 was being calculated at less than five.

Whether that's a blip or a trend remains to be seen. In any event, how Africa's rising population can be turned from trouble into triumph remains a conundrum of truly global proportions. The youthfulness of Africa's 54 nation states holds out the promise of exponential growth and development, but it also threatens greatly increased famine and armed conflict.

Right now, Africa's demography is more a problem than a promise of better times to come. Half of all Africans are under 25 years old, and only one in six of these young people has work in the sense of a regular full-time job. Matching Africa's rapid population growth with far more employment opportunities seems a distant, almost Utopian hope. Greatly improved agricultural output to feed a hungry world is an obvious answer, but the tide is running against that. Africa's smallholder farmers are leaving for the cities, so the third of Africans who are urban will within a few decades have grown to two-thirds.

A revolutionary introduction of modern farming techniques and effective storage and transport is needed if Africans are to feed themselves, let alone others. As to industrial growth, for all the upbeat talk of 'Africa Rising', the reality is that poor infrastructure and limited electrification have choked back investment. In the 1990s, manufacturing accounted for 17 per cent of African GDP, and since then it has sunk to 11 per cent.

The demography of the Arab world, meanwhile, can best be described as similar but very different. Population increases in many Middle Eastern and North African nations will be no less disruptive, but their improved levels of education and long-established urban infrastructures offer a sounder base for economic development.

The combined populations of the 22 Arab countries more than doubled in the quarter-century since the mid-1990s, rising from around 180 million then to 415 million in 2020, and are projected to reach a half-billion by 2030. The region's political volatility and religious frictions make these rapid population increases quite literally explosive.

Latin America, the Caribbean and the US

The picture in the Americas is markedly different to that of Africa and Asia. National populations have increased, but at a steady arithmetical rate rather than at the geometric speed of China, India and the Arab world. In richer northern America, where low fertility has been similar to the trends in Europe, immigration is doing much to reinvigorate their populations. For many poorer southern and central American countries, emigration northwards is a vitally important economic safety valve.

At the 20th century's midpoint, the inhabitants of South America, Central America and the islands of the Caribbean numbered 200 million. The population of the US was 150 million and that of Canada 14 million. All have increased at a manageable speed. Seventy-five years on, the Latin American population has risen threefold to 660 million, en route to 780 million by 2050. That of the US has rather more than doubled to 335 million – with much of the increase due to immigration from its southern neighbours, and there are almost 40 million Canadians thanks in large part to policies that encourage immigrants. By 2050, there are expected to be 400 million Americans and almost 50 million Canadians.

Donald Trump's 2016–20 presidency saw the northward flow of migrants slow markedly. This was partly caused by his much-derided wall along the Mexican border, but most of all by the Trump administration's equally controversial clampdown on 'illegals'. But with America's fertility rate down to 1.73, labour market experts are warning of the consequences of further reduced immigration.

Contrasting effects of the global baby bust

The wealth gap is widening between the rich nations grouped in the G20 and the overwhelming majority of poorer countries that make up the bulk of the UN's 200 members. Despite the many concerns over runaway population growth among the latter, attention increasingly centres on the different impacts of the worldwide baby bust.

The World Bank reports that the global birthrate has fallen sharply over the past 50 years, from an average of just over five children per woman to 2.4. This is why demographers generally agree that humanity will reach 'peak population' at some point in the next 30 to 40 years. The long-standing UN forecast of the world's population reaching 10.8 billion has therefore been revised on the basis of declining birthrates in even the poorest countries. It's now estimated that a high point of 9.7 billion may be reached in 2064, and will slide down to 8.8 billion by the end of this century.[13]

Concerns over humanity's responsibility for climate change rightly dominate the global agenda. But influential analysts have also begun to warn of the perils of population decline. There will be a marked contrast between poor countries grappling with population explosions and rich ones assailed by shortages of workers and consumers.

What they will have in common is a global economy suffering from the ill-effects of demographic fluctuations. In countries where ageing is diverting more spending to pensions and away from investment and savings, some experts believe the result will be higher interest rates and inflation. Others advance an opposite scenario of deflation and excessive savings that dampen consumption. Opinion is divided over the degree to which less-developed countries will suffer from the demographic upset. Some argue that in our interdependent world they'll be hit by the global baby bust along with more advanced ones. Others say their continued population growth will sharpen their competitive edge.

Falling demand resulting from fewer consumers was certainly John Maynard Keynes' worry. He feared this would trigger more unemployment and therefore lower growth. Rather than higher interest rates, Keynes pointed to a long-term decline in interest rates that would discourage investment. His view is being echoed almost a hundred years later by academic researchers in the US. Emphasising that the over-fifties will rise from 25 per cent today to 40 per cent of the global population by 2100, they argue that ageing at this rate will increase savings, and this in turn will depress both inflation and interest rates.[14]

The reality is that no one knows where the global economy is heading. New technologies, the reordering of geopolitics, climate change and the impact of future pandemics that potentially could be more devastating than COVID-19 are all wild cards to upset the forecasts. But in the absence of any radical changes, there seems a degree of consensus in two broad areas: deteriorating fiscal trends in rich countries and improved living standards in poorer ones.

Researchers at the IMF, the European Commission and universities around the world point to big changes in tax policies and social benefits in developed countries. The OECD's richer countries are expected to see a huge increase in yearly health costs that currently average $4,000 per head, and by mid-century these could rise in some countries by six percentage points of GDP. Healthcare costs will overtake spending on pensions.[15]

Despite fears in lower-income countries of the widening wealth gap between themselves and richer ones, there are signs that demography may be coming to their rescue. Whereas more advanced economies are slated to see per capita GDP slip by between 0.5 and 1.0 per cent by 2050, in poorer ones the opposite may be true. A wide-ranging 2022 global study has suggested that in almost all of Latin America, Africa and South

Asia, 'there will be a tailwind of growth' that will add up to 1.0 per cent growth to GDPs.[16]

Europe's diverging demographics

Demographic change looks to be the greatest threat of all to the economic and political integration of the EU's member states. The EU is urging ever-closer common energy, defence and economic policies to confront global pressures, but very different national population trends are instead pushing them apart.

Diverging demographic patterns within Europe threaten to fatally weaken the EU's efforts to build its internal strengths and global clout. They reflect the increasingly fluid nature of European society, with substantial movements of people – especially younger ones – from the east and the north to the west and the south, and most of all from the countryside to towns and cities.

Decades of convergence and regional policies at both EU and national levels cannot stem these flows. Yet it's clear that some wide-ranging policy rethinks are needed. The drift from rural to urban life may become a stampede if the structural disadvantages besetting so many farming communities are not tackled.

Two-thirds of Europe's farmers are older than 55, and many have no one to take over from them. The sagging profitability of all but the largest agricultural holdings bodes ill for inheritors or potential buyers. The EU's farm policies are themselves a discouragement, with the latest 'Farm to Fork' reforms of the Common Agricultural Policy aimed at cutting back output so as to meet ambitious new environmental goals.

Europe's huge regional variations make it hard to generalise, but across the EU farmers and those whose livelihoods depend on farming account only for 2 to 5 per cent of the population. Farmers' waning political weight is disguising the importance of preserving rural economies from the Aegean to the Arctic. Policies to counter the pronounced effects of population decline in rural communities should be given much higher priority.

These imbalances are equally visible in Britain. Wealth and human capital has long been drawn to the London region and south-eastern England at the expense of the rest of the UK, and it's getting worse. A report by the Resolution Foundation identified two key drivers in these regional imbalances: 'Young people are leaving rural and coastal communities, which are already older on average than other locations, for urban areas, and low birth rates are a key factor in the ageing of older communities.'[17]

A Eurostat scenario published some years ago underlined this. The population of inner and outer Greater London is expected to be 60 per cent larger by 2060, with other capital cities like the Paris region, Prague and Copenhagen 50 per cent larger. During that time, 15 major regions of Europe stand to lose over a third of their present populations.

The black swans of COVID-19 and Putin's war against Ukraine have reawakened EU policy makers' sense of urgency. Yet the most striking feature of the policies being rolled out is the absence of a demographics-based approach. Taxes and benefit arrangements need to be tailored to encourage investment and jobs in regions that have been haemorrhaging young people.

What, then, will European society look like in 20 years' time, when this century's midpoint is coming into sight? Will Europe, including Britain, have become more cohesive through a deepening of its integration in defence of its global interests? Or will demographic divisions have hardened nationalist fault lines? The answer will depend on whether national leaders recognise, and react to, the fact that deep-seated change is to be forced on European society by generational imbalances.

Europeans are going to see their living standards under serious pressure, bringing to an end decades of steadily improved conditions for all, including the unskilled and less educated. Nobody can say where the line will be drawn between comfortably off Europeans and vulnerable underprivileged ones, but it's plain that education and know-how will be key.

In the years to mid-century, Europe's population will probably hold steady at around 0.5 billion people, but its active workforce will have shrunk by 50 million. Perhaps new technologies will come to the rescue and dramatically boost productivity, enabling Europe's dwindling manpower still to produce the wealth needed to fund the growing legions of pensioners.

So far, despite much hype and many confident forecasts, the Digital Age and its fourth industrial revolution hasn't moved the dial on productivity. It looks as if the deciding factor on whether Europe can cope with ageing will be its degree of awareness of the challenges. If politicians grasp the reality of accelerating demographic change, society could reorder itself to cope with it. Failure to recognise the ways that ageing and infertility will upset delicate social structures threatens chaos and conflict.

5

Gen-Z: golden or blighted youth?

The Gen-Zers and millennials who must bear the brunt of ageing's costs have yet to grasp its threat to their careers and lifestyles. Burdened by mounting debt and rising taxes to pay for their elders' pensions and healthcare, their lot has so far been low wages, insecure jobs and the housing crisis. Are millennials and 'zoomers' 'the unluckiest generations'?

A generation usually defines people born within a period of 25 years; in other words, the average time span between their parents' birth and their own. It's a term that can both confuse and clarify, but it's impossible to avoid using it in any discussion of demographic change and the 21st century's disruption of once immutable generational rhythms.

Nowadays, each generation has its own distinctive label. This started with the 'lost generation' of the 1920s in the aftermath of the First World War, and was followed by the 'baby boomers' who enjoyed the golden years that followed the Second World War. There's some disagreement about the precise time frames since then, but they are broadly as follows.

From the mid-1960s into the 1980s, there was 'Generation X' – so called, perhaps, because it lacked a clear-cut identity. Its successor was dubbed 'Generation Y', but its members were soon being called 'millennials' because they were born and matured in the years spanning the new century. They were followed, of course, by 'Generation Z' – also known as 'Gen-Z' or 'zoomers' – who like the millennials have been born into an era of volatile and largely unpredictable change. Their successors, born from 2010 onwards, are Generation Alpha.

As well as being prey to the upheavals of new technologies and dramatically shifting geopolitics, these generations must bear the brunt of ageing. By 2050, the youngest millennials will be in their fifties, and most zoomers in their forties, but both will have to fund Europe's snowballing elderly population. The costs of retirement and healthcare will be severe in most parts of Europe, and not least in the UK. Ageing's impact will also be global, particularly in China although not so much in the US.

Different characteristics are often attributed to each generation, though they tend to be fictions invented by advertising copywriters. Over the years, some generations have been branded as 'inventive and adventurous' while others were 'conventional and disciplined'. Such labels are about as instructive as zodiacal horoscopes. The real differences are the socio-economic conditions into which successive generations were born, and the ways they respond to pressures and opportunities.

In broad terms, millennials have been dealt the most difficult hand of all, and are waking slowly to the realities of Europe's weakened international clout and its diminishing wealth. Gen-Z, too, will suffer the effects of an ageing population, but being so much younger seems more carefree and optimistic. It could be nicknamed Generation Zzzzzz because it seems to be sleepwalking towards victimhood. It's possible that it may somehow emerge in the 2040s as the beneficiary of a gloriously wealthy and productive Digital Age, but right now the zoomers risk being the luckless inheritors of an environmentally ruined planet and worsening economic turmoil.

Whether they are millennials in their thirties or teenage Gen-Zers, the cultural references of both generations can baffle their elders. That has always been the way, but the difference now is that today's young people must face a world where the once unchangeable balance between generations has been dislocated. Longer lifespans are altering the equilibrium between youth, people in their middle years and those entering old age.

This is especially true in richer countries, but not exclusively so. Demographic change is global. Our greater life expectancy has made us all aware of this shift, but we are less familiar with its many associated problems. Younger people tend to be more conscious of these because they are already having to contend with lower living standards than those of their forebears.

Today's lower wages, higher housing costs and dimmer career prospects for many young people are harbingers of worse to come. The proportion of older people in our populations is growing so fast that today's underprivileged youth is doomed to pay for soaring pension and healthcare costs. The full effects of these handicaps lie several decades ahead, but these are accumulating costs. Mid-century seems the point at which separate trends will combine into full-blown crisis. The speed with which today's decision-takers wake to these darkening clouds and seek shelter will determine whether society takes steps to soften the impact.

Unlike national governments, whose political leaders pander most to older voters, it is unelected and 'faceless' international institutions that have tried to sound the alarm. They have shown themselves to be more alive to intergenerational tensions than the member states. In Brussels, a 'Cult of the Young' is trying to take root inside the EU. Ambitious 'youth strategies' and a plethora of youth organisations and projects are being financed by the European Commission, whose officials recognise that Europe's ageing is a threat to living standards and political stability.

The goal of the 'Eurocrats' is to help young people have a stronger voice on economic strategies and priorities for the future. So far, this debate has been dominated by middle-aged politicians who too often seem out of touch with the problems of younger people. In the European Parliament, the spotlight is turning towards younger members with fresh ideas. These are badly needed, as the proportion of young euro-parliamentarians in relation to all the older MEPs is 1:15, even though their ratio in the overall European population is 1:5. The 2024 European elections saw a slight improvement, with the under-39 MEPs going to 25, from 19 in the previous parliament.

In general, though, it's too soon to say whether the EU's progressive efforts to empower youth will add up to much; they date back to 2010 or so when the global financial crisis was triggering national austerity programmes that hit younger people the hardest. And although programmes such as the EU's 2019–27 'Youth Strategy' are well intentioned, they tend to suffer from leaden and unimaginative thinking.

What the EU's growing focus on youth has yet to achieve is a starkly honest picture of the difficulties that older Europeans are handing down to younger ones. A Europe-wide focus is needed on the youth policies that should be actively promoted and concrete ways to tackle these unfairnesses. Most of these social and economic problems are national, and beyond the EU's remit, but Brussels could do much more to highlight them.

Critics of the EU often present it as all-powerful while also wholly undemocratic and unaccountable, and claim it's determined to build a European 'super state' that would challenge its member states' sovereignty. That's a travesty of the facts, and it also disguises the EU's lack of powers in almost all the areas associated with ageing.

European governments, including the UK's, would nevertheless find it easier and more effective to use the EU's various frameworks to collectively adjust their tax and spending policies that relate to ageing. There's little likelihood of this at present, yet separately or together Europe's national governments must act speedily if their young people are to avoid being unfairly penalised by the costs of ageing. Economic and social policies require years to be formulated, applied and take effect, so tough choices must be made in the years up to 2030 if the problems of 2050 and beyond are to be addressed.

How different are millennials and zoomers?

New technologies are upending communications, media, workplaces, working practices, consumer patterns, transport and education, and the generations born into the Digital Age are at the sharp end. While much is expected of them, they're comparatively ill-equipped to protect Europe's interests in a global economy that's more competitive than ever.

Some of these young people are highly educated, with a string of degrees and diplomas. But too many have been the victims of education budget cuts that stemmed in many European countries from post-2010 austerity policies. Millennials and Gen-Zers lack many of the advantages enjoyed by earlier generations.

Their incomes are on average lower, housing is more expensive, employment is less secure and their child-raising years are fewer.

They are also far more socially aware and environmentally conscious than their forebears, which may at some point translate into greater political activism that will disrupt the tenor of present-day society. That they haven't yet done so is no guarantee that they won't, and it's arguable that socio-political upheavals of some sort would be preferable to inaction and stagnation.

Today's young will have to contend with particularly acute economic and political difficulties. The generalisations used to characterise millennials and Gen-Zers around the world can be meaningless, but it may nevertheless be instructive to look at how those generations see themselves. In Europe, youthful optimism seems to be blinding young people to political realities. Their political inertia and growing disdain of the ballot box is compounding the problems they must face in the years ahead.

The future is daunting for millennials now well into their thirties and the zoomer generation that's beginning to enter labour markets in substantial numbers – more so perhaps than many of them realise. That's certainly the case for Generation Alpha, whose birth years span 2010–25. Their lack of awareness is understandable because younger people have been presented with a deceptively optimistic vision of their future.

It's hard to grasp the idea of darkening storm clouds when one's elders paint rosy pictures of the world that awaits. Governments and business corporations are often at pains to reassure voters and savers, consumers and investors that tomorrow will be sunnier than today. Their message is that while living standards may have slipped, this is a blip and not a trend.

It's unrealistic to expect politicians or business leaders to be voices of doom, but the bright images they promote can be dangerously misleading. Young people are featured in official and corporate brochures with dazzling smiles and confident body language. They are presented as a blessed generation whose superior skills and higher education assure Europe of a golden future.

The reality is that, far from being blessed, the zoomers are on course to become a blighted generation. Their millennial elders are already finding their prospects dimmer than those of preceding generations, with income levels below those of younger people in Europe's buoyant post-war economies. The lowest rungs on the housing ladder are prohibitively expensive, and at the same time fewer and fewer companies offer job security. As France's president Emmanuel Macron put it in a remarkably frank televised address to the nation in 2022: 'We are living through the last days of the Age of Abundance.'

Most Gen-Zers ignore these unwelcome truths and are more concerned with climate change, pandemics and the uncertainties of the 'metaverse' being created by AI and the digital revolution. The zoomers' outlook is sometimes even one of unbridled optimism: when pollsters interviewed a representative sample of Canadian under-25s, 88 per cent characterised their outlook as 'extremely positive'. That may be the excessive overconfidence of youth in a country of abundant resources, but it's also indicative of widespread insouciance.[1]

The heavy pressures that ageing societies will impose on young people as they reach maturity are the result of a demographic crisis that began to take shape 50 years ago. For decades, shifting birthrates went largely unnoticed and smaller families were hailed as a sign of social progress and rising living standards. Few analysts considered the implications of rural depopulation and shrinking workforces. Demographic change will in any case be only one of their handicaps. The hopes and ambitions of the children of the 'Internet Age' must also be set in their wider context of climate change and unpredictably disruptive technological developments.

Sociologists have scrutinised millennials and Gen-Zers far more closely than they have preceding generations, but much less attention has been paid to the way Europe's ageing will affect them in economic terms. Here, the two generations are frequently lumped together, despite their differences, because many studies and scenarios are commercially motivated. These focus on spending power, and banks and multinational corporations prefer upbeat messages, even when they differ markedly from the more down-to-earth findings of a growing number of researchers and think tanks.

The reports favoured by commercial interests are skewered in a thoughtful analysis by one of Britain's leading pollsters. Ben Page of the Ipsos-MORI organisation in London pulled no punches in a pamphlet he entitled 'Beyond binary – the lives and choices of Generation Z'. He wrote that 'generational analysis is developing a bad name. And fair enough because a lot of it is poorly done, aimed more at getting headlines or hits for simplistic interpretations of difference than providing true insight.'

Page went on to say that 'bad generational research is a tendency to segment everything into boxes – this idea that the next cohort will be either this thing or that'. His more nuanced view of Gen-Z is that it's 'the first truly fast-Internet enabled generation', and therefore more open to ideas because it has 'more ways to connect, see and experience more things'. The downside, he suggests, is that technology also carries the risk of fragmenting Gen-Zers into 'bubbles and echo chambers'.[2]

Despite some very different characteristics, zoomers and millennials tend to be seen as one because together they constitute the bulk of our active workforces. By 2030, three-quarters of both Europe's and America's working populations will be millennials and zoomers. Europe's over-65s, meanwhile, who may or may not continue in paid work after reaching retirement age, will have exploded from being roughly a fifth of the present European population to almost a third in the 2030s.

Why the crystal ball for zoomers is so clouded

Gen-Zers' experience differs significantly from that of the millennials. Born fully into the digital age, they were immediately at ease as children or teenagers with the 'virtual' elements forced on society by the COVID-19 pandemic. None of them is able to remember the dramatic events of 9/11 in September 2001, but they grew to adulthood in the austerity years that followed the 2008–10 financial and economic crisis. Zoomers are said to be more money-minded than millennials, while sharing the same climate change anxieties.

An important caveat at this point is that much of the research into younger people's attitudes has been conducted among students and professionals rather than unskilled workers, even though they too are going to be of crucial importance. Seen through this distorting lens, the more privileged members of Gen-Z inevitably harbour high hopes of a glittering career. Other analysts are less optimistic, and fear the focus on zoomers will be counterproductive. Marc Loriol of the University of Paris-

Panthéon-Sorbonne has argued that emphasising generational differences is slowing the integration of younger people into the workforce.[3]

A survey of American college students saw a quarter expecting a starting salary of $60,000 a year 'straight out of school'. Two-thirds cited a good salary as their key objective, with only a third or so opting for an agreeable work–life balance. America's zoomers say they are fully prepared to work hard to achieve these objectives.

As teenagers, they do twice as much evening homework as was the norm in the 1990s. On getting to college, they soon start looking around for possible employment after graduation. By their senior year, three-quarters are job hunting, and just one student in ten waits to have graduated before looking for work.[4]

In spite of this drive and ambition, there's also anxiety. When COVID-19 was raging, a quarter told a poll organised on behalf of the Dell computer company that they expected their generation to be hit the hardest of all by lay-offs or wage cuts. They were also uncertain about how new technologies would affect the shape of jobs, with 59 per cent saying they didn't think their present employment would take the same form in 20 years.

This awareness of unpredictable change is leading some zoomers to worry most about their future finances. The Center for Generational Kinetics in the US believes that 35 per cent of Gen-Zers intend to start their own private pension plan while still in their twenties. A spokesman for First Dollar, a US savings fund catering specifically for zoomers and millennials, has said, 'Gen-Zers do not want to end up like their parents.' The reference was to the years of austerity after the 2008 global financial crisis, but it also spoke volumes about an uncertain future.

Pensions were at that time less immediately affected by the economic stringencies that hit many on both sides of the Atlantic, but zoomers' faith in the financial underpinnings of their own retirement has been shaken. The authors of a book entitled *The Gen Z Effect* found that almost a third of zoomers say they expect never to be able to retire, and among the 22–32 year olds that proportion rose to almost half.

This partly reflects their mistrust of increasingly overburdened pension schemes, but also Gen-Zers' belief that they must be self-reliant. Six in ten of the young people questioned for the book expect to start their own business – often through crowdfunding.[5]

Millennials are labelled 'the unluckiest generation'

If tech-savvy Gen-Zers look like being condemned to tough times, with only a small proportion reaping rich rewards, spare a thought for the millennials. They are already suffering unfairly from the aftermath of the 2008 financial crisis and the ensuing austerity policies, while the demographic deficit threatens worse to come for those already in their mid-thirties and struggling.

An influential report that pulled together analyses from around Europe called the millennials the 'Unluckiest Generation'. Under the headline 'Ten shocking statistics about Millennials and money' it noted that people born between 1982 and 2004 are 'the first modern generation to be worse off than their parents'.

The study cited British, Italian and Luxembourg statistics, and noted that in the UK a third of millennials will probably never be home owners. It also found that almost a third of them complained of 'income discrimination' in the shape of the poor deals offered to them when applying for mortgages, loans or even credit cards.

Like Gen-Zers, these millennials were well aware of the need to start saving at an early age for their retirement, with only one in four failing to do so. Significantly, they are seen by bankers as saving too little because future conditions threaten to make such heavy demands on them. Millennials' chief concern seems to be with ethical investment, and they are well known to favour sustainable 'green' funds far more than previous generations.

Millennials defy easy categorisation. Worried though they may be about their financial situation, they are at the same time far more maverick than previous generations. The report's authors say many millennials are disillusioned with political or religious leaders, looking instead to private sector bosses to create both ethical and sustainable business models. 'They want business to take a much more aggressive stance towards making a positive impact,' the report says.[6]

In the US, bankers paint a similarly mixed picture. On the optimistic side, the authors of a Morgan Stanley study threw caution to the winds with a glowing description of the new era that will unfold thanks to the arrival on the labour market of a talented generation of young people. 'With Millennials overtaking Baby Boomers as the most populous generation in the US, and Gen Z close behind,' they wrote, 'the country could see the dawn of an economic "youth boom" with significant implications for retailers, the food and beverage industries, electronics and travel – and opportunities for investors.'[7]

Elsewhere on Wall Street, analysts at Charles Schwab, the investment and financial services company, have been less bullish. They reported that only 38 per cent of millennials in the US are 'financially stable' and warned that the remaining 62 per cent are 'living from paycheck to paycheck'. Experts at Bank of America echoed that cautious note with a forecast that by 2031 average incomes of Gen-Zers will be overtaking those of the millennials.

The providers of financial services are as volatile and unpredictable as financial markets, so it's unsurprising their studies show no consensus. A common thread can be found, though, in public domain statistics prepared by governments, NGOs, think tanks and academic researchers. The overall picture presented by this heterogeneous range of analysts vividly illustrates the threat levels to the underprivileged young on both sides of the Atlantic.

The barriers younger people have to face on leaving school or university are considerably higher than any their elders had to contend with. They form a daunting obstacle course for men and women in their twenties and thirties, and will often dog their careers and financial prospects well into middle age and beyond. These of course don't affect all young people everywhere in Europe. But they suggest diminished prospects for a substantial majority of young Europeans, and are a catalyst that's widening divisions between 'haves' and 'have nots'.

Jobs are the first hurdle. When the gig economy first began to gather momentum, the availability of more flexible employment for young people was hailed as a positive development. Since then, zero hours contracts, unsocial hours, low pay and the growing absence of employment security has dramatically altered that view. Most European countries' labour markets are not efficient enough to 'clear' all the people wanting work by matching them with employers looking for workers. That failure can be put down to inadequate training and to technological change that's moving so much faster than before.

Wages for entry-level jobs are lower on average than in the past, and that is hitting younger people's lifestyles and career prospects. The ripple effect of poorer pay in many sectors is braking economic growth and creating an array of other problems that affect younger people. Inadequate housing in the UK and throughout Europe is doing serious damage to society. As well as discouraging larger families, higher housing costs are depressing regional development and in many regions of Europe compounding the problem of rural 'desertification'.

Socio-economic class divisions that policy makers have striven to narrow throughout the post-war years are instead widening. Squeezes on jobs, wages, housing and childcare may not be felt acutely by the offspring of wealthier families, but they sap the social and educational progress of less privileged young people who had expected to benefit from a more meritocratic society.

This reversal of the social progress achieved, albeit unevenly, over the last half-century risks coming at a high price. The strategy of 'Social Europe' prized so highly by the EU in the closing decades of the 20th century may turn out to be no more than a flash in the pan rather than a sustained achievement. Yet addressing the difficulties of young people as they enter adulthood is vitally important for all in Europe.

Global youth, and China's *jiulinghou*

What is the global outlook for younger people in a world that's becoming polarised between predominantly elderly rich countries and overwhelmingly youthful poorer ones? An insight into attitudes beyond the confines of Europe, the US and most OECD member countries is provided by a report called 'What the world's young people think and feel'.

Commissioned by the London-based Varkey Foundation, the study was based on a 2017 survey carried out in 20 countries by the Populus polling company. It offers an unusual portrait of the attitudes of 15–21 year olds to largely social questions. The report is part of a project reflecting the concerns of Sunny Varkey, an

Indian-born billionaire philanthropist who vigorously promotes global education projects.

The Varkey Foundation initiative set out to answer fundamental questions about youthful attitudes around the world. 'Are they disengaged teenagers lost in their smartphones and their immediate social network with no thoughts beyond? Or are they smart, informed citizens with just the qualities needed to address the world's most pressing problems?'

The answers it came up with are downbeat and upbeat in more or less equal proportions. 'Although their desire to contribute is a source of hope,' the survey says, 'Generation Z are pessimistic about the future – and overall seem unhappy with the state of the world that they have inherited.' More than two-thirds fear there's a worldwide lack of children's education, and roughly the same proportion cite climate change and pandemics as major worries. Surprisingly, four-fifths thought extremist terrorism an even greater threat. Only in China did young people put climate change at the top of their concerns, with 82 per cent saying it's the greatest challenge of all.

China's *jiulinghou* as Gen-Zers are known, nevertheless came out at the top of the more optimistic part of the Varkey survey, with 53 per cent saying the world 'is becoming a better place'. India's young people were just behind at 49 per cent. In stark contrast, young French and Italian respondents occupied the far end of the spectrum, both with 53 per cent believing the world is getting worse.

A broad theme in this unusual survey is a global tendency towards more liberal attitudes that seems in direct contradiction to the observable shift towards autocratic governments and populism. In 14 of the 20 countries, young people favoured easier living and working conditions for migrants. Getting on for half the respondents criticised their own government for doing too little to resolve the global refugee crisis.

On religion, there's a clear split between the 77 per cent of young Africans for whom it's important and the majority of young Europeans and Japanese who say it has 'no significance'. Where young people were evenly, and unexpectedly, divided was over freedom of speech. When religious or political sensitivities risk being offended, as many young people defended freedom of speech as opposed it. Support for free speech was alarmingly lukewarm, however, in France, the UK and even the US. The Varkey Foundation's survey found almost four-tenths of young Chinese saying they believe in freedom of speech, something that the country's communist leadership should ponder because it points to interesting future developments within Chinese society.[8]

Like Europeans and Americans, the Chinese stick labels on successive generations, so the *qilinghou* are those born during the Cultural Revolution in the mid-1960s, the *balinghou* during the years of one-child families and now the *jiulinghou* who are often presented as symbols of China's new vitality and creativity. Despite that upbeat tone, more and more are reportedly calling themselves 'Foxi', which roughly translates as laid back. This is part of a trend that's reportedly worrying Beijing's policy makers because it advocates 'lying flat', and is associated with young professionals opting out of stressful jobs.[9]

Also called *tang ping* – voluntary laziness – this rejection of the Chinese ethos of 'struggle and endeavour' went viral in mid-2021 on the Douban social network, and following that on even more popular Weibo. Perhaps these are no more than straws in the wind, but they suggest that China's young adults are reconsidering their social attitudes and consequently their political views. China's active workforce recently peaked, and is starting to decline sharply in relation to its ageing population. These mood shifts among the young seem likely to be a potent new factor.[10]

How useful are analyses of Gen-Z?

Looking back over the years since the Second World War, it's unclear whether generational tags or nicknames have ever offered useful clues to how young people will behave in adulthood. Many of France's famously rebellious 'soixante-huitards' – the rioting student dissidents of May 1968 who hastened the downfall of General de Gaulle's conservatives – became prominent industrialists, political leaders and journalists.

So too did members of Italy's 'Brigate Rosse', the far-left Red Brigades movement whose campaign of terror in the 1970s included the murder of former prime minister Aldo Moro. And in Germany the activities of the similarly violent Red Army Faction lasted until the dawn of the 1990s. In all these cases, those youthful activists became pillars of society, as did America's 'flower power' generation of hippies and Vietnam War protesters.

Millennials and Gen-Zers could be said to be more responsible and open-minded than previous generations. Of course, appearances can be deceptive, but so far those who are more educated seem to share liberal social attitudes, a hard work ethic and an admirable degree of respect for the environment. Less progressive are the younger voters in a number of European countries whose response to narrowing opportunities has been to back hard-right populist parties.

In developing countries as well as in wealthier industrialised ones, pollsters have found widespread tolerance among younger people for hitherto unacceptable practices such as same-sex marriage. Their tolerance of other religious faiths is also strikingly at odds with the militancy of some Islamic as well as Christian sects. If there's hope for a cooling of jihadism and Christian fundamentalism, it may lie with younger people.

So much for the prospect of a more enlightened 21st-century world. The financial and economic outlook for zoomers and millennials is far less encouraging, and their living standards and those of their children are inextricably tangled in the fraught debate over the future of market economies, and of a global economy in which the benefits of globalisation are not merely being reassessed but angrily challenged.

The three-quarters of a century that followed the Second World War saw the capitalist model prevail, but now its shortcomings are all too evident. The gaps between the rich and the poor, the haves and have nots, are increasingly criticised as unsustainable, whether between countries, between regions of the world or within nation states. The task of overhauling and streamlining the international economy will to a large extent fall on today's under-fifties, so their challenge will be to maintain the wealth-creating elements of capitalism while reducing its characteristics of 'winner takes all' and 'devil take the hindmost'.

Reshaping capitalism is a tall order. Demographics is at the root of the geopolitical tensions created by exploding populations in the world's poorest regions and rich countries that although shrinking in size are determined to defend excessive privileges and wealth that are rooted in the 18th and 19th centuries.

Potentially dangerous tensions will demand unpopular political compromises, yet the most notable feature of Europe's younger generations is the absence of a strong interest in politics. Parliamentary democracies are disappointing many voters, and above all the younger ones. At a global level, international institutions are seen as powerless to deliver on peace and security and on credible responses to climate change, but national politicians, too, are dismissed as ineffective and self-interested.

This is the legacy being handed down to the world's young people. In addition to the burdens of demographic change, particularly in Europe, millennials and Gen-Zers may well have no choice but to become radical reformists. They must help to adapt the political economies of richer nations to the needs of poorer but larger ones. It's too soon to speculate on how Generation Alpha will respond to these pressures, but they will have to wrestle with unprecedented geopolitical and intergenerational problems.

Europe's political leaders are in search of a new global role, partly as a reflex of the EU's long-standing ambitions, but most of all as a response to this century's growing confusion and contradictions. 'Big Power' geopolitics involving America, China and Russia have been pushing Europe to the wings of the world stage, in spite of its trade and economic weight.

Championing the rebalancing of intergenerational influence in both rich and poor nations could do much to restore Europe's standing. Global demographics are reshaping our world, and Europe's comparative advantage in today's fast-changing international political economy is the EU's reputation for constructive cooperation.

Thanks to the more Europe-minded generations of zoomers and millennials, and perhaps the alphas who will follow them, the EU is arguably better placed than, say, the UN to launch a global debate on reconciling the needs of ageing richer nations now shrinking in size with those of poorer ones beset by population explosions. That's the ambition advanced by some EU policy analysts, but whether Europe can put it into practice remains to be seen.

6

The young need better pay

Ageing's costs will be unaffordable in low-wage economies. But hiking pay scales risks stoking inflation. The erosion of many people's purchasing power is an increasingly widespread problem across Europe. Social safety nets are essential, but sometimes discourage people from entering the labour market. The uncertainties of digitalisation and AI underline the need to rethink employment and defuse the demographic timebomb.

Young people in Britain and across Europe too often get a lousy deal at work. Compared with earlier generations, their job opportunities are bleaker and salaries lower. This is not just unfair; it's also unwise. Living standards in general, social benefits for the needy along with healthcare and pensions for the elderly, all depend on the ability of today's young to pay tomorrow's sky-high taxes.

Millennials now in their thirties bore the brunt of austerity in the wake of the 2008–10 global economic crisis. Now it's Gen-Zers who are on the threshold of an increasingly chaotic labour market. Both generations face far tougher conditions than their predecessors, yet are doomed to bear the mounting costs of an ageing society. Their disposable incomes are appreciably less than those their parents and grandparents enjoyed, yet they will be asked to pay proportionately more tax to fund the costs of ageing.

Both the millennials and zoomers were born into the new era of digitalisation, and, just as revolutions are said to devour their children, they are its victims. The insecurities of the gig economy and zero-hours contracts together with the impact of de-industrialisation on manufacturing jobs are seeing wages plummet in real terms for all but a handful of the highly educated or technically proficient.

The young people of the rich Western world are no longer privileged in the way they once were. Competition from developing countries, chiefly in Asia, has upset many of the trade and investment advantages that made Europe and America wealthy. If Europe is to afford the costs of its ageing, the employment conditions and prospects of younger generations must be radically improved.

That younger people are getting an increasingly unfair deal has been evident for at least a quarter of a century. It's itemised in reports by governments, and was highlighted by the EU's proposed job guarantees scheme. But identifying the difficulties younger people face hasn't resolved or even diminished them, nor has it lessened the chances of today's young becoming a blighted generation.

The case for overhauling wage structures and employment practices is all too familiar. Politicians pay lip service to the idea of making labour markets friendlier to the young, but it's complicated and politically unrewarding to restructure any market in which supply and demand determine prices.

Relatively short-term factors like skills shortages or discouragement to work have shaped labour markets across Europe, and have distorted their efficiency. In the longer term, this will inevitably sap European countries' ability to fund rising healthcare and pension commitments.

There are two parallel challenges. One is strategic; the other is more immediate. There's the demographic timebomb that's set to explode with destructive force several decades from now, and there's the problem of intergenerational unfairness. Researchers tend to focus on the latter rather than on society's wider need to defuse the timebomb.

In Britain, the Intergenerational Foundation is one of the loudest voices championing a fairer deal for younger people. When it opened its doors in 2011, it unveiled a novel unfairness index to show the sharp rise over 20 years of the handicaps that young people will have to contend with. 'It's only fair', said its introductory report, 'that younger generations should have the same standard of living as generations who have gone before.'

The foundation's warnings have been widely echoed by other analysts. When pollsters at Ipsos-MORI commented on the findings of one of their own surveys, they wrote, 'The economic context in which western Millennials have matured is characterised by uncertainty and stagnation,' adding that 'the employment struggle has created … an adult purgatory'. Their underlying message was that job difficulties delay and even discourage parenthood, and thus exacerbate demographic decline.

Looking at intergenerational fairness across Europe, EU officials in Brussels warn that there's 'a generation gap in labour markets that if not addressed may undermine social cohesion, support for reforms and trust in the system and institutions'. The Eurocrats said there's a need for changes in the welfare state that would 'facilitate intergenerational solidarity'.[1]

Young Europeans starting out on their working lives have for a decade or more been hit by a double whammy. First there was the 'Great Recession' triggered by the worldwide financial crisis of 2008, and then there was the COVID-19 pandemic. In both cases, the prevalence of 'last in, first out' hiring and firing practices saw youthful employees being laid off in their millions and first-time jobseekers turned away.

The economic crisis that followed the near-meltdown of financial markets in 2009 pushed the unemployment rate among Europe's under-25 year olds to 26 per cent. Mercifully, that high point didn't last very long, but the discouragement of so many young people has had lasting consequences. Long-term joblessness has spread and become rooted among millennials, who were hit the hardest by recession and austerity policies. Sociologists say that a pattern of lower ambitions and reduced earnings has visibly gained ground.

The COVID-19 lockdowns that paralysed people's lives a decade later compounded these troubles. At the pandemic's height, almost 3 million young people in the UK were unemployed, and had it not been for furlough schemes to maintain jobs and wages the total would have been far higher. In Italy, Spain and Greece, the toll on jobs was greater, and throughout developed countries the impact was similar. The OECD calculated that as well as temporarily closing down all but essential services, among its member countries the lockdowns destroyed forever nearly one job in ten.

These two shocks to the system have coincided with three other factors – digitalisation, working from home (WFH), made possible by instant telecommunications, and the growing reluctance of people to accept rigid working hours. Labour markets are becoming more flexible and multifaceted as game-changing technologies transform manufacturing economies into service-based ones.

The so-far unanswered question is whether this quiet revolution will deliver enough new jobs to improve overall living standards. The picture isn't encouraging. The dislocations caused by two major disruptions only about ten years apart have accelerated structural changes to society that were already taking place beneath the surface.

Whether they are school leavers or university graduates, too few young Europeans are being equipped with the skills and know-how employers need. Educational systems have not been restructured quickly enough to adapt, and that's as much a comment on the conservative attitudes of Europeans as a criticism of governments.

Meanwhile, the mismatch problem is growing; more and more job vacancies remain unfilled, with jobseekers failing to find work because they lack the right skills. There's also much regional mismatch. Just as there are too few workers to meet employers' needs in Europe's cities, there are too few available jobs in poorer regions, especially rural ones. There's a disproportionately high number of unemployed would-be workers, especially younger ones, in the less-developed areas.

For policy makers, the great conundrum is how to reconcile the pressures that aggravate unemployment with Europe's dwindling manpower resources. The big picture is that there aren't enough rewarding and well-paid jobs for young people, yet there's not enough manpower to meet employers' needs. Media reporting, and therefore most people's awareness, concentrates on jobless figures, but ignores all the pointers to growing labour shortages.

When the pandemic's hiring freeze began to hit hard in the summer of 2020, a Düsseldorf-based specialist at the Boston Consulting Group made an astute observation. 'A large number of organisations have recruitment bans,' Rainer Strack told the *Financial Times*, 'but if you look ahead to 2030 Germany will have a shortage of millions of employees. So students should use this time to improve their digital skills as there will be fantastic opportunities in a few years.'

That's not only true of Germany. Universities in the UK and continental Europe are widely seen as failing to supply enough high added-value graduates with strong technical and intellectual skills. Higher education is criticised for resisting modernisation, while it's also recognised as having been severely handicapped by budget cuts. Radically improving the situation would require courageous measures by governments that are under pressure to reduce state spending.

In many European countries, secondary education, too, has been slow to adapt to the requirements of the knowledge society. Employers who complain of the failings of education systems as a whole point especially to inner-city schools, where there are large and seriously underprivileged immigrant populations. How much blame teachers should accept is debatable when the more deep-seated problem is low wage levels for young jobseekers. Many face the prospect of a lifetime in semi-skilled or unskilled work, with considerably less spending power than that of their parents.

This should be a massive incentive for younger people to embrace digital training or reskilling, but the evidence so far suggests the contrary. Less educated millennials seem prone to discouragement, and are opting out of the workforce. The safety nets of social security and unemployment benefit make life in the black economy feasible, but at a substantial cost to society. As well as adding little value through their work, they will be weighing on the system rather than contributing to it. The conditions that discourage them from the active labour force don't save taxpayers money but create an expensive fiscal burden for the coming years.

How realistic is a 'jobs strategy' for young people?

Glued to screens of one sort or another, the young people of the TikTok generation are a paradox. Their lives often revolve around their smartphones, but at the same time would-be employers complain these youngsters lack technical know-how. Familiarity with social media and all its apps apparently has little to do with acquiring marketable skills.

The importance of technical training, and the cost of its scarcity, is illustrated by some national statistics. In Germany, 8.6 per cent of under-thirties are either jobless or without an apprenticeship of some sort, whereas in France it's 14 per cent. Young Germans are far less likely to find themselves discouraged from finding a decent job than their French or British counterparts, because they generally arrive on the jobs market with useful qualifications.

So what sort of strategy should other governments be putting in place to fix the skills shortages that risk making European companies less and less competitive in world markets? And how can doing so get more young people into good jobs with solid enough prospects to afford a home and start a family? There's no magic wand for governments to wave over increasingly chaotic and inefficient labour markets, but it's clear they should be redoubling their efforts to address the challenges of youth employment.

That would mean levelling with public opinion – which is to say voters – about the challenges that lie ahead. More taxes will be needed to fund the costs of ageing, and that will mean higher wages. A Scandinavian-style high-wage economy for the whole of Europe sounds attractive, but how can that be achieved without first undergoing an inflationary spiral that would weaken many EU countries' international competitiveness?

How serious is the underpayment of today's younger workers? It's often argued that their low levels of pay are only temporary, and that their situations will improve once they step into their elders' shoes. It's a dangerously misleading assumption because low pay for young people is at the root of Europeans' economic problems. The widening gaps between haves and have nots, reduced competitiveness and drooping productivity can all be traced back to persistent wage disparities.

But identifying the wage problem doesn't resolve it. Over 90 countries around the world – almost half the UN's membership – have introduced minimum wage levels of one sort or another, none of them very satisfactorily. The EU is proposing a Minimum Wage Directive, but its usefulness is disputed. Its opponents claim that wage increases spur lay-offs and thus lead to more unemployment. They also say that because there are so many more 'self-employed' workers in the gig economy whose zero-hours contracts aren't covered, minimum wages don't improve matters for the truly low paid.

Opposition to this EU project isn't voiced only by employers and right-wing conservatives. Scandinavia's trade unions are solidly against it on the grounds that it weakens their bargaining power. In Germany, where a minimum wage was belatedly introduced in 2015, researchers found that its chief effect was to encourage employees to move from small companies to bigger ones.

None of this rules out substantially higher minimum wages. Ranged against the doubters is a formidable body of largely left-wing opinion that at times recalls Henry Ford's thoughts a century ago. When America's pioneering automobile tycoon was asked to explain why he'd doubled his workers' wages, Ford said: 'If I don't pay them well, who's going to buy my cars?'

Campaigners who urge higher wage levels for the poorly paid and for young people make precisely the same point. As British trades union leader Frances O'Grady put it: 'Better workplace conditions and wages would help attract and retain staff.' She was commenting when she was secretary-general of the Trades Union Congress (TUC) on the post-COVID-19 labour shortages that many British businesses were bitterly complaining of.[2]

A blanket approach to wages would probably be ill-advised, given all the variables that exist within different sectors and industries. But looking at the general wages situation, it's certainly possible to say that too many people in Britain and in continental Europe are underpaid. The delicate equilibrium between the financial responsibilities of the state – meaning the need for more taxpayers and revenues – and those of individual employers is out of kilter.

Are taxpayers subsidising low-paid jobs through benefits?

Low pay hasn't kept up with inflation, which is why the cost of living crisis is a burning issue in so many countries. Diminished spending power is a very real problem in rich and poor countries alike. It fans the flames of discontent that benefit populist politicians, and slows economic growth by depressing consumption.

This can sometimes tempt governments to subsidise wages, but doing that is far from straightforward. Businesses that have been assailed by austerity policies and by COVID-19 may welcome social benefits that top up their employees' wage packets. But these benefits can have an opposite effect of encouraging people to be unemployed and withdraw from the active workforce.

Another perverse effect is that smaller companies may be tempted to take advantage of these subsidies and underpay their employees, who thus join the ranks of the 'working poor'. There's a counter-argument, which sounds much more theoretical than practical: it is that if social security benefits shrink the pool of available labour, wages will in the longer term be pushed higher.

In the US, where labour markets although less regulated are still broadly similar to European ones, the federal government's Bureau of Labor Statistics has come up with some significant findings. Looking at the federal minimum wage of $7.25 an hour, it calculated that to maintain an employee's spending power it should rise to $20. Over the 50 years since the 1970s, its authors reckoned the earnings of 'middle class workers' have declined in real terms by 11 per cent.

Leaving competing theories aside, the reality is that low pay has become a deep-seated structural problem in many parts of Europe, not least in Britain. Disposable incomes had been so eroded by mid-2021, when the UK economy was emerging from the COVID-19 lockdowns, that real wages were back to 2008 levels. Some 3.6 million employees in Britain, said the TUC's Frances O'Grady, are in precarious and insecure jobs, while the UK's Living Wage Foundation has put the number of seriously underpaid people at 5 million.

The ebb and flow of economic migrants within Europe and from beyond blur the picture, but overall it's plain that too many occupations are no longer adequately paid, and that technological change is deepening labour market uncertainties. Young entrants to these markets are regrettably among the first to suffer, but it's also entirely predictable because they are the least experienced and often the least skilled.

Landing one's first job is usually a short-lived 'frictional' problem. Far more worrying is the longer-term outlook for today's unemployed youngsters. Sociologists warn of the consequences of lengthy periods of unemployment, and that's especially true of the young. People who are between jobs for a few weeks or months are frictionally unemployed, and even if a bit bruised by the experience usually look back on it as a stepping stone to better things. The victims of such larger pressures as the closure of 'rust bowl' industries or business collapses risk becoming 'structurally' unemployed, which can mean long-term joblessness. This fate, once largely reserved for older employees such as miners and steelworkers, now threatens the young too.

Discouragement from the labour force is becoming a striking feature of rich Western economies. It was thought that discouragement levels were only briefly exaggerated by COVID-19 furlough schemes that replaced wage packets with welfare cheques. But the 'Great Resignation' of people ducking out of formal employment seems more than a temporary blip. The overall trend is that people increasingly prefer to work from home or find flexible employment. Some settle for gig jobs such as driving for Uber or pedalling for Deliveroo.

Others fall back on social security schemes offering basic support that can occasionally be complemented by casual work in Europe's thriving black economies. As well as depriving governments of tax income, this discouragement is contributing to manpower shortages in key services. From healthcare to transport and from retailing to hospitality, low-paid jobs are being shunned because often they offer people little more than 'working poverty'.

The speed of the post-COVID-19 jobs recovery has varied considerably across Europe and North America, but the common denominator has been a dawning awareness that labour shortages will continue to grow. Before the pandemic struck, an important study warned of a future in which Europe would be more preoccupied with finding people to fill jobs than with creating jobs for the unemployed.

In collaboration with Google, researchers at the McKinsey Global Institute think tank looked at over 1,000 regional labour markets across Europe to measure the likely shortfall in available jobs over the next few years. The answer was that although automation is clearly introducing change, it won't make up for workforce shrinkages. By 2030, there will be 6 million unfilled vacancies in the EU. The study underlined the 'churning' that will revolutionise occupations and skills; over 20 million jobs in Europe will vanish and 90 million people will need to acquire 'significant new skills' if they are to keep their jobs.[3]

That research was carried out in 2020, and predated not just the pandemic but also the upsets caused by war in Ukraine. It nevertheless reflects the growing alarm with which policy makers see Europe's digital shortcomings. The survey's focus on no-skills and low-skills labour markets demonstrated that despite all the upbeat talk of the Information Age, society still relies on 'essential' low-pay jobs.

Garbage collectors and sanitary workers along with nurses and home carers became the new heroes of the COVID-19 period, reminding locked-down populations of services that are taken for granted and whose providers are undervalued. Whether that awakening will eventually lead to a more realistic and well-deserved round of pay rises remains to be seen. Market forces should at some point play in their favour because poorly paid jobs in healthcare and construction are occupations where society's ageing will inevitably increase demand.

In many parts of Europe and in the US, employment recovered well once the pandemic receded. But not in the UK. In the year after lockdowns eased, there were half a million fewer people in work than before COVID-19. Britain's registered workforce was almost a million people smaller than had been forecast before COVID-19, a downwards trend that's prompting concerns about an economic version of 'long COVID'.

The furlough schemes introduced in Britain and across continental Europe were essential to maintaining jobs and the economy, but they may backfire in the longer term. The major German insurer Allianz reckons that 9 million jobs in European services sectors will disappear in the wake of COVID-19's furlough subsidies. The withdrawal of wage supports may signal the disappearance of vulnerable jobs in the tourism and hospitality sectors. On the other hand, the good news could be that the younger workers released from these jobs will be available to other sectors that are starved of manpower.

Labour shortages are unlikely to be temporary

There's much debate about how serious Europe's labour shortages are, but little illumination. Governments' statistics are a hodge-podge of different scenarios and assumptions. The skills shortages that can thwart a major industrial company's expansion plans should not be misleadingly lumped in with the absence of seasonal fruit pickers caused in the UK by Brexit, or elsewhere in Europe by anti-migrant policies.

Shortages of people who would have been available to fill jobs reflect a wide range of political and economic factors. The common denominator is that there are fewer youngsters entering the labour market than before. Demographic decline has brought about a tailing-off of new workers, and this is going to be a long-term challenge to economic growth throughout Europe.

The problem is being compounded by labour market mechanisms that haven't been adapted to 21st-century needs. The OECD says a major problem for Europe is the lack of qualified teachers, managers, health carers and high-tech boffins. It has also found that seven university graduates in ten, with science as well as arts degrees, struggle to find work in their specialist field.

Skills shortages result from mismatches as well as from insufficient supplies of qualified young people. European labour markets often fail to fit young jobseekers into appropriate occupations. This pattern of square pegs and round holes is especially problematic in high-skilled areas where, the OECD finds, five out of ten jobs are hard to fill. One of the larger pan-European employers' groupings – Eurochambres, which represents some 20 million businesses – complains that the lack of skilled workers is 'one of the biggest challenges faced by European companies'.

Eurochambres says 'we are sleep-walking into a highly damaging socio-economic crisis by failing to address growing skills mismatches'. Such warnings should be taken very seriously because its members are often the small specialist companies and high-street retailers that form the backbone of Europe's consumer-led economies.

There's a temptation to see jobs in 20th-century terms rather than as part of a fast-changing picture driven in unpredictable directions by new technologies. So, what *is* a job in the new era of teleworking, and for that matter what is work? If some people can perform their allotted tasks remotely, how should they be rewarded – with a flat salary or as piecework? And if office work patterns are to be revolutionised, what sort of time commitment should be expected of employees?

As well as responding to social pressures that see people demanding a better work–life balance, employers are having to look harder than ever at productivity. Among the attractions of teleworking there's the promise of greater output per worker because the unproductive downtime of travelling to work is reduced. But mankind is a social animal, so where does that leave all the essential dynamics of human intercourse – innovation, morale, corporate identity and drive, to say nothing of friendships, romances and advancement up the corporate ladder?

We know what telecoms can do for a business that was originally conceived and structured conventionally, and was then streamlined by technology. But what would an entirely virtual company look like? There's no crystal ball to tell us what the world of work will look like by mid-century, but some trends are fairly clear.

In all the confusion created by the COVID-19 pandemic's lockdowns, a picture has emerged of more casual employment and fewer reliably secure jobs that would take an employee through to retirement. Even before COVID-19, one of Britain's best-known labour market economists pointed to a future of scarcer permanent jobs. 'It's probably safe to say', comments Prof. Diane Coyle of Cambridge University, 'that at least a quarter of the UK workforce is not in a traditional full-time permanent job.'[4]

Some experts recommend doubling down on this trend. Prof. Robert Skidelsky urged a 35-hour week in Britain's public sector in a 2019 report for the Progressive Economy Forum commissioned by one of the Labour Party's more radical left-wingers. Lord Skidelsky is an eminent economist and historian and the author of an authoritative biography of John Maynard Keynes. His thinking, shared by a good many others, is that employers should share with their employees the productivity improvements derived from new technologies.[5]

Teleworking is seen as another way of boosting productivity, but its big disadvantage is that it widens the gap between white-

and blue-collar jobs. WFH is beyond the reach of key workers in hospitals, transport, supermarkets and local authorities whose essential services were highlighted by COVID-19's lockdowns.

Their occupations are in the main poorly remunerated, and the pay gap separating them from the WFH brigade looks likely to widen. On the other hand, if teleworking were to deliver substantial productivity improvements, some of that wealth might boost economic growth and be to the general advantage of all.

Could greater productivity compensate for fewer workers?

It sounds a very attractive proposition: don't worry about the shrinkage of our workforces, say some experts, because digitalisation's revolutionary impact is going to raise output so dramatically that fewer workers will be required.

If this turns out to be the case, a brighter future beckons. Although smaller workforces mean fewer taxpayers and fewer salaried consumers, more output per person in both manufacturing and services would help to compensate for demographic shrinkage. There might even be so much more cash per head of population that problems such as housing deficits, education shortcomings and bankrupt pension systems could be tackled.

That presupposes a substantial improvement in productivity, so it's useful to look at the picture so far and the predictions being made. Politicians talk airily of productivity when advancing their policy ideas, but in truth recent years have seen little sign throughout the industrialised Western world of a productivity bonanza. On the contrary, output per person has registered only minor improvements or has stagnated. The 'Fourth Industrial Revolution' has yet to generate wealth on the scale that had been hoped for.

The heyday for productivity growth in Europe came long before microelectronics and the labour-saving gadgets it spawned. Fifty years ago, in the early 1970s, European productivity as measured by relating economic growth to hours worked peaked at more than 5 per cent yearly. That then nosedived to 1.5 per cent as a result of the 'oil shock' triggered by the Arab-Israeli conflict of 1974, and for the following quarter-century it bumped along at between 2 and 3 per cent.

Happy days! Buoyant economic activity rather than technology's magic wand was at the root of those enviable improvements in productivity. The gradual decline in productivity growth in Europe continued into the 21st century, and then plunged to zero and below in 2008 with the worldwide financial crisis. Since then, a single percentage point improvement every year has been the European average, and the UK has lagged below even that.

How to recover those glory days is widely referred to as the 'productivity puzzle'. The confusing factors involved were marshalled by Andy Haldane when, as the Bank of England's chief economist, he delivered a paper at the London School of Economics in 2017. 'Productivity', he said, 'is a gift for rising living standards, perhaps the greatest gift. It is not, however, one that keeps on giving … If history is any guide, there is unlikely to be any single measure that puts productivity growth back on track.'

Haldane separated possible measures into three broad categories: first, showering money on better infrastructure; second, more specific policies to promote high-tech innovation; third, encouraging non-tech companies to adopt new equipment and methods. Among these low-productivity companies, he reckoned, even modest improvements could bring dramatic results.

The nature of productivity and how to measure it has been a feature of economic policy discussion for decades, and the arguments have been getting more vexed and intense as productivity growth slowed and then flatlined. The winner of the 1987 Nobel prize for his work on economic growth theory neatly summed up the problem. 'You can see the Computer Age everywhere but in the productivity figures,' said the late Robert Solow of MIT.

'Solow's Paradox', as it's called, has become the curse of advanced industrial countries. No one can say whether future technological breakthroughs will transform working lives and resolve our thorniest social problems. Perhaps AI and Big Data will in some unimaginable way revolutionise societies, just as nuclear fusion, as distinct from fission, it is hoped will eventually deliver limitless, clean and very inexpensive energy.

But maybe not. As things stand, total factor productivity measuring output growth in relation to employees and money invested in an enterprise remains stubbornly low and shows no signs of recovering its mid-20th-century mojo. The internet is failing to deliver the powerful new dynamics its champions had expected, and it looks as if the telecoms revolution is more peripheral than central to economic growth.

The bottom line is that for the foreseeable future technology won't be coming to the rescue by compensating for Europe's declining workforces. It may introduce efficiencies that benefit start-up companies as well as internet giants, but it's unlikely to improve the lives of the many young people who will be stuck in low-wage work with minimal job security.

Stagnant productivity is a global challenge. Britain may lag behind much of continental Europe, and Europe behind the US, but globally the booby prize for really poor productivity coupled with workforce shrinkage goes to Japan. By 2030, as many as 9–10 million Japanese will have left the active labour force, while for productivity Japan ranks lowest of all the developed countries.[6]

Even though productivity is a global challenge that goes far beyond labour markets, it has somehow to be fixed. Sluggish productivity will exacerbate threats such as climate change because it's a brake on wealth creation, forcing governments to prioritise immediate needs to the detriment of strategic environmental goals. The key question, meanwhile, is whether there will be enough well-paid work for younger people in the UK and around Europe; and enough workers to fill those jobs.

Women and older workers, the underprivileged keys to growth

The future roles of women and older people are crucial. Their manpower is badly needed if labour markets are to be restructured and made more efficient, yet when it comes to finding work they are too often second-class citizens.

Women and older people are key to defusing the demographic timebomb. If working conditions for women can be made more attractive – and that usually means more flexible – they will be able to have more children. It's not too late to create a surge in the number of jobseekers entering the labour market of mid-century. If that were to happen, demographers' dire predictions would be confounded. But first there has to be a massive upheaval in the way women are treated in the workplace.

Enhancing the role of older people is no less important, although different. Attitudes to the employment of people in their sixties and seventies still lag far behind the revolutionary changes to lifespans and lifestyles that have occurred in the past half-century. Older people are still forced into retirement by outdated statutory rules, and face bureaucratic barriers and prejudices when they look for work.

The reality of the huge under-used labour reserves of women and older people is sometimes obscured by media spotlights that illuminate high-profile exceptions. The financial pages of the more serious newspapers often feature stories about octogenarian tycoons and powerful female CEOs that paint a misleading picture of the degree to which the 'diversity gap' of gender, racial and age inequality is being narrowed.

Women are usually paid a good deal less than men, and often tend to be found in low-status service jobs that are either part-time or precarious. While the female share in Europe's active workforces has risen steadily over the past 50 years, these improvements still fall short of what's needed. To meet Europe's labour shortages and address the infertility crisis, there needs to be a radical rethink of the training and education of women, along with their pay and employment conditions.

At the top of Britain's educational pyramid, women make up only a fifth of graduates in scientific and high-tech disciplines. In what are known as the STEM qualifications – science/technology/engineering/mathematics – that are fundamental to future economic growth, female students are disproportionately few. The picture is marginally brighter in the US, with women STEM students at around a third.

Where women *do* predominate is in lower-paid sectors such as health and retailing. There, the difficulty is in Britain and most parts of Europe that low wages mean female workers can't afford to take time off for childbearing and the rearing of larger families. Healthcare, and above all care for the elderly, is set for massive growth, yet its structures aren't being adequately modernised and streamlined. Demand for health workers is soaring everywhere, but working conditions remain unattractive.

Tackling such a deep-seated problem as gender imbalance can only be done through much closer public–private cooperation; governments and employers have to approach female discrimination hand in hand. A handful of large companies are doing that, but they are still very few.

In Sweden, Volvo Cars offers new mothers and fathers six months' paid parenthood leave and is extending this to its American and Chinese employees. Other corporations such as drinks giant Diageo and the global investment company Abrdn, formerly Standard Life Aberdeen, have similar schemes.

These ideas may seem unaffordable for most employers, and ultimately for national economies. But the example of Sweden perhaps presents gender equality in a different light. Sweden tops the Women in Work Index presented yearly by the PwC consulting and accountancy group, and derives much economic advantage from doing so. If the UK, which comes in around midfield at no. 16, were to match Swedish practices and boost women's pay by 20 per cent, it's reckoned that would add almost £200 billion to Britain's GDP.[7]

Getting more women into better jobs isn't an impossible dream. It requires a judicious mix of policies and tax measures that would compensate employers and allay their fears over the cost and inconvenience of granting maternity leave. Europe needs to reverse the trend towards women having fewer children. Yet it also needs more women at work to stem the shrinkage of well-remunerated, tax-paying workers who are so important to our consumer-led economies.

Highly subsidised crèches and child-caring facilities, along with carefully targeted tax benefits, could do much to help women pursue worthwhile careers rather than accepting menial work or becoming so discouraged they no longer see themselves as part of the workforce.

Overcoming cultural discriminations against women at work in many parts of Europe, including Britain, would deliver a huge economic bonanza. It could also deliver a new baby boom that would do much to head-off demographic disaster. It's not too late to transform Europe's increasingly ingrained infertility into a soon-to-be-forgotten blip.

Keeping older people in work is essential, too, but less clear cut. At one end of the scale there are the corporate executives and professional people whose retirement is eagerly awaited by their ambitious juniors. At the other end are manual workers tired by a lifetime of toil. The former must make way to successors, but in this day and age they are still healthily energetic and in need of stimulating roles. The latter, whose work and life choices have been limited, have looked forward to pensionable freedom but may also welcome a defined role in society and a financial supplement.

Retaining both white- and blue-collar retirees in the active workforce demands different solutions. Imaginative thinking that could channel retired high-flyers into unpaid charitable work – maybe the opposite of a youth corps – might be worth developing. For older manual workers and the unskilled, tax breaks that would encourage employers to hire pensioners as part-timers should be encouraged.

For those who have retired for no other reason than that they reached pensionable age, there's a simple way to keep them active. Backloading pensions so that the later they are claimed the more they pay out would do much to slow workforce shrinkages.

Extending the statutory age at which state pensions can be claimed is an inevitable consequence of longer lifespans. It's also one of the most explosive issues facing political leaders. France's president Emmanuel Macron tried to raise the pensionable age in his first term, got a bloody nose politically but pushed forward on it after winning his second term. It remains among the most divisive issues in France, and in much of Europe.

Some political leaders are unconcerned that their national pension arrangements risk being overwhelmed by their fast-growing population of the elderly. Populists see resistance to pension reform as a sure-fire vote winner. Hungary's unashamedly populist prime minister Viktor Orbán even increased state pension payouts, although his financial advisors warned him that the workforce there is shrinking so fast the pensionable age should be 72.

The greatest barrier to rethinking employment conditions for older people and women is cultural. Over many years, unemployment statistics have made headlines and served as an instant guide to economic success or failure. But this preoccupation with joblessness obscures the fact that there are fewer and fewer workers to fill the available jobs. The days are gone when it was the other way around, with too many people chasing too little work.

In the wake of the COVID-19 pandemic, the British labour market chalked up a notable but widely misunderstood first – there were more job vacancies across the UK than there were jobseekers. The then government in Westminster crowed that thanks to its policies unemployment was at an all-time low. It's much the same story across the Channel, with some European politicians greeting post-COVID-19 disruptions and labour shortages as proof of their employment policy successes.

It's nothing of the sort, and points instead to continuing economic decline. There are few if any examples of countries able to combine enviable economic growth with a contracting workforce. On the contrary, it's more or less an iron rule that a growing workforce is an essential precondition for economic dynamism. Common sense tells us that more people with more wage packets means more revenues to pay for public services. China's extraordinary 21st-century growth provides an excellent example of the benefits of harnessing a rising proportion of the population into active employment.

The reality of Europe's shrinking workforces acting as a brake on economic growth was highlighted two decades ago by one of the EU's most senior officials. Klaus Regling headed the European Commission's economic affairs directorate when he warned in 2006 that growing labour shortages would place a ceiling on growth.

Regling said that GDP growth in the EU's 15 richest members would therefore be limited to an average 1.8 per cent from 2010 to 2030, and to no more than 1.3 per cent from 2030 to 2050. That was in the boom years before the 2008 financial crisis, and his warning was greeted with widespread disbelief. Today it's all too clearly an integral part of Europe's economic malaise.[8]

Yet the idea persists that unemployment is the chief enemy. That's in some ways admirable because it shows concern for the less fortunate and underprivileged. But it's also a negative influence because the focus on joblessness has the effect of hardening outdated and wrongheaded prejudices about the nature of labour markets.

Fact and fiction about youth unemployment

Unemployment statistics are, and have always been, an unholy mess, and that's true most of all for joblessness among the under-25s. It's obviously right to worry about youth unemployment, but wrong to present it as so overwhelming a problem that it defies solution. Young people aren't nearly as vulnerable to unemployment as is generally believed. What they need most of all is higher wages and greater security, rather than the extra jobs governments promise to 'create'.

Youth unemployment is presented statistically in two ways: the rate and the ratio. They sound similar but give very different results. The EU's Eurostat service publishes both – the rate of joblessness as a percentage of all under-25s in the workforce and as a proportion of everyone in that age group, including those still in education or training. Then there's the ratio, which is the proportion of the 16–24-year-old population without a job.

Across the eurozone, youth unemployment rates generally average around 20 per cent, whereas the jobless ratio for young people is about 9 per cent. That's high but not disastrously so, as the young tend to move around between jobs while still finding their feet.

The political problem with all this is that because European voters are assailed by dramatic unemployment statistics, they have come to believe there's a finite number of jobs to be competed for. In fact, jobs are a very elastic part of an economy, so if there's more growth and dynamism there are more jobs, but if there's a slump employers won't be hiring as much.

Much of the antipathy to migrant workers in Europe and elsewhere reflects this widespread public belief in what economists have long called the 'lump of labour fallacy'. It's not only migrants who stand accused of wanting to 'steal' someone else's job; older people looking for post-retirement work or women seeking better hours and pay are often presented as competing unfairly with a male head of household who is thought to deserve a better paid job than a part-timer.

The idea that women and older people should accept handicaps in the jobs market to ensure middle-aged males enjoy some notional advantage is plainly absurd. The fundamental point here is that the more people are in work, the higher will be overall living standards. This is especially true at a time when Europe's active labour force is shrinking fast, and that of Britain faster still.

Politicians and the voters who elect them cling stubbornly to the idea that youth employment problems will somehow be resolved during the years ahead. The assumption is that while younger people may be underprivileged now, they will sooner or later step into the shoes of their elders and enjoy similarly high incomes.

Would that it were so. The reality is that the world of work is being blurred by new technologies, and that experts are divided over the shape of things to come. What we *do* know about the way our economies work is that today's young people will not automatically become richer when they reach middle age. Their lower wage levels will have slowed economic growth over the coming decades, so they may be getting a marginally bigger slice of a much smaller cake.

Some young people will nevertheless prosper. In the higher reaches of medicine, the law and major corporations, today's young professionals are set to outperform their seniors. But these beneficiaries of the knowledge economy look to be exceptions to the rule. Stable hierarchies and predictable career patterns are being broken down by new technologies, and younger workers should not expect their future seniority to deliver a much higher standard of living.

In bigger companies, information and communications technologies are disrupting managerial functions and reporting lines. Smaller retailers are being outgunned by hypermarkets, and both are increasingly menaced by the shift to online buying. It's impossible to say what sort of jobs will be on offer in the 2030s and beyond, but it's a fair bet that they'll be very different from those of today.

The more optimistic forecasts point to new and transformative technologies showering jobs and higher salaries on our stagnating economies. Researchers at MIT point out that two-thirds of today's jobs didn't exist before 1940, and are post-war 'inventions'. A more measured view is that of David Autor, a leading employment policy expert at MIT, who comments, 'The sky hasn't fallen in, but it is getting lower.'[9]

Other specialists who echo this put forward a variety of solutions to soften the impact of demographics and inadequate technological training. Major international institutions ranging from the World Bank and the IMF to the OECD and the World Economic Forum, as well as a slew of banks and think tanks, have been urging some abrupt policy U-turns.

McKinsey, the international management consultancy, has called for a doubling of investment spending by what it labels the 'digital laggards' – manufacturing, mining, healthcare and education. If this had been done in 2020, it estimated that by 2025 something like €2.5 trillion would have been added to the collective GDPs of the EU combined with the UK. As it is, the absence of some 10 million skilled high-tech workers and the persistent lack of political will means the laggards are falling ever further behind.[10]

Assuming they can summon the courage to level with their electorates, could Europe's governments counteract these pressures and thus maintain jobs and living standards? Could they unscramble the omelette of inefficient labour markets, old-fashioned work practices, unscrupulous internet giants and wholly inadequate education and training sectors?

On present showing, it seems too daunting a proposition for all but a few northern European and Scandinavian countries. Yet it should be attractive to mainstream political parties, beset as they are by populists, to tell voters that as matters stand young people will not be wealthy enough to fund more and more pensioners.

Incumbent governments should appeal to common sense rather than any political ideology. The plain fact is that without radical improvements to young people's job prospects there won't be enough wealth to pay for the costs of Europe's ageing. Without a radical rethink of employment, everyone will be the loser.

7

For homeless, read childless

Over 150 million Europeans are reported to be impoverished by the costs of housing. The young are the worst hit, with three-quarters of millennial couples saying home ownership is out of their reach. A massive 25 per cent increase in affordable social housing is needed. But without hugely expensive government-backed housing drives, Europe will be dogged by low birthrates and inflexible labour markets.

It's obvious when you think about it: housing shortages hit the young hardest, and thus discourage parenthood. With demographics at the root of Europe's problems, scarce and expensive housing is turning ageing from a quiet but seemingly unthreatening phenomenon into a politically explosive catastrophe.

Overhauling property markets to ensure affordable accommodation for everyone is vital, and it's where governments on both sides of the English Channel and the Atlantic are failing dismally. The ways housing is both taxed and subsidised has to be rethought, and housebuilding given a far higher priority. It holds a vitally important key to tackling the ageing crisis.

The conundrum, whatever a government's political hue may be, is that policies that would make housing more affordable would hit property prices and thus devalue homeowners' primary asset. People who have scraped and saved for years to buy their house or apartment would suffer a tough financial hit. Dramatic government measures to ease housing shortages and prick property bubbles would penalise the thrifty, especially older people who sooner or later would exact their revenge at the ballot box.

The lack of adequate housing stems in part from population growth outstripping supply. From 1965 to 2015, Europe's overall population grew by 25 per cent to just over half a billion, and that exerted huge pressure on property markets. Europe's population has now peaked, so those pressures will eventually ease and by the end of this century there will be about 80 million fewer people in Europe. But that's in the long run. As things stand, there will be little change in Europe's headcount before 2040, even if many of those heads will be greyer.

Social change is greatly aggravating the housing problem. An older person whose partner has died either moves to a much sought-after smaller apartment or remains in housing that in many cases could accommodate a family. Rising divorce rates have seen one-parent families increasing in number and as a proportion of the overall population, with the separated partner doubling housing demand by needing his or her own premises. Fewer young people want to remain in the parental home until they find a mate, so competition for single occupant units is intensified by both the elderly and the young.

Designing housing policies in these days of shifting demographics is complex, and not just because of the rising numbers of people to be accommodated. Home ownership is about much more than shelter; it's the basis of most people's wealth and is often crucial to their work and their children's education. One's home denotes social status and financial security – where you live is who you are.

Housing in Britain and most of Europe has been transformed from a solvable challenge into an impossible Catch-22. Young couples and newly-weds who in years past got their feet onto the property ladder with a small, modestly mortgaged apartment today face almost insuperable barriers to reaching even the lowest rungs. If they manage to scrape together an initial down-payment, up to two-thirds of their wages can be swallowed by accommodation costs.

The pressures created by scarce and inadequate housing depress birthrates, and so are now a major infertility factor. Young people in cramped housing whose cost mops up the bulk of their modest wages are putting off parenthood until they reach their thirties. Even then, family sizes are being constrained by housing considerations.

To defuse the demographic timebomb, young Europeans must reverse the infertility trend that has set in so solidly over the past half-century. If the present rate of around 1.5 children per couple could be turned around to an average of 2.5 or even three children, then the labour shortages set to squeeze the economic life out of mid-century Europe could be reversed. But bringing about such a significant change would require a judicious mix of tax incentives and imaginative home-building strategies. Nevertheless, it could be done.

A giant misconception stands in the way of building more homes: it's the widespread conviction, in Britain especially, that we are already overbuilt. The spectre of tarmac inexorably spreading out over green fields, stifling nature and turning virgin countryside into ugly estates, is a powerful brake on housing projects, but it's misguided. In the UK, according to the Office for National Statistics, only a shade over 5 per cent of the land area is taken up by homes and gardens.[1]

There's no getting away from the reality that more homes are needed in and around towns and cities where accommodation is already limited, and therefore expensive. That's where the jobs are, so it's where more housing is essential. Increased construction is only part of the solution. There must be a more imaginative approach to converting existing buildings to the needs of changing societies. This should include tax benefits that encourage the elderly occupants of large houses to exchange them for purpose-built flats with suitable amenities.

Interfering in the free market for housing is politically super-sensitive, and is a risk that vote-seeking politicians are understandably reluctant to run. Yet the scale of housing shortages across Europe is so great it's a step that must be taken. If present market forces are left untamed, the immediate victims will be today's underprivileged young, and eventually society as a whole.

Why housing shortages are so deep-seated

Housing statistics are confusing, and can easily be misleading. Economists warn against 'adding apples and oranges' – conflating unrelated data – and housing statistics are a real fruit salad.

The owner-occupier figures bandied about relate both to homes that are owned outright and those that are heavily mortgaged. When rented accommodation is cited, that can refer to subsidised public housing as well as to outrageously overpriced short rentals. The advent of online services such as Airbnb is adding another, and often volatile, level of confusion to the swirl of housing statistics.

Statistical trends on property that at first point policy makers in one direction can, when looked at more closely, provoke an abrupt U-turn. A good example of how bust can turn to boom was Britain's housing market after the economic crisis of 2008. At first, living standards were hit so hard that demand for property sagged. Then, inexplicably at first, the housing market went into overdrive. It turned out that investors were deserting unrewarding financial markets and instead putting their money into 'buy to rent' housing deals.

The overall picture now seems clear: in Britain and throughout continental Europe people invest more readily in bricks and mortar than in stocks and shares. Property has become the savings vehicle and financial market of choice, with housing widely seen as the preferred way of safeguarding savings, often with the added bonus of substantial profits.

Governments are wary of reform policies that, although primarily designed to put roofs over heads, will adversely affect homeowners' prime investments. They fear that interfering with housing markets risks depressing property values. From the politicians' standpoint, there are more votes to be lost than won through reforms as there are many more homeowners than would-be buyers.

Despite these sensitivities, housing shortages are a growing menace to Europeans' quality of life. If not addressed, people of all generations stand to pay a heavy economic, social and political price. There simply aren't enough dwellings and a rising proportion of people are paying sky-high rents for sub-standard housing. The European Investment Bank says investment in affordable social housing projects needs to rise by 25 per cent, and puts the investment deficit on affordable housing at €57 billion a year.[2]

For many people, the cost of a roof over their heads has become a huge burden. Something like a third of all households are having to spend far more on accommodation than they can reasonably afford. Out of Europe's 220 million or so households, 82 million are 'overburdened by housing costs', according to the Housing Europe Observatory.

This Brussels-based NGO has warned that a substantial number of rent-paying households are so financially precarious that they live with the constant threat of eviction. Unaffordable rents have the knock-on effect of making people on low wages – the 'working poor' – worse off than ever. Out of the EU's population of roughly 500 million, over 150 million people are either poverty-stricken, or teetering on its edge, because of housing difficulties.[3]

Britain's housing situation is especially alarming. Homebuilding in the UK has for the past 30 years been running at less than half the rate of the previous three decades. Paul Cheshire, who is at the London School of Economics (LSE) and is one of the foremost experts on Britain's housing policies, says 'we have systematically been building the wrong sort of houses (too small) in the wrong sort of places'.

After the Second World War, in which well over a million buildings were destroyed by Luftwaffe bombing, house construction was a high priority. At first, flimsy 'prefabs' were hurriedly erected, and these were later replaced by a concerted drive on apartments and council housing. Homebuilding became a strong feature of the UK economy, so from 1959 to 1988, some 7.5 million houses were built in England.

Those years are now looked back on as a golden era when providing more homes was among the top priorities of both central and local government. But from 1989 to 2018, the rhythm of construction dropped vertiginously, with only 3.3 million homes built over that period.

That works out at roughly 100,000 homes a year, when those that were demolished are subtracted. Over that same period, the working age population jumped from 36 million to 42 million, a rate that was double the number of new homes being built. Add in the steadily rising numbers of economic migrants and periodic refugee surges, and it's plain that Britain's housebuilding has for more than 30 years been totally inadequate.

Prof. Cheshire's research shows that successive British governments aggravated the housing problem by building new homes in areas where employment is shrinking, and neglected construction in those where jobs are booming. From 1980 to 2018, the industrial graveyards of Barnsley and Doncaster benefited from almost 60,000 new homes, double the 30,000 allotted to the university towns of Oxford and Cambridge, whose combined populations grew by almost 100,000.

Cheshire's study makes two further points that bring Britain's housing muddle into sharp focus. The first is that fewer new homes means the proportion of old, cramped housing has been growing so fast that getting on for two-thirds of Britain's houses are now more than half a century old. He says these elderly buildings remind him of Cuba's 'clapped out and polluting' vintage American automobiles. His other point is that housing as an investment has outperformed almost all other assets: 'With policy-imposed long term restrictions on housing supply, the British have performed the alchemy of converting houses into gold.'[4]

Similar mistakes are being made elsewhere in Europe. Fewer new homes in regions where services jobs are booming has meant higher house prices and runaway rents. The foremost example of this is the Netherlands, where accommodation shortages have for more than a decade been outpacing the rest of Europe. The ABN AMRO bank has warned that a million new homes should be built by 2030. For a country of around 17 million people with limited land space, that looks a tall order.[5]

These are not isolated instances of housing in crisis. In March 2021, angry protestors in Madrid defied COVID-19 lockdown restrictions and took to the streets to demand fairer housing costs. In Sweden, the issue of capping rents contributed to the mid-2021 toppling of Sweden's government, and in Germany rent controls have become massively divisive.

The European Index of Housing Exclusion reported in 2015 that the 21st century has seen housing costs rise faster than household incomes everywhere except Germany, Finland and Portugal. The Council of Europe Development Bank echoed this when it reported in 2017 that housing costs have become 'an excessive burden' for almost a third of low earners.

In Britain, the Institute for Fiscal Studies (IFS) has said that these rising costs are having a disastrous impact on young people. 'Even the cheapest homes are out of the reach of at least 40 per cent of young adults,' it has reported. The IFS study of barriers to home ownership makes it clear that this has not always been the case, and that until fairly recently younger home buyers earned enough to routinely qualify for a mortgage from a bank or building society.

In 1996, mortgages were granted to nine young applicants in ten. Financial support for first-time home buyers was more or less automatic. Now, warns the IFS, the reduced earning power of younger people coupled with soaring property prices has shrunk their successful mortgage applications to three in five nationally, and one in three in London.[6]

Zoomers fear they'll be 'Generation Rent'

The cards are stacked against the young in a number of ways, whether they are house-buyers or renters. The barriers they must overcome should be reduced by policy makers, but that would first require a coherent plan. So far, there has been no sign of one at either European or national levels.

Generation Z is becoming known as 'Generation Rent'. Even when young couples can raise the down-payment of a tenth or so of the purchase price, the mortgage they need to finance buying their home is often unavailable or financially out of reach. If they turn to the rental market, soaring demand means that there too they face sky-high housing costs.

Renting has long been more popular in continental Europe than in Britain. In Germany and other parts of northern Europe it's frequently the norm. In the UK it is a comparatively recent development. The traditionally placid and predictable British market for rented accommodation has become a rollercoaster of rising prices because disappointed would-be home buyers are forced to settle for renting.

The Victorian era's industrial revolution saw the construction of endless rows of workers' cottages. Miners, dockyard workers and factory hands had little choice but to rent these from their employers as part of a mine or mill's package deal. This tradition of renting persisted right up to the Second World War and even beyond, to judge by the 'Coronation Streets' that are still such a feature of industrial towns in northern England.

About two-thirds of all accommodation in Britain was privately rented during the interwar years of the Great Depression. After the Second World War, however, the situation was rapidly transformed by post-war social housing reconstruction and by building societies that could offer affordable mortgages. By the early 1990s, only 5 per cent of Britain's housing was privately rented.

That was the point at which the nationwide slowdown in home construction began to reveal its full effects. Over the three decades to 2020, when the building of new houses had shrunk to half the rhythm of the previous 30 years, private renting shot up to a fifth of home occupation in Britain.

This surge is being supercharged by the 'buy to rent' phenomenon in which home owners are able to use the collateral of their primary dwelling to finance another. The post-2008 austerity measures pressured people to look for additional income by becoming landlords, and there seems little chance of a let-up. The same financial pressures are unlikely to ease with the aftermath of COVID-19 and the unfolding Ukraine crisis. By the early 2020s, rather more than a tenth of British households owned at least one additional property, and that trend seems to be accelerating.

In continental Europe, renting has long been viewed as a more flexible way of meeting accommodation needs, and of encouraging greater mobility for people who are willing to move to find work. The rental market functioned well for a good many years, but shortfalls in house construction have begun to upend hitherto stable property markets. Seventy-seven German towns and cities warned in the aftermath of the 2015–16 'migrant crisis' that they no longer have spare housing capacity for newcomers. By way of explanation, they cited a collective shortfall in available accommodation of 2 million homes.

Berlin is, unsurprisingly, the epicentre of Germany's housing crisis, and the German capital is also an object lesson in the intractable politics of capping rents. Efforts to alleviate Berliners' rent burdens triggered political turmoil and ended in an embarrassing climbdown.

Germany's planners were hoisted by their own petard when they launched a bold modernisation drive in Berlin. Wrecking balls demolished many of the older, unoccupied buildings that were relics of East Berlin's communist past, and the destruction was also prompted by a growing awareness of Germany's demographic decline. Berlin's 150,000 unoccupied dwellings in the closing years of the last century were seen as an expensive glut on the housing market.

The authorities seriously miscalculated cosmopolitan Berlin's powers of attraction to Europe's young, and its runaway success as an economic hub. Some 300,000 newcomers arrived between 2014 and 2020, and the city is now flailing desperately to find housing for annual influxes of 50,000 people when only 10,000 new apartments come onto the market every year.

Berlin's left-wing local councillors voted in mid-2019 to freeze skyrocketing rents in an attempt to alleviate the financial squeeze on Berlin's younger newcomers. Within two years the measure was dropped, partly for legal reasons but also because of the measure's inherent disadvantages. Germany's constitutional court in Karlsruhe overturned the five-year rent freeze because it contravened federal law, but the chief lesson was that rent caps discourage house construction. Private investors quickly began to lose interest in Berlin.

That lesson wasn't learned in Paris, where in the same year the French government reintroduced the rent controls of 2015 that an administrative court had overturned in 2017. Dubbed by some 'the world's most expensive city alongside Hong Kong and Singapore', Paris was anxious to stamp out blatant rent profiteering that it feared was provoking social unrest.

Opponents of rent controls in France and elsewhere point out that they discourage private sector housing investment and therefore aggravate housing shortages. Ranged against them are rent control advocates who argue that it's important to limit landlords' power to exploit tenants. Even if rent controls dampen private sector investment, they say, they increase the pressure on public authorities to deliver on their promises to build more social housing.

The UK is the only major European country to eschew outright rent controls, or even some form of rent moderation. Spain, Portugal, the Netherlands, Poland and Italy limit rents, while Ireland and Sweden cap rents, and presumably watch with interest as Germany and France tussle internally over the issue.

The bottom line in this unsatisfactory debate was drawn not long ago in the pages of *The Economist*: 'If politicians really want to help renters,' wrote one of its journalists, 'they should favour concrete-mixing, not price-fixing.' The point is well made, because the slowdown in house building lies at the root of Europe's, and Britain's, housing shortages and ultimately of their demographic difficulties.[7]

The great social housing boom that never was

Social housing in Britain and throughout Europe has a long history, but its past looks brighter than its future. In the early 1980s, a third of the UK's housing stock was publicly owned, chiefly by town or county councils, and in the mid-2020s, that share has more or less halved to around 16–17 per cent.

Unless public authorities invest substantial amounts of taxpayers' money in affordable new homes, the vice-like grip of private property markets will condemn the less well-off, especially younger people, to declining living conditions and even outright homelessness.

Queen Victoria was still on her throne in 1898 when pioneer urban planner Sir Ebenezer Howard published his visionary paper entitled 'Garden cities of tomorrow'. His plans for simply designed housing in green spaces led first to the Letchworth project in Hertfordshire and by 1920 to the nearby and better-known Welwyn Garden City. Some 30 other similar developments followed, in the UK on sites donated by municipalities, and abroad in Canada and Australia as well as Japan, Brazil and Poland.

Ebenezer Howard's dream was by no means the first example of social housing. In 16th-century Bavaria, the immensely wealthy Fugger banking dynasty built the Fuggerei complex for Augsburg's poor. In Britain and France, 'company towns' sprang up, the best-known examples being Cadbury's Bournville model village, Lever Brothers' Port Sunlight and Chocolat Menier's '*cité ouvrière*'. The unchallenged prize for government-backed housing remains with the ambitiously monumental Karl-Marx-Hof built in socialist-controlled Red Vienna in the late 1920s to spearhead a construction drive that created 60,000 new apartments.

Housing experts talk wistfully of recovering that spirit of enlightened public construction, but the barriers to doing so are high, and despite much brave talk are getting higher. In any case, the heartening examples from yesteryear were all about philanthropy, not economic policy.

For the UK to embark on a grand strategy capable of building enough affordable homes sited close to employment hubs, schools and hospitals would require nothing short of a revolution. Britain's planning laws have been tinkered with for years, but what's really needed is radical liberalisation.

The system has been captured by big business, and needs much more public money if it is to shake off the inertia of a planning system that can postpone decisions for years on end. The British Property Federation warns that since 2010 spending on planning has been cut by 55 per cent, even though the decade to 2020 saw housing targets rise by 50 per cent.

It's not just bureaucracy and government penny-pinching that's at fault. Greed plays a major role: once land has been granted permission to be built on, it can be worth as much as 100 times more. The construction of new homes in the UK is caught in a high stakes scam worthy of Russia's oligarchs.

Thanks to the 1961 Land Compensation Act brought in by Harold Macmillan's Tory government, big companies with their armies of lawyers began to dominate the speculative acquisition of land suitable for construction. Giant building conglomerates like Taylor Wimpey, Barratt and Persimmon are now accused of hoarding large tracts of land and waiting for house prices to rise higher still before they build on them in earnest.

During Britain's post-Second World War boom in homebuilding and reconstruction, smaller builders dominated the industry and delivered the goods. Until 2008, they built three-quarters of all the UK's new homes. Whether the buyers were young married couples intent on rearing a family or older people being rehoused because of slum clearances or war damage, Britain's proud new home occupants had up to that point been crossing the thresholds of 10,000 freshly built properties every week.

Since then, the big corporations have gradually taken over, and now account for about two-thirds of all new private house construction in the UK. Their behaviour has been devastatingly described by Alex Morton, a former senior civil servant in the 10 Downing Street office of Britain's prime minister: 'Planning permission is a one-way gift which boosts the value of land from more or less £20,000 per hectare to £2–3 million in return for no obligation to do anything beyond breaking ground ... As a result, housebuilding is largely in the hands of a few large builders. The current system incentivises these large corporations to acquire and control land. The six largest have holdings of over a million plots, 90 per cent of them controlled by Taylor Wimpey, Barratt and Persimmon.'

Morton left Downing Street to become a think tanker at the Right-leaning Centre for Policy Studies, where he drew up a plan he believes could increase Britain's housing stock by more than a quarter of a million homes a year. He doubts that the country's cumbersome planning system can ever be scrapped, but suggests that it could be substantially modified. Planning permissions, Morton argues, could be turned into 'delivery contracts' that commit builders to a completion deadline, failing which they would have to sell on to another builder. The new system would be deliberately angled towards smaller building firms.

There's no shortage in the UK of studies and research papers on housing policies; it's the homes themselves that are in short supply. One of the most prominent figures in the debate is Dame Kate Barker, at one time the chief economist at the Confederation of British Industry, the leading UK employers' organisation, and latterly a tireless advocate of better housing policies.

In 2004, her authoritative Barker Report was hailed as the first significant analysis of housing needs since a long-forgotten 1977 government Green Paper. The gap between the two dates shows the low priority Whitehall's mandarins have given to homebuilding. The absence of concrete results illustrates the indifference of successive UK governments.

Often lauded as a 'crusader' for affordable housebuilding, Kate Barker's 36 recommendations were in fact modest enough to be easily implementable had there been the political will. She proposed an extra £1.2–1.6 billion a year to meet predicted social housing needs, a new Regional Planning Executive to decide where more homes are needed, and a mechanism for releasing any additional land that would be needed. The dividend she promised was that these extra private housing starts would calm Britain's spiralling property prices.

Indefatigable in her efforts to bring about change, Kate Barker returned to the fray in 2014 with a book called *Housing: Where's the Plan?*, which looked not only at planning and construction but also at the growing social inequalities penalising the young. Building on her report ten years before, Barker called for other changes such as easing green belt building restrictions, promoting self-build projects and compensating people affected by new developments. Above all, she wanted to see more new towns.

The chorus of voices urging more determined action on housing is getting louder, both in Britain and on the continent. It would be more accurate, though, to call it a cacophony, as there's little agreement on what exactly needs to be done, by whom and with what resources. Yet if consensus plans were to emerge at regional, national and EU levels, Europe's housing shortages could be rapidly addressed.

In the UK, much criticism is levelled against local authorities, who are said to stand in the way of ambitious building projects through their application of planning rules. It's an accusation the Local Government Association (LGA) roundly rejects. 'Between the late 1940s and 1950s councils built more homes than the private sector,' it said in its paper 'House building in England'. 'Until the late 1970s local authorities were building 100,000 homes a year … until a suite of (central government) policy measures.'

The LGA puts the blame on the public sector's withdrawal from homebuilding and says it is itself working with partners to release land for at least 160,000 new homes to be built on. It underlines the economic importance of boosting construction, pointing out that the housebuilding sector contributes almost £20 billion a year to GDP and gives work to 600,000 people.

In mid-2020, a White Paper from the UK's then Conservative government promised to boost the construction of new homes to 300,000 a year, and said that among the measures that would deliver this would be reforms to the 'archaic planning regulations' that created on average a seven-year hiatus between a project's conception and its completion. The reception given to the White Paper was at best lukewarm. Critics complained of its lack of focus on repurposing or modernising older buildings and the lack of support for small building firms, a fifth of which have since collapsed.

By 2022, Boris Johnson's beleaguered and ill-fated government had identified housing as an important vote winner, and announced its revival of Margaret Thatcher's 'Right to Buy' scheme of the 1980s. Young people would be helped onto the home-owning ladder because 2.5 million households currently renting would be able to buy their homes at discounted prices. This apparently attractive proposal was quickly revealed to be a remodelled version of an earlier Tory government's abandoned 'Help to Buy' scheme in 2013, of which the *Financial Times* had commented, 'This is good politics and horrendous economics.'

The fundamental problems facing house construction in Britain and Europe are easy to summarise: Insufficient housebuilding is caused by inadequate public and private investment, and that in turn has led to labour shortages in the building industry. All are fixable.

Policy mixes for Europe's ill-housed young

One of the most striking aspects of the housing shortages and soaring costs facing younger people is the similarity of national crises across Europe. The UK's situation may be slightly worse than some of those on the continent because London's magnetic pull is a big factor. But all European countries arguably require similar policies to address comparable handicaps.

The questions confronting them aren't complicated. Are there basic do's and don'ts for central and regional governments? How national in character are guidelines (and pitfalls) when designing a housebuilding strategy? And given the rising costs of construction materials, is there a pan-European dimension to be developed, both physically and financially?

The first observation to be made is that housebuilding is incredibly old-fashioned – slow, complex, stubbornly resistant to new techniques and materials. Pause at the roadside to take a look at most construction sites and it's evident that the majority of methods are still rooted in the late 19th century. Yes, plastics and hybrid metals have replaced lead, plaster and some of the more artisanal elements, but the business model of a building that grows slowly upwards from a basement or the ground, with specialist trades observing their critical path of installations, hasn't changed in centuries.

Prefab buildings got a bad name when they sprung up on both sides of the English Channel after the Second World War. Flimsy, damp and draughty, they had been badly needed by Europe's bombed-out or displaced millions, and were replaced as soon as possible. The prejudice against prefabrication remains, with few people well disposed to the idea of a home delivered in ready-made slabs straight from the factory floor. Yet prefabricated homes frequently feature in architectural journals and even glossy interior-decor magazines, and raise few eyebrows in Scandinavia or the US.

If mass housing projects could be prefabricated, the speed and cost of housing would be transformed. Instead of being increasingly unattainable, home ownership could be within easy reach of most people. It's not impossible: the Chinese have for some time been erecting skyscrapers at the rate of one Manhattan every two years, and while the featureless urban landscapes of their megalopolis cities are anathema to most Europeans, China's construction methods are instructive.

They are in any case beginning to arrive in Europe. Russia's PIK company built 40,000 housing units in 2020 at its factory in south-west Moscow, using robots to cut production costs by 30 per cent. The company's boss, Sergei Gordeev, says that PIK can produce a prefabricated block of flats in just a fortnight. 'It's a fundamental technological shift,' he has told the *Financial Times*. 'Construction won't be hand made and you won't have all those people on the building site because all buildings will be manufactured in factories and built in a matter of days.'[8]

There can be no doubt that Gordeev's analysis is correct: in Europe at any rate there are no longer enough skilled construction workers to produce housing for the growing numbers of ill-housed or homeless. Only the efficiencies offered by a massive switch towards prefabrication can narrow this widening gap. The National Housing Federation in the UK has said 'building homes in factories out of materials such as timber frames and assembling them on site' could multiply homebuilding by a factor of four.[9]

In the US, 3D-printed house construction has made a modest start, notably in Florida, where a company called Icon has printed two dozen new homes. But for a nation that's famous for its enthusiasm for innovative ideas, the take-up is proving slow. As one commentator put it: 'So far, 3D-printed construction has generated more headlines than buildings.'

Attractive as a switch away from traditional bricks and mortar methods sounds, it's not something 'the market' can deliver. Only the substantial funding and tax incentives available to governments will be enough to encourage major corporations to invest in the factories that would build these homes. In the meantime, social housing is in full retreat across Europe.

In France, where low-rent, high-rise *'habitation à loyer modéré'* (HLM) subsidised apartments ring the outer suburbs of most cities, the drive to build affordable accommodation has slowed almost to a standstill. Much of the state spending that was to fund new apartment projects has been sidetracked into the 'greening' and decarbonisation of existing buildings. Many flats intended for students and younger workers are therefore going unbuilt. Between 2016 and 2020, such projects shrank by 29 per cent.[10]

There are some signs that a more 'European' approach to the continent-wide housing crisis is beginning to take shape. The EU Commission plans to fund a strategy for renovating old buildings that would involve some of the heavy hitters in the European construction sector. The EU executive has pledged eye-watering financial support for the repurposing or modernisation of older houses and industrial buildings, which could create 35 million new homes by 2030. By integrating this into its hugely ambitious Green Deal for achieving carbon neutrality by mid-century, the EU is promising almost €60 billion for renovations and new buildings, with much of that coming from the €1.8 trillion 2021–27 COVID-19 economic recovery and stimulus budget.

On top of that, Housing Europe, which groups social housing organisations, aims to refurbish 4 million homes by 2030 at the rate of 400,000 a year. It acknowledges that to do so requires an extra €13 billion in yearly investment up to 2050 on top of the €23 billion already pencilled in.

These are enormous sums, and nobody seems sure where they might come from. Advocates of housing drives on such a scale underline the fact that construction accounts for almost a tenth of Europe's collective GDP and is an obvious means of kick-starting recession-hit economies.

Leaving aside the pros and cons of pump-priming Keynesian economics, the focus is increasingly on the plight of people who either have nowhere acceptable to live or who must spend so much on accommodation that they are condemned to lives of penury. No one can gauge the extent to which Europe's housing shortcomings contribute to the rise of political extremism and volatility, but it's clearly a potent factor.

There's certainly a growing awareness that European countries cannot economically afford persistent housing shortages, and certainly they can't allow the shortfall to keep on growing. Fifty or so private sector associations and trade federations have come together in its project 'Construction 2050 Alliance: Building tomorrow's Europe today' that calls on the EU to create a coherent new policy framework. They want to bring a greater sense of purpose and urgency to homebuilding, and suggest a starting point would be for Brussels to take the lead with a strong EU political initiative.

Led by the European Construction Industry Federation and a slew of similarly muscular pan-European bodies, this initiative may eventually make a dent on housing shortages. But the EU has neither legal competence nor political clout in the housing sector. 'All politics is local', as a veteran US senator once said, and nothing is more local than housebuilding. Brussels can sound the alarm, but the call to arms has to come from national capitals.

Local schemes abound in the UK, but their delivery of new homes is poor and getting poorer. London's stock of council housing stood at 400,000 in 2019, and two years later was almost 4,000 homes smaller thanks to demolitions and 'right to buy' sell-offs that transferred social housing to the less affordable private property market. The Homes for Londoners scheme unveiled in 2016 that had promised to spark the construction of 116,000 'genuinely affordable' new homes in fact yielded only 954, with a further thousand or so existing ones that were acquired by the Greater London Council rather than built.[11]

Instead of wrestling with the intractable difficulties of building more inner-city homes, pressure groups urge the development of heavily protected green belts around London, Manchester, Birmingham, Newcastle and Bristol. An organisation called Centre for Cities has a plan to build more than 2 million new homes, all within walking distance of suburban railway stations. Its report by the LSE's Prof. Paul Cheshire and Boyana Buyuklieva of University College London says the profits from selling these new 'climate friendly' homes should be invested in improving commuter rail infrastructures and in more social housing.[12]

Comparable schemes have been springing up in continental Europe. France's municipal authorities have been seizing the initiative out of frustration with the pettifogging slowness of the country's notoriously centralised decision-making in Paris. In cities as diverse as Saint-Nazaire on the coast of Brittany, Tours on the river Loire and Seine-Saint-Denis on the capital's eastern fringes, mayors and local councillors have begun working in close collaboration with private property developers to break bureaucratic logjams and get construction moving.[13]

These initiatives reflect an awareness across Europe that housing shortages are a fundamental problem that must be addressed to avert dangerous social and political consequences. A joint paper from the EU-backed European University Institute near Florence and Oxford University has suggested that housing problems are fuelling support for far-Right populist parties. 'We found strong evidence at the aggregate and individual levels', its authors said, 'that housing markets shape voting for populist campaigns.'[14]

Ambitious local housing initiatives are little more than gnat-bites when set against the speed with which the problem is deteriorating. COVID-19 greatly aggravated the situation of both the housing sector and commercial property. From high-rise office buildings to high street shops, the property market is in turmoil, with the young and the underprivileged the first and greatest victims.

Reversing the deepening housing deficit

The COVID-19 pandemic's lockdowns shook the foundations of society's approach to work and to property. Its tremors are widening the gap between WFH 'knowledge society' teleworkers and 'essential' workers who must be physically present, and the aftershocks are more damaging still. The hitherto stable equilibrium between property that houses people and property where people work is being upset; there are too many offices and shops and not enough homes.

Some office buildings can quite easily be converted into apartment blocks, with the added advantage that doing so would regenerate activity in city centres whose business districts become soulless morgues after dark. But the WFH trend will inevitably create more demand for housing, driving up prices that have in any case been fuelled by half a century or more of inadequate construction.

Number-crunching by backroom boffins at *The Economist* magazine in London suggests that over the years since 1960 the number of new houses being built in rich countries in relation to their populations has fallen by half. The magazine also reported that 30 years ago the last of America's baby boomers – the generation whose median age in the 1990s was 35 – owned a third of US real estate by value. Younger people's share has since shrunk dramatically, with millennials now owning only a tiny 4 per cent of property in the US.[15]

The overall picture is much the same in Britain, where the proportion of younger people among home owners has suffered a sharp drop over the last three decades. In the closing years of the previous century, 25–34 year olds accounted for almost a fifth of home ownership, and that has since fallen to around 8 per cent.

Property-owning millennials and Gen-Zers have been declining relatively and in absolute numbers right across Europe. In France, surveys say that although three-quarters of under-35s aspire to home ownership, a majority of them acknowledge that financially this is beyond their means. Germany, often held up as a model because property prices have been comparatively stable in relation to the UK, has seen home ownership among the under-35s decline by over a third since the 1970s.[16]

With fewer and fewer new houses coming onto the market, and with longer life expectancies slowing the rate at which existing properties are put up for sale, younger people with slender means are finding it harder than ever to own their home. There has been a sharp rise in Britain and elsewhere in the proportion of young people whose home ownership relies on family help. The 'Bank of Mum and Dad' is among the top ten UK property funders, with more than half of under-35-year-old home buyers saying that loans and gifts from relations had been essential.

The slowdown in housebuilding in Europe and America is, of course, all about money. Home owners don't want the value of their property to be diminished by what they would see as the too ready availability of more housing. Objections to development projects are often presented as safeguarding the environment, but they also reflect local concerns that existing properties will be worth less if the supply of housing is increased.

Banks are reluctant to tie up funds in mortgage lending when they can earn bigger profits in financial markets. That's why Jamie Dimon, boss of JP Morgan Chase and one of Wall Street's most famous wolves, explained back in 2016 that he found the mortgage business less attractive because of 'increasingly low returns' on financing home buying.

A host of subsidiary pressures stem from these two principal dampeners on homebuilding. They include planning restrictions, investment limitations, regional development policies and interventions by state authorities. The question that civil society across Europe and in America must address is whether these pressures should be confronted by radical new policies, even if these might have unsettling political consequences.

It's useful to look at countries that have resisted the pressures to freeze or cut back on homebuilding. Switzerland's federal government uses tax breaks to encourage cantonal authorities to allow housing developments. As a result, the Swiss build twice as many houses per head of population as the Americans and three times more than in Britain. In Japan, a similar approach has seen Tokyo alone putting up as many new homes in recent years as are built in the whole of England.

Tax has been the decisive factor in these cases, but it's not the only instrument available to governments. Housing problems have become so widespread and central to people's socio-economic futures that far more comprehensive policy mixes are needed if they are to add up to a strategy.

The cornerstone of a housing strategy in Britain and elsewhere would be a more coherent approach to planning, and most of all to the granting of permission to build. 'Planning' is shorthand for decisions on who builds what, and where, and therefore has long been a bone of contention between local authorities and central government. Grassroots democracy and the devolution of powers to elected local representatives, combined with stubborn small 'c' conservatism, has produced a nightmare kaleidoscope of different rules across England.

When the Tory government's 2022 White Paper on 'Planning for the Future' proposed a rules-based system with a standard format for assessing planning requests, even the most forthright critics of Britain's patchwork of planning regulations gave it grudging approval. The LSE's Paul Cheshire called it 'the first serious attempt to reform our dysfunctional land use planning system since its inception'.

There's widespread agreement that local decision-making and 'nimbyist' (not in my backyard) resistance to development has been a massive brake on homebuilding. 'The planning system in the UK', commented the authors of a paper by the Policy Exchange think tank in London, 'has little relevance to the country's 21st century liberalised economy … although regularly tinkered with, its fundamental principles are the same as when it was established in 1947.'

Their recommendations were broadly in line with those of the then government: clear new rules to prevent local authorities from limiting the allocation of land, and a strong shift in favour of increasing housing and office development instead of stifling it. A major clarification of green belts and national parks would be accompanied by a bonfire of red tape, forcing local authorities to boil their planning rules down to just a few pages instead of several hundred.[17]

Other elements of an overall housing strategy would include regional and industrial policies. The long-standing conundrum of whether policy makers should prioritise taking the jobs to the people or the people to the jobs is more crucial than ever thanks to the shift from manufacturing to services in the new 'knowledge economy'.

The emptying out of rural areas and the spread of industrial wastelands is increasing the demand for subsidised social housing at a time when its supply is dwindling. The UK, along with highly developed economies elsewhere, needs a much more holistic approach to both public housing and private homebuilding.

Then there's the environmental question. Everyone knows that old-fashioned and uninsulated buildings are major contributors of CO_2 and greenhouse gases, but it also seems widely accepted that this huge problem defies practical solutions. Greening could nevertheless be the lever to move the mountainous problem of inadequate housing. Grants to fund environmental overhauls would act as financial flywheels that set in motion ambitious home improvement and construction drives.

The rewards would be huge. A determined housing strategy could do much to revive sluggish post-COVID-19 economies still in the throes of recession. The drag effects of housing shortages are widely recognised, but have made little impact on governments whose fiscal rectitude has often outweighed calls for deficit financing.

The World Bank is just one of the international institutions arguing for proactive housing policies to counter the inflation of costs, particularly those that damage the prospects of younger people. Its report on the Europe-wide affordable housing crisis warned that accommodation costs are at the heart of growing economic divides. More residential construction, argued the World Bank, would have positive knock-on effects for social mobility and productivity. The study's authors made three key recommendations: earmark public land for new housing; improve transport links around big cities; and ensure price transparency by creating public registries of house sales.[18]

The long saga of housing gloom

The most striking feature of the housing crisis hitting young people so hard isn't its complexity and its damaging effects, but rather the sheer length of time during which housing shortages have persisted and deteriorated. The legacy of half a century or more of political short-sightedness and neglect risks being another 50 years of housing gloom.

The expert analyses and warnings published across Europe and by authoritative international bodies have made remarkably little impact on national decision-making. Instead of accepting the idea that housing and property are fundamental to economic well-being, the different levels of government in the UK and most of the EU continue to view housing-related policies as ancillary to economic governance.

The breadth of the problem in Britain has been neatly encapsulated by House of Commons library researchers. 'Housing need manifests itself in a variety of ways,' they reported in January 2021, 'such as increased levels of overcrowding, acute affordability issues, more young people living with their parents for longer periods, impaired labour mobility resulting in businesses finding it difficult to recruit and retain staff, and increased levels of homelessness.'

The British parliamentarians' report looked back at several different governments' pledges to fix the problem. In 2015, the goal had been to add a million net new homes by 2020, and in 2017 that was raised to a further half-million by the end of 2022. These receding targets also have to be set against a background of under-building over several decades. Instead of the 300,000 new homes every year that successive Conservative governments had promised, the reality for 2010–20 was 130,500 a year.

That was the record of a Tory party ignominiously ousted in the general election of July 2024. Whether its successor Labour government will opt for the streamlining of what it labelled as 'archaic' planning methods remains to be seen. It's doubtful, in any case, that the reform of planning would ever be enough to deliver a huge increase in housing.

When the LGA had fought back against the Tories' criticism of planning procedures, it said that to blame local authorities was to 'duck the big issue'. It pointed out that in mid-2021, permits for over 475,000 new homes had not been acted on, and said the real culprits are withdrawals of public housing, shortcomings of the land market and shrinkage of the construction sector's manpower. It traced the origins of today's severe housing difficulties back to the 1980s, when public housing construction began to fall sharply. Even when the post-Second World War public housing boom had subsided, the LGA pointed out, local councils were contributing 100,000 new homes yearly to the housing stock, but that was snuffed out by central government in the late 1970s.

The lesson is clear. Policy makers in Westminster and most of Europe's capitals must radically rethink their approach to housing and to the degree that generational imbalances are making matters worse. On top of decades of laissez-faire neglect of younger people's housing needs, the retention of homes by older people is aggravating undersupply.

Tax incentives to encourage the transfer of existing housing to younger buyers, and to improve care facilities and health services for the elderly, should be crucial to an overall strategy. Overhauling housing should be seen as key to improving the fertility of younger couples as well as an essential factor in addressing the needs of ageing populations.

Above all, a broader appreciation is needed of housing's role in the transformation of European society. As well as shifting economically from the making and trading of things towards the creation and diffusion of ideas, the upsetting of millennia-old intergenerational balances is exerting huge pressures on where people live, and how. Without deep-seated change, the outlook will get grimmer year on year.

8

Older voters' 'silver stranglehold'

Pensioners, already powerful, are getting stronger still. The over-sixties increasingly dominate Europe's democracies and have been fuelling populism, including Brexit. Older voters will outnumber the young for the foreseeable future, and will want to protect their welfare and healthcare interests. This strengthening is paralleled by youth's political apathy. Electoral reform needs to loosen the 'silver stranglehold' with policies that counteract the effects of ageing.

We in advanced Western democracies look to our political systems to resolve conflicts. It can be a messy process, but by and large it has served us well. Whether nationally or at a European level, the power of electorates has been a force for good.

But we can no longer take this for granted. It may sound a dangerous heresy, but Europe's parliamentary democracies risk being part of the problem and not the solution. Ageing and demographic change are skewing voting patterns and sapping the ability of younger people to influence policymaking. As Europe ages, it's the elderly who will call the shots.

With the average age of Europeans by mid-century knocking on 50, up from around 43 today, more tax money will be needed to pay for rising welfare spending that chiefly benefits the retired. These taxes are overwhelmingly to be paid by younger workers. Politicians seldom highlight this growing conflict of interests because they fear that warning of trouble ahead is a mug's game electorally.

Around the world, 2024 was the 'Year of the Ballot Box', with more than 2 billion people in a hundred or so countries exercising their right to vote. In Europe, snap general elections in France and Britain followed the scheduled five-yearly election of MEPs to the European Parliament. However, a notable feature of the electoral campaigns across Europe was the silence of politicians on the political implications of ageing.

An unwillingness to heap future problems on top of present ones is understandable. But the unavoidable truth is that tomorrow's politics will be uglier than ever. Diverging interests will pit wage earners against pensioners, while the over-fifties will be able to outvote their taxpaying juniors. As well as being more powerful politically, older Europeans will remain wealthier than the young. They not only draw a pension and benefit the most from social security and healthcare, but they are also the greater owners by far of property, investments and savings.

Seen from younger people's standpoint, the elderly want to have their cake and eat it. There's a widening chasm between the young who are taxed and their seniors whose pensions and healthcare are funded by those taxes. This hasn't yet hardened into opposing political parties defined by age, but it's beginning to confuse voting patterns.

Democracies are in theory well placed to deal with the upheavals triggered by demographic change. Government by the people for the people should mean flexible decision-making to ensure that those most affected by shifting conditions are adequately protected. But not in practice.

How well such adjustments work differs across Europe. By and large, the post-Second World War years saw most parliamentary systems perform satisfactorily. Democracies have grown substantially in number thanks to the collapse of the Soviet Union and the rebirth of many of its communist satellites as EU member states. Liberal democracies and market economies are now the European norm.

Yet ageing Europe stands on the threshold of disruptive new pressures. Nobody can say how resilient the EU's political structures will be, but to resist ageing's pressures, Europe's nation states must reorder their social welfare and tax raising arrangements. And that will come down to votes. EU governments must secure democratic mandates to reverse fiscal policies that currently hit youthful earners much harder than their less active elders, who may not work but own so much of Europe's wealth.

Older voters easily outnumber younger ones in most parts of Europe, and will do so for decades to come. Paradoxically, the elderly are likely to resist the radical tax and benefits reforms that Europe's ageing will demand. They will probably also oppose moves to rebalance democratic decision-making in younger voters' favour. This 'silver stranglehold' is set to be a major factor in the European political landscape of the 21st century, and one that risks seriously exacerbating the problems that stem from ageing.

The rising tide of retirements in most European countries is already shifting taxation onto the shoulders of the under-fifties. And because it's such a long-term problem, it will by mid-century begin to weigh heavily on the members of Generation Alpha who are still in kindergarten.

The preferred solution would be to refashion our democracies in ways that ensure younger taxpayers cannot be systematically outvoted by their elders' electoral majorities. But that's easier said than done as the choice is between root and branch reforms, or timid changes that would be no more than minor adjustments.

The political auguries aren't encouraging. Europe's national democracies are so different that it's hard to see how they might be adapted to ageing without first streamlining EU decision-making. The EU's 27 member states are currently stalemated over mooted improvements to their intergovernmental arrangements. Although more majority voting in the Council of Ministers is opposed by only a few member states, achieving it would require unanimous approval.

British politics, meanwhile, are beginning to recover from the chaos of Brexit, but show no sign of avoiding the fate of becoming a gerontocracy. There doesn't seem much appetite for change. Many Britons still revel in the Victorian grandeur of the Houses of Parliament and the confrontational drama of the two largest parties on their opposing benches. Only more radical voices warn that the system is outdated, inefficient and at odds with public opinion.

On the continent, most European countries have remodelled their democracies over the last three-quarters of a century. Perhaps this could make them more prepared to accept a rebalancing of the powers of younger and older voters, but there too the appetite for reform seems muted.

There is nevertheless a growing consensus between political scientists that demographic shifts are going to upset familiar voting patterns. That doesn't mean there's any consensus at all on how to reform national parliamentary democracies or how to upgrade the European Parliament. As to getting EU countries to discuss common measures that would address the political imbalances of ageing, so far that's been a non-starter.

Europe's track record on constitutional reform has been mixed, so the likelihood of redressing demographic change's electoral imbalances is slim. Less dramatic shifts stand a better chance of eventually being adopted by some countries, either whole or in part. Suggestions for this come in the main from smaller fringe parties or from NGOs.

It's too early in the scattered national debates on electoral reform to gauge the reactions of the larger mainstream parties. It is harder still to say whether European politics will ever mature in ways that can handle the challenges of demographic change. Pessimists say that although national parliamentary democracies are structured very differently across the EU, their common denominator is that all are too sclerotic to be reformed or to be welded into a more coherent whole.

Top of the list of suggested reforms is the lowering of voting ages and the introduction of 'youth quotas' in parliaments and even local councils. Others include whether digital technologies could have a role in the creation of new parties and voting blocs. There are also ideas that interactive online techniques could bring democratic decision-making closer to the public, especially to its younger members. A number of studies and research projects have begun to explore the European political landscape up to mid-century, but to date there are more questions than answers.

The truth is that young people are political outsiders

It won't be easy to convince Europeans that their political systems are no longer fit for purpose. Their parliamentary democracies are evidently incapable of delivering the reforms and compromises that could defuse Europe's demographic timebomb. On the contrary, the polarisation of the extreme Left and hard Right is exacerbating the ageing problem.

Politicians have had little success in engaging young people's support for policies that could address their own future. At first sight, this would seem to reflect a youthful disdain for politics, the proof being low voter turnouts. In fact, the picture is more complicated. A growing number of younger voters have been backing populist parties, raising questions about the part age plays in voters' susceptibility to simplistic slogans.

Europeans' politics are on the move, and in many countries they are shifting rightwards – the wrong direction in terms of tackling the growing demographic crisis. Populists woo older people with promises of earlier retirement and lower taxes, and younger voters apparently fail to understand that they will be the eventual victims of these pledges.

The familiar Left–Right pattern looks as if it will be merged with, and perhaps even replaced by, Young–Old politics. The conflicts of interest between younger Europeans and their elders will not be resolved within existing parliamentary democracies. With the gap widening between the needs of outvoted under-40 year olds and the self-interests of their elders, something has to give.

This problem has been staring politicians in the face for many years, but it has been too uncomfortable to confront. Back in the relatively good times of the 1990s, international bodies like the Council of Europe (CoE) in Strasbourg and the Paris-based OECD were trying to draw attention to the declining earning power of younger people and their lack of political clout.

The CoE issued a report warning that fewer than one young person in ten in Western Europe belonged to a political party, and put the figure at one in a hundred for Eastern Europe. The only youthful political activism the report's authors could detect was Green. These warnings of apathy if not downright hostility to politics failed to provoke any significant reactions by governments or civil society organisations.

In 2008, youth ministers attending a CoE conference admitted their inability to strengthen young people's political clout. They acknowledged the 'precariousness' of younger people to be a major challenge, and added that responsibility for the problem didn't lie solely with the young. The ministers' reluctant conclusion was that youthful voters are becoming 'a less important focus for political parties, and are potentially peripheral to public policy'.[1]

That ministerial meeting took place as the crisis in global financial markets was deepening and austerity policies were beginning to hit younger people hardest. Across the EU, 15–24 year olds were proportionately losing the most jobs and were also beginning to suffer the 'scarring' effects of the ensuing decade-long 'Great Recession'. They either became so discouraged that they joined the ranks of the long-term unemployed, or they found themselves forced to accept low-paid jobs and thus qualified for membership of the new category of 'working poor'.[2]

Could the politics of age displace those of the Left–Right?

The 2008 global economic crisis that almost melted down the financial markets was at one point thought so devastating that it would force Europe's political structures to be rebuilt. To the relief of some and the despair of others, that didn't happen. Instead, the post-crisis years saw austerity rather than reform dominating the policy debate.

But beneath the surface a quiet revolution was taking place, with age rather than long-standing Left–Right pressures beginning to influence governments' decision-making. Although this sounds encouraging, it's not. Instead of younger voters waking to the opportunities offered by the ballot box, it was the grey electorate that began to mobilise and defend its own interests when social benefits and healthcare were being threatened by cash-strapped governments.

Young people's apathy has exacerbated the problem, with voter turnout among 18–24 year olds some 16 percentage points lower than among people aged 25 to 50, according to the OECD. This indifference of younger voters is disquieting, but less so than developments within the so-called silver vote. Older voters haven't yet formed sizeable political parties of their own, but that looks to be only a matter of time. In the Netherlands, the 50Plus Pensioners' Party seems likely to be the forerunner of others elsewhere in Europe.

Governments are increasingly aware of their need to satisfy older voters' demands. The disproportionate political power already wielded by pensioners and those nearing retirement is going to increase over time. Older people's concerns rather than those of child-rearing taxpayers look set to dominate governments' spending agendas. Politicians know that older people can be relied on to turn out to vote, whereas younger voters are not only fewer but are also fickle and unreliable at election times.

When by 2030 the last of the baby boomers has retired, millennials and Gen-Zers will constitute the majority of active workers in the EU. But because retired people remain voters, the young people's workforce majority won't save them from being an electoral minority. Younger people will be outvoted until at least mid-century, and so will very probably have a tough time advancing policies on the issues that affect them most.

In wider European terms, the question analysts are asking is whether geopolitical change will invigorate younger voters' interest. Putin's war against Ukraine has arguably done more to drive home to European public opinion the link between responsible environmental policies and energy reform. Political analysts in most Western European countries are watching closely to see whether environmental issues will also rally younger voters and thus dilute the influence of their elders.

Populism's triumphs across Europe clearly reflect the way political opportunists pander to older voters, even if some younger people have counter-intuitively succumbed to their blandishments. Brexit heads the list of ultra-conservative voting by older people that has been at the root of political upsets in Italy, Sweden, Hungary and elsewhere in continental Europe. These victories have not always proved durable, but so far they have been a persistent trend. The mid-2024 European Parliament elections saw a quarter of the newly elected MEPs representing a Eurosceptic standpoint of one sort or another.

Hard Right populists such as Poland's Law and Justice (PiS) party and Hungary's Fidesz led by Viktor Orbán rose to power by appealing to older Eurosceptics, and once in government rewarded their supporters by legislating earlier retirement. Although PiS was ousted in autumn 2023, it remains a formidable factor in Poland's politics.

In France, Marine Le Pen's nationalistic and anti-immigrant Rassemblement National was rebuffed in the 2024 general election, but expects to rely heavily on the support of the over-fifties in the forthcoming 2027 presidential election. In Germany, a similar electoral profile brought the right-wing Alternativ für Deutschland out of obscurity and into a challenging position in frontline politics.

Germany is looked to as a bellwether for the future direction of European politics, and there have been warnings from senior figures in Berlin that the age factor is a growing concern. Georg Thiel, the federal official supervising elections, has cautioned that voting patterns are changing. He noted that turnout by over-sixties in the 2019 European elections was around two-thirds, far higher than that of younger voters. 'Owing to these differences in voter turnout and the demographic trend,' he commented, 'the 60-plus generation has an increasing influence on election results.' Thiel's remarks echoed those of the late Roman Herzog, who as President of the Federal Republic had warned of a 'pensioners' democracy'.[3]

It is harder to draw useful conclusions from the British political scene. The Brexit referendum's mid-2016 upset was undoubtedly an example of populism that sparked a nostalgic form of nationalism, evoking the supposed glory days of empire. The Conservatives had come to power in 2010 in the wake of the 2008–09 global financial crisis, and their extended 14-year rule saw the Tory party move steadily to the Right as it sought to buttress its waning electoral support.

In the UK, a changed pattern is becoming clearer; class loyalties are being upended by age considerations. The Brexit referendum was narrowly won by older voters from across the socio-economic spectrum who hoped that a break with the EU would somehow relax the constraints of UK austerity policies. These gut instincts trumped younger Britons' view that their country's future lay within the protective strengths of Europe.

An interesting comment on that – and an indication of the speed of demographic change – is the calculation that if the Brexit referendum had been held two and a half years later, the UK would still be in the EU. 'Assuming constant voting patterns,' wrote Niall Ferguson and Joseph de Weck in the influential American magazine *The Atlantic*, 'by January 2019 enough Remainers had reached the voting age and enough Brexiteers had died to reverse the 2016 result in the event of a new referendum.'[4]

Age had a limited influence on voters' choices until comparatively recently. In 1970s Britain, the roughly 40 per cent of the electorate who voted Labour came from all age groups, with working-class voters three times more likely to support Labour than the Conservative party. Fifty years on, a 70-year-old is three times more likely to vote Tory than Labour and a 30-year-old is twice as likely to vote Labour rather than Tory. Labour's July 2024 landslide victory seemed to suggest that dissatisfaction with the Conservative government transcended age differences, although it's noteworthy that only 52 per cent of the electorate voted, making it the lowest turnout since the 1928 introduction of universal suffrage in England, Wales and Scotland.

Britain's post-Brexit and post-COVID-19 woes crowded out age-related issues, but these nevertheless remain the most important underlying trend. 'Older people are massively outvoting the young,' according to the Intergenerational Foundation, a London-based organisation concerned with demographic problems. Its co-founder Angus Hanton commented that baby boomers such as himself are changing the age profile of voters and 'leading Britain towards a gerontocracy run by the old for the old'.[5]

Not everyone agrees. British sociologist Jennie Bristow has advanced a spirited argument against it in her book *Stop Mugging Grandma*. 'I have no interest in defending the interests of one generation against another,' she wrote. 'My argument is that generations do not have competing interests, and that it is very dangerous to pretend they do. The aim of this book is to cut through this phoney generation war, to understand why these poisonous myths have taken such a hold.'

Bristow believes that 'the generational split in voting and values is far less clear-cut than has been presented'. Yet despite devoting substantial sections of her book to electoral issues, she repeats some telling statistics, notably that half of Germany's electorate is over 50 while under-thirties voters make up only 15 per cent.[6]

It's obvious that today's advanced societies share a common interest in strengthening intergenerational bonds. Unfortunately, that's not the way democratic politics work. The temptation for both voters and candidates for office is to favour highly specific issues or sections of society rather than to prioritise the common good. The price to be paid for doing 'the right thing' in pursuit of a country's general wellbeing can be daunting. The year after Emmanuel Macron won election to his first term in the French presidency, he learnt this lesson the hard way.

When Macron became president in 2017 after having created a new centrist political movement, he embarked on a radical reform programme to improve opportunities and living standards. He soon met a storm of angry protests and civil disobedience when dissident *'gilets jaunes'* in bright yellow high-vis jackets blocked major road junctions and rampaged through some of the wealthiest districts of Paris. Macron reluctantly diluted his reform plans.

Many of the *gilets jaunes* were middle-aged protesters from rural France objecting to a well-intentioned but clumsy 'green' tax hike on diesel fuel that hit country folk hardest. They also opposed a planned shift in social security contributions that would reduce the burden on young people with low salaries. Instead, Macron proposed an increase in contributions from middle-income pensioners.

More a technocrat than a dogma-spouting ideologue, Emmanuel Macron is very aware of ageing's threat to France's, and indeed Europe's, future. He envisaged across-the-board reforms to his country's tangle of special pension and benefit arrangements. Although branded by opponents as the 'president of the rich', he also took aim at the tax privileges of the wealthier, many of whom are either pensioners or are approaching fairly comfortable retirement at the age of 62.

Re-elected in April 2022 to a second five-year term, Macron soon found his reform drive draining support for his own party. In short order he lost his majority in the Assemblée Nationale, suffered a drubbing in the June 2024 European elections and then found himself confronted with a Left–Right impasse following the snap election he'd called to 'clarify' matters.

Macron's gamble had been whether his reforms could kick-start jobs and growth quickly enough to quell opposition from older voters. Other European governments preferred to duck such a high-risk approach. In August 2019, Angela Merkel's 'Grand Coalition' of Right and Left eased access to pension payments, and the coalition government led by Social Democrat

Olaf Scholz since December 2021 was equally cautious. Scholz had pledged to maintain pensions at 48 per cent of the average wage by borrowing fresh money to pay for a special €200 billion fund, but critics pointed out that this would also entail increased contributions by younger Germans.

In Poland, the former populist PiS government's 2017 reduction in the retirement age left its successor led by Donald Tusk with a fait accompli that's difficult to retreat from. Men can draw their pension at 65, two years earlier than before, and women five years earlier at 60.

Italy's political conundrum over pensions is arguably the most dramatic in Western Europe. Ever since Georgia Meloni took office in autumn 2022 as leader of the Brothers of Italy party, her right-wing coalition government has been dodging and backtracking on issues ranging from welfare to pensions to voting qualifications. Italy's index-linked pensions can be worth 90 per cent of the average wage and are bankrupting the country: they absorb 15 per cent of its GDP, and by 2042 that will have risen to 17 per cent.

Whether Italy can resolve its pensions problem is keenly watched by other EU countries with similar difficulties. The European Commission is concerned that more than half of the EU's member states have unsustainable state pension systems. It has been chiding them and urging reform since 2019, but the electoral consequences of overhauling retirement ages has dampened many governments' enthusiasm.

Vote-seeking politicians have unashamedly solicited the votes of older people, and in doing so they have brazenly ignored the impact on their own public finances. The consensus view among policy analysts is that unless Europe can shorten pensionable retirement years, the strains will cripple future welfare arrangements.

If democracy is failing us, can we not improve it?

Despite the enormity of the demographic challenge, Europe remains saddled with inappropriate political systems. Once quite efficient, these are now creating more problems than solutions. The squeeze between governments' spending needs and their financial resources means democratic decision-making is certain to grow in importance, and is very likely to result in the wrong choices.

At the heart of the problem is the age-old debate in many countries about 'big government' versus 'small government'. The former is all about state-led economic development and hands-on management of infrastructure and welfare. Advocates of smaller and more libertarian government call, in contrast, for a light touch approach to the market economy.

Instead of a straightforward question over how parliamentary voting can be rebalanced to ensure younger people's interests are safeguarded, there's the even bigger question of what governments should and shouldn't control. The shadow of COVID-19 is lifting, but the pandemic has done much to focus public attention on the role of the state. Beyond issues surrounding healthcare and emergency financial bail-outs rage other arguments that are very relevant to any country that faces ageing's snowballing social costs.

Advocates of 'freedom', generally on the centre-right, insist that the powers needed by central governments to manage COVID-19 lockdowns and vaccinations must be speedily relinquished so that smaller government can be restored. Ranged against them are those who see the strains created by the pandemic as pointers to the greater responsibilities society must accept when catering for so many more elderly people.

In truth, big government never really went away in Western industrialised countries – whatever admirers of Margaret Thatcher in the UK and Ronald Reagan in the US might claim. The three decades since the end of the 1980s saw successive crises force governments to bail out motley collections of banks, industrial giants and mortgage holders large or small. Financial rescue packages for COVID-19-hit businesses and their employees have been only the latest of these.

The nadir of the pandemic saw the extra fiscal and monetary help given by governments in some developed countries reportedly bring total social spending to an astounding 40 per cent of their GDPs. COVID-19 aside, when societies become more advanced and socially progressive, the role of the state inevitably grows. More social equity demands higher tax revenues, and the two feed on one another in either a virtuous or a vicious circle, depending on the political prism through which they are viewed.[7]

It's often said that governing is fundamentally about choosing, and often that means between the bad and the less bad. In fact, the choices that try to reconcile social fairness and freedom have so far been handled more or less satisfactorily in Britain and continental Europe. But it's hard to see the democratic structures that did so surviving in their present form. Once demographic shifts begin to seriously disrupt the balance of intergenerational interests, the pressures for change will intensify.

Younger Europeans need – and will no doubt eventually insist on – a fairer share of resources and wealth than they receive at present. Their needs range from greater job security and higher wages to cheaper housing coupled with incentives to raise more children. Above all, there must be a revolutionary new approach to building up and guaranteeing their pensions.

This daunting list of demands in the name of fairness has long been largely ignored in most parts of Europe. As matters stand, older Europeans will continue to have the necessary political and democratic clout to deny the young these crucially important policy changes. But depriving the young of these improvements is in no one's interests. Society as a whole will suffer if the young become a blighted generation.

A more progressive political narrative by politicians across the spectrum should explain why a better deal for younger people is in the interests of all. Cushioning older people at the expense of younger ones condemns Europe to long-term economic and social decline.

It won't be easy, to say the least, to persuade Europeans of all ages to address these difficulties by upending familiar democratic structures. Voters by and large approve of their existing parliamentary systems, even if they don't necessarily admire their politicians or welcome the laws handed down by them.

Electorates have shown themselves reluctant to endorse radical change, so to achieve that would require an extraordinary shift in the public mood. A first step would be sustained and skilful information campaigns to create a greater public awareness of the plight of the young who are Europe's future.

Europe's plethora of democracies – Gordian knot or hopeless muddle?

Generalisations about democracy in Europe are complicated by the differences between national systems. The 'party list' form of proportional representation is by far the most common, with 31 generally smaller countries other than Poland and Spain adhering to the system in which voters opt for political parties rather than candidates.

Parliamentary candidates are selected and ranked in preferred order by behind-the-scenes party apparatchiks. Voters choose the party they support, and the total number of votes cast for it determines how many of the prospective MPs who stood for that party will be elected.

Two EU countries, Ireland and Malta, use the single transferable vote (STV) method, and two others, Germany and Hungary, use mixed member proportional representation (PR), sometimes known as the additional member system. Parallel voting in various mixed forms is used by five electorates, with Italy making an odd bedfellow with Andorra, Ukraine, North Macedonia and Lithuania.

The UK has long stood out as the 'awkward squad' in any discussion of PR, because in all its various guises this is designed to produce consensus-seeking coalition governments. Britain's long-standing 'first past the post' is intended to avoid them.

Scotland and Northern Ireland, however, use the STV to elect Scottish local councils and the Northern Ireland Assembly and its councils. The centrist Liberal Democrats have ceaselessly campaigned for the nationwide introduction of STV, but it's anathema to the Labour and Conservative parties. That's because Westminster's first past the post system favours the two largest political parties and discourages coalitions that might reconcile different interests and ideologies.

Far from being widely admired, the rest of Europe tends to look askance at the bellowing and jeering antics of MPs in the House of Commons. Britain's confrontational system produces the sort of stop–go policy hiccups that most countries are at pains to avoid. The only other European nations to eschew PR are far from democratic Belarus along with France.

There are other variables in Europe's confusing pot-pourri of national democratic systems, so overhauling them to create more 'youth responsive' structures seems a distant prospect. Some systems are federal, notably those of Germany and Belgium where there's greater regional autonomy, or Spain that has moved towards it. France, like Britain, heads the list of strongly centralised countries that have been wary of greater devolution.

On top of these differences, which are often emblematic of national cultures, there are various voting age rules and in some countries mandatory voting. Making it illegal to refuse to cast one's vote has advocates and opponents, and it certainly confuses analysis of voter turnout levels across Europe. Confusion is in any case a hallmark of European democracy. Quite apart from all the question marks over EU-level voting and the role of the European Parliament, there's little consensus on the value of parliamentary democracies.

That's true of Western democracies as a whole: 30 years ago, two-thirds of the people interviewed in Europe, North America, Northeast Asia and Australasia were satisfied with democratic government, but now a majority is not. The UK, Spain and Greece join the US, Japan and Australia in having swung onto the list of dissatisfied electorates, according to a global survey in 2020 by Cambridge University.

When pollsters examine views on politics, it can be hard to distinguish between responses that assess a democratic system and those that reflect their own personal fortunes. So it was perhaps predictable that this survey also found that smaller, high-income democracies enjoy rising confidence among voters. Forming 'an island of contentment' in a sea of growing discontent, Switzerland, Denmark, Norway, the Netherlands and Luxembourg registered all-time highs, in which more than three-quarters of respondents claimed to be satisfied.[8]

Public confidence in government ebbs and flows across Europe and beyond. The basis of citizens' approval reflects their perceptions of corruption or impartiality among decision-makers, together with governments' performances at times of crisis. The COVID-19 pandemic reduced concerns over corruption in a number of EU countries and in others may have helped to boost confidence in governments' effectiveness, according to a University of Gothenburg European Values Survey.[9]

How younger people's voting power could be boosted

Creating a more homogeneous Europe-wide parliamentary democracy is clearly impossible. The best approach to the problem might be to introduce common features adaptable enough to fit in with the different national systems. Voting ages and party funding are the most obvious areas where consensus could be found.

Financial contributions to political parties' campaigns are a running sore in the sides of almost all Western democracies. Limits on private donations, rules limiting corporate support and strict regulations imposing transparency are regularly flouted by ambitious politicians and secretive administrations. In France, former president Nicolas Sarkozy was sentenced to a one-year term in jail – served as house arrest – for illegal funding practices. In Britain, long before Vladimir Putin's invasion of Ukraine provoked rising anti-Russian sentiments, sleaze allegations swirled around Russian oligarchs' funding contributions to the Tory party.

Successive crackdowns in European capitals on party financing abuses have mostly been whack-a-mole exercises, with successes making only temporary dents in the wider problem. The difficulty in relation to younger voters, meanwhile, is that illicit party financing is inevitably aimed at maintaining a status quo or advancing specific industrial interests, rather than bolstering progressive policies.

If limiting the funding of centre-right political parties risks being a lost cause, that's not necessarily true of lowering the voting age. Millions more young people could be enfranchised if the issue were to be tackled by a cross-border alliance of political parties.

In most of the EU's 27 member states the voting age is still 18, but the trend to bring it down to 16 is gathering pace. Austria was the first to lower it to 16 in 2007, followed by Malta in 2018. In Greece it's 17. Thinking may be influenced in other EU countries by Germany's decision to move to 16, because part of the negotiations leading in late 2021 to the 'traffic light' coalition of Social Democrats, Liberals and Greens was an agreement to reduce the voting age of 18 by two years.

Belgium moved to allow 16 year olds to vote in the 2024 European elections, which the European Parliament endorsed as desirable for the EU as a whole. In the UK, voting in local elections is open to 16 year olds in Scotland, Wales, the Isle of Man and the Channel Islands, although these liberalisations seem to reflect devolutionary pressures rather than a focus on younger voters' socio-economic interests.

It may be that the subtle influence exerted by public opinion in this age of youth cultures will lead to lower voting ages around the world. This has already taken place in some regions, notably in Latin America, where voting at 16 has prevailed for a good many years in Brazil, Argentina and smaller nations. But it may also be that more conservative countries and political parties will continue to oppose lower voting ages because young people have tended to vote Leftwards.

How an across-the-board enfranchisement of 16 year olds might alter the landscape of politics in Europe is anyone's guess. Experts at Population-Europe – a network of demographers – took a stab at the question when they developed their Generational Power Index (GPI) that used a 'Brexit scenario' to judge the impact of enlarging electorates to younger voters.

The UK voting patterns that produced an almost 52 per cent majority in the Brexit referendum are now widely understood. More than two-thirds of younger voters wanted to stay, but were far outnumbered by older 'leave' supporters. The key to Brexit was that at 5.3 million voters, the 18–24s were less than half as many as the 11 million over-65s. Harald Wilkoszewski of Population-Europe commented, 'Even a 100 per cent turnout by young Brits, or lowering the voting age, could not have prevented Brexit.'

The GPI compared outcomes in 19 countries when the minimum voting age stayed at 18 and when it dropped to 16. Nineteen mostly European countries were surveyed, but the US, Canada, Australia and Japan were also included. For statistical purposes, voter turnouts were put at 100 per cent. The demographers found that in only five countries – Ireland, Poland, the US, Australia and Canada – did voting at 16 shift electoral power to younger age groups. In the remaining 14, it reduced older people's voting supremacy but by no means vanquished it.[10]

If admitting 16 year olds to Europe's electorates wouldn't be enough to sap the power of older voters, what other devices are available? Among the ideas being put forward there's that of weighting votes so those of older people are handicapped in relation to those of, say, the under-fifties. But penalising citizens who have already contributed to society in one way or another seems a non-starter.

A more fruitful area would be to boost the turnout of young voters, while also encouraging the creation of 'youth agendas' within political parties. These would help to shape pre-election manifestos and thus exert greater influence within the coalition governments that are so common in Europe.

The inertia, indeed indifference, of younger people at election times tempts some commentators to conclude that 'it serves them right'. It's a short-sighted view because skewing politics in ways that favour older voters is creating a problem for all. In this 'Asian century', Europeans risk becoming technologically backward and industrially sclerotic when their international competitors are getting stronger. They cannot afford to compound their problems by favouring conservative social policies at the expense of more progressive and productive ones.

Using social media and new information technologies to boost youth voting could pay handsome dividends. It's also possible that the cumbersome voting methods of ballot papers in curtained booths still prevalent in many European countries could be revolutionised, and with them the machinery and structures of democracy.

It's hard to tell how much appetite there might be for a digital overhaul of voting methods. Younger people who are children of the Information Age would surely welcome ways of making themselves heard, especially if new features such as Swiss-style referendums were to be introduced for social and even local questions.

For older voters this might well be anathema, especially if it were made plain to them that established privileges ranging from pensions down to bus passes could be challenged more easily. On top of that, Americans' disputes over voting machines, mail-in voting and the corruption of electoral processes could well prejudice more Europeans against the introduction of high-tech voting.

The chances of meaningful changes to voting methods in Europe seem slim, and slimmer still are those of EU-wide electoral reforms. Yet Europe needs change that will pave the way to a democratic rethink of how to tackle ageing's problems. On present showing, our social and fiscal policies will not merely exacerbate intergenerational conflicts but are putting young and old on a collision course. Deeply pessimistic as this will sound, the alternatives are worse. Ignoring the problems now accumulating so rapidly guarantees Europe will become poorer, and younger Europeans the poorest of all.

9

Ageing's costs are youth's burden

The costs of ageing are soaring while Europeans' currently hard-hit economies risk even greater stagnation. By mid-century, a quarter of their GDPs will be taken by pensions and healthcare at a time the IMF warns workforce shrinkage will limit growth rates to 1.2 per cent a year. Only higher taxes can pay for rising social spending, and that burden will fall on the young.

Ageing is the 'ostrich issue'. Few people acknowledge its scale, even though they may be dimly aware that its disastrous costs threaten us all. It's a crunch that lies in the future, so is little heeded. Out of sight is out of mind. Ageing also highlights a major drawback of democracy: because political power lies with the majority, younger generations are an increasingly impotent minority.

The young will be poorly placed to address the two chief burdens on European society: snowballing healthcare costs and tectonic shifts in the number of pensioners. Younger people will have to fund the lengthening retirement years of their elders while accepting greater handicaps on their own future prospects. In crude terms, anyone now under 40 years old will need to work until their eighties to enjoy the same pensionable income as today's 65 year olds.

We must expect shocking changes to the shape and structure of European economies. If independent projections such as those of the Paris-based OECD – the so-called rich countries club – are any guide, far fewer taxpayers will be supporting many more welfare recipients and pensioners. By 2050, warns the OECD, pensions will amount to 12 per cent of its member countries'

GDPs. Other experts forecast that healthcare and social costs will by then average around 15 per cent of national GDPs.

Around a quarter of the European economy is going to consist of pensions and healthcare, with ancillary social services coming on top. Non-productive state sectors will in most countries dwarf those of today. These are the predictable consequences of ageing, but they have yet to emerge as divisive Left–Right political issues. It has seemed unrewarding for politicians to raise problems that in electoral terms lie in the future, so Europe's national political processes have not focused on the overarching strategies needed to deal with them.

This inaction, despite mounting evidence of ageing's dire consequences, may also reflect the way planners seem dumbstruck by the sheer size of the problem. Their response to looming dangers has been to file and forget. Some policy makers are nevertheless beginning to tread cautiously in the foothills of change, and are well aware that climbing gets harder as the mountain steepens. It would be easier if governments and civil society started to tackle the problems of ageing while still on the nursery slopes, yet so far there have been few signs of this.

Defusing the demographic timebomb requires national authorities to address a range of sectors. This means substantially greater investments in the amenities needed by the elderly, along with the hiring and training of more healthcare personnel. Doing so today may be controversial and politically risky, but within a few years it would prove to have been worthwhile. As well as helping to kick-start presently stagnant economies, investing in ageing's greatest challenges is the only way to head-off their explosive consequences.

Many more hospitals, care homes, doctors and nurses are needed. This means far better training and reskilling of older people so they can continue to earn their own livings. There also has to be a revolutionary shift in the way new technologies are harnessed to the workplace and to healthcare. As well as a greater use of e-health techniques to monitor and treat elderly patients at a distance, older people could be encouraged to telework. When the COVID-19 pandemic led to a surge in working from home arrangements, the young and digitally skilled were the first to take advantage, and now it should be the turn of their elders. Distance working could be ideal for the less mobile but more experienced.

Strategies to improve older people's lives should not be restricted only to them. Younger people are essential to the equation. The root cause of Europe's demographic imbalance is the fatal mix of infertility and longevity. Falling birth rates demand a strategic rethink because shrinking family sizes are a major contributor to the demographic crisis. If European countries are to get on top of their demographic deficits and defuse intergenerational tensions, a first step is to increase the number of children being born. That means reversing the accelerating trend of recent decades that has seen women postponing childbearing until their thirties.

Encouraging couples to start a family in their twenties calls for an array of incentives and more imaginative policies. These range from better housing to cheap or free childcare and should include more flexible and generous employment conditions for women, along with improved transport and schooling infrastructures. These prerequisites underline the way comparatively wealthy Western European countries – and perhaps the once energy-rich UK most of all – squandered their 20th-century wealth instead of investing it in younger generations.

The absence of pre-planning in most parts of Europe beggars belief. In Austria, a country that prides itself on its socially responsible institutions, four in ten doctors are to retire by 2030. That's just a microcosm of the Europe-wide manpower shortage in healthcare. When in 2020 COVID-19 was spreading like wildfire, 230,000 medical practitioners left the EU workforce, reducing Europe's doctors to 1.57 million from 1.8 million.

Where are their replacements to come from? From the world's poorer countries, where higher European salary levels are a powerful magnet for newly qualified doctors in countries that themselves desperately need them. Replacements for European doctors now taking retirement should have come from European medical schools, but penny-pinching and the medical profession's conservatism have frozen, and in some cases reduced, the quotas for medical students despite the obviously expanding healthcare needs of Europe's ageing populations.

The dearth of qualified nurses is more dramatic still, as is the absence of less qualified or even unqualified carers who see to the needs of the elderly and bedridden. Carers are needed as home visitors and staff at retirement homes and geriatric clinics, but recruitment is increasingly difficult. Low pay is at the root of high staff turnover rates, with leavers often replaced by less competent personnel.

A quarter of care workers are reckoned to stay less than a year in their job before either finding more congenial work elsewhere or falling back on state benefits. This discouragement from active participation in the labour force, coupled with growing anti-immigration pressures, presages a disastrous Europe-wide labour shortage in healthcare.

Paying for ageing's multiplying costs

It is almost 20 years since researchers at the IMF published a detailed analysis of the speed at which Europe is ageing, and the likely economic impact. Looking towards mid-century, they saw the EU's working-age population shrinking by almost 50 million, and the over-65s increasing by nearly 60 million.

Because the IMF's focus is economic performance, the study zeroed in on areas such as employment, productivity, GDP growth and the outlook for EU governments' spending commitments. Its conclusions weren't encouraging as they predicted a fall in the number of working-age Europeans whose taxes fund national budgets, coupled with a dramatic rise in older people who receive benefits and pensions. A grim combination, warned the IMF.

Called 'Can Europe afford to grow old?', the IMF report forecast a halving of the maximum possible rate of GDP growth, saying this would drop from 2.4 per cent to just 1.2 per cent, and that age-related spending throughout the EU 'would be equivalent to a 10 per cent increase in the size of the government sector'. It commented bleakly that in a number of EU member states the only source of economic growth would be through improved productivity, and said that this combination of demographic trends posed a long-term threat to Europe's single currency, the euro.

This 2006 bombshell from one of the most highly respected international institutions provoked barely a stir of interest. Those times were, despite the US-initiated war raging in Iraq, still economically golden. Policy wonks may have nodded sagely when reading the IMF report's recommendations, but Europe's politicians took little note of the warning that called for 'substantial policy reform and adjustment'.[1]

Reports of this sort are sometimes seen by only a few specialists, and therefore fail to make an impression on the public consciousness. That was not the case with this one, which the IMF published in its widely distributed quarterly magazine *Finance & Development*. It was also promoted by the European Commission, which had collaborated in its preparation. Although it subsequently unleashed a spate of national analyses, they too have had only a limited impact on public opinion.

The body of evidence to show that Europeans are heading into deep trouble has since then grown almost exponentially. At first, universities and think tanks led the rush, with studies showing how smaller workforces can never yield the economic growth needed to fund ageing populations. Now, governments are taking up the cudgels as they strive to explain the policy dilemmas that confront them.

In 2021, the French government set out in stark terms the pressures that must somehow be reconciled. Its in-house think tank, France Stratégie, raised uncomfortable questions about who should pay for the costs of ageing. Noting that combined healthcare and pension costs that 30 years ago absorbed 25 per cent of France's GDP now account for 31 per cent, the study emphasised that three-quarters of this huge sum is spent on the over-sixties, and is rising fast. Its conclusion was that older people in France must be asked to contribute more in taxes.[2]

In Britain, a chorus of voices has warned of ageing's fiscal implications. In the chaotic years that followed Brexit, an influential core of Conservative politicians insisted that the UK's future was as a low-tax Singapore-style economy. This preoccupation eclipsed many pressing issues, but could not hide Britain's deteriorating tax position. Ageing is hitting the nation's finances hard, and will cripple its growth prospects unless tackled with realistic policy measures.

Healthcare costs in the UK have been rising faster than elsewhere in Europe. Germany tops the EU's spending league table, with 11 per cent of its GDP going to the health sector, and Britain is racing to catch up. Its soaring healthcare costs are, though, unrelated to the quality of healthcare; the UK's independent watchdog, the Office for Budget Responsibility (OBR), has identified low productivity as the chief culprit.

Getting on for three-quarters of a typical hospital's budget goes on staff costs. The OBR applied the 'Baumol effect' – a widely used formula when costing healthcare – to show that labour costs will inevitably push NHS financial needs higher and higher. Named after the late William Baumol, a prominent American labour economist, its central argument is that sluggish productivity improvements in hospitals lead to ever-larger staffing levels.[3]

In 2017, the UK's Institute for Fiscal Studies looked 50 years ahead and reported that by 2067 some 26 per cent of the country's population will be over 65 years old – more than double the 1966 level of 12 per cent. The message was clear: healthcare and welfare costs will soar.

The OECD in Paris has made its own health spending projections, and they underline the national studies published around Europe. Because the OECD 'rich nations club' extends outside Europe, its figures include countries such as the US, Japan, Mexico, Australia and New Zealand. They therefore broadly reflect the trend in the developed world: healthcare that in 2015 averagely mopped up 8.8 per cent of the GDPs of the OECD's 38 members will by 2030 climb to over a tenth.[4]

These runaway costs don't fit very well with widely held complaints in Britain and elsewhere that health services are deteriorating. People know that more tax money is being poured into healthcare, but they also know that getting an appointment with specialist consultants means joining a lengthening queue, and that emergency services are at breaking point and sometimes fail when most needed.

Governments' spending cutbacks are the obvious reason for this. Less apparent is the rapidly increasing cost of treating the elderly. The OECD says that the over-65s who presently make up around 15 per cent of the European population account for 60 per cent of total health spending. With advancing years, the cost of treating the elderly rises higher still. Some analysts point to the 'cost of dying', saying that in budgetary terms it's almost prohibitively high because a patient's financial burden on the system often triples in the last year of life. The legacy of the large baby boomer generation will be a greater number than ever of people who suffer from chronic ill-health but will not succumb as quickly as previous generations.

People in richer countries have come to insist on ever higher standards of medical care, and this comes with a hefty price tag. Greater longevity resulting from breakthroughs in the treatment of once fatal diseases has conditioned patients to be more demanding. Anecdotes about the closure of hospitals and the shortages of doctors and nurses are counterbalanced by stories recounting near-miraculous recoveries at death's door.

Hospitals are expensive and getting more so, while general practitioners are getting fewer. Old-style family doctors retire earlier than before, often for tax and pension reasons, while newly qualified graduates of medical schools reportedly find a GP's financial rewards unappealing. The area that could conceivably yield improvements and significant cost savings is specialised care for the elderly, which is public health's fastest growth sector. It is also at the centre of heated debate over the question of whether means-testing patients should be used to help fund their long-term care.

Policy prescriptions for more affordable healthcare

Controversy rages in Britain and a number of European countries over whether older people's assets should be seized by the state to help pay for their care. In simple terms, the question is about the forced sale of property owned by widows or widowers who are very unlikely to return home. This raises deep-seated issues about where socialised medicine begins and ends, and also touches on the vexed question of inheritances as a driver of widening inequality in society.

There's an urgent need to reduce the numbers of elderly patients who occupy hospital beds because there aren't enough available places in care homes. This problem of 'bed blocking' by older people who don't need the sophisticated and expensive facilities of a hospital is compounded in Britain by a bureaucratic process that could easily be reformed. The financing of social care is integrated within the overall funding of the NHS, and has thus become the 'poor relation' for budgetary allocations.

To release social care from this armlock would require little more than a ministerial signature. Far more difficult is the restructuring of a care sector that's going to be swamped until it's disastrously under water. The OECD has calculated that a 60 per cent increase in care workers will be needed by 2040, and if the shortage of care workers is daunting in the UK it's more alarming still in many continental neighbours. The over-85s in France, for instance, currently number 1.5 million, but experts grappling there with the lack of care homes – Ehpads in the jargon (Établissement d'hébergement pour personnes âgées) – say that figure will rise to 4.8 million by 2050.[5]

The answer could be a radical overhaul of Europe's largely centralised social care systems. In the Netherlands, where long-term care for the aged already accounts for almost 4 per cent of GDP, an innovative approach is beginning to deliver results. Called the 'Buurtzorg model', this takes the reins of decision-making away from the administrative hierarchy of local authorities and hands them to small and highly autonomous neighbourhood teams of carers. The financial dividend from this more flexible arrangement has been a cost saving per head of one-third, so the Buurtzorg model is being looked at in 25 other countries.

Cash-strapped governments are often reluctant to listen to ideas that cost them more money. Yet the only lasting solution to the problem of insufficient care workers is to invest more. It's a sector that will inevitably have to be expanded to accommodate more old people, and it offers the advantage of being far cheaper than falling back on institutional healthcare facilities. At present, though, instead of growing in number, care homes for the elderly have been closing because of staff shortages.

The rapid turnover in personnel at care homes clearly reflects the poor conditions and pay levels on offer. The result has been severe staffing difficulties that inhibit the sector's long-term growth. Britain's social care sector is desperately trying to recruit more staff – relying often on immigrant labour – and warns that the 2 per cent of the working age population currently employed as carers will have to rise to 4 per cent by 2033 to meet demand.[6]

Potential recruits as carers are scarcely queuing up to be hired. In the UK, the government-appointed Migration Advisory Committee complains that carers earn only 71 per cent of the average wage. The EU average is slightly higher at 79 per cent, but continental Europe nevertheless faces a similar shortage of carers. France has only four-fifths of the carers it needs, and in Germany a third of those taken on as carers for the elderly leave after a year or less.[7]

As with public health in general, many of Europe's governments have taken the easy option and squeezed budgets for carers, even though doing so is short-sighted and in the end more expensive. Chronic ill-health has pushed half a million British workers out of the active labour force, proportionately the most in the OECD's 38 member countries. That's an argument some other countries are beginning to heed. Sweden offers free day care to the elderly – much the same as its childcare arrangements – and Switzerland operates day care centres with special transport arrangements for older people.

Restructuring care for the elderly is only part of the intensifying debate on the overall cost-benefits of healthcare spending. The OECD estimates that 37 million working days are lost every year to easily treatable diseases, and says this is braking economic growth because ill-health is compounding Europe's labour force shrinkage.

Looking beyond Europe, the McKinsey Global Institute – the international management consultancy's in-house think tank – calculates (or perhaps guesstimates) that the world economy would be 15 per cent larger if the drag effects of poor health could be removed. It reckons that $12 trillion could be added by 2040 to the planet's gross domestic product because every dollar invested in better health would bring a return of between $2 to $4.

Who will pay when healthcare costs double?

When economists at Bruegel, a Brussels-based policy think tank, looked at the likely trend in healthcare costs, they confirmed in stark terms the more discreetly worded warnings of the EU. By mid-century, they said in a 2016 report, healthcare in Europe is set to cost twice as much unless a radical reform strategy is introduced that creates greater flexibility, less fragmentation and duplication of effort, along with a regulatory overhaul.

Britons have been wont to boast of the treatment they get from the NHS, and are proud of the way its post-war launch blazed a trail for other European countries to establish their own socialised medicine and healthcare systems. The NHS is always a central element in Britain's sometimes frenzied political debates, and its independence from commercial influence is fiercely defended. So it would doubtless surprise many people in the UK to learn that the NHS in fact delivers fewer services and is less efficient than many of its counterparts in continental Europe.

Healthcare costs in Britain were ruthlessly reined back over the decade before the COVID-19 pandemic. Conservative governments pared NHS services wherever possible, and by 2017 had reduced health-related spending to 9.6 per cent of GDP from the 2013 level of 9.8 per cent. As a result, Britons receive markedly cheaper healthcare than people in, say, France or Germany. In 2017, healthcare in Germany cost almost £4,500 per person, in France £3,750 and in the UK £2,900.

Older people naturally account for the bulk of these costs. Health spending on a 65 year old is roughly double that of a 30 year old, and for people aged 70 it's three times greater. By the time someone reaches their nineties, their healthcare costs are almost eight times those of a 30 year old.

Europe's ballooning population of over-eighties will see today's figures pale in comparison with projected mid-century costs. By 2050, there will be 40 million Europeans over the age of 80, up from 14 million in 2010. Because older people – and especially those in their last years of life – account for such a disproportionate share of healthcare spending, more than 16 per cent of Europe's GDP will have to go on health costs.

This prospect is beginning to spark discussion – dissension would be a better word – about who should pay, and for what. Europeans delight in comparing their safety nets of social benefits and healthcare arrangements with those of the US, but the viability of socialised healthcare is increasingly coming under scrutiny. Suggestions that access to 'Social Europe' should be means tested so that prosperous people contribute more are buttressed by a growing tendency in some countries for the well-off to go private.

There's a beguiling idea that the rising costs of healthcare could be slowed or even frozen by privatisations and by charging richer patients for services that poorer ones get free. At a time when widening wealth gaps are polarising politics across Europe, imposing hefty fees on those who can afford them has obvious attractions. A glance across the Atlantic might, however, dampen enthusiasm for this.

At first sight, the US model looks attractive. Private equity finance has been pouring into American healthcare, spurring investment in advanced medical technologies and life sciences. In the two decades to 2020, private equity investments in various US healthcare sectors increased 20-fold. This money was, though, looking for fairly immediate profits rather than an overall improvement in the quality of clinical services.

'Think about how private equity will make money in something like a hospice', comments one of the authors of a research paper on the 'financialisation' of US healthcare. 'They'll cut the seasoned staff trained to help families understand and cope with the process of dying, and hire people who might be able to help clean the house.' The longer-term result, as a New York-based *Financial Times* commentator put it, is that 'the unprecedented sums of money sloshing around a complicated and opaque system will undoubtedly make the rich richer, and the sick sicker'.[8]

Where the US public health system is headed is anyone's guess; to European eyes its eye-watering medical charges are as incomprehensible as America's lack of gun control. But with two-thirds of bankruptcies there citing medical costs as a major factor, there's an unmistakable shift in public opinion. For the first time, a 60 per cent majority of those questioned for a 2017 poll by the Pew Research Center said it's the US federal government's responsibility to ensure access to quality healthcare.

How that can be reconciled with the promises of America's populist politicians is perplexing. It seems more likely that the answer in the US will be an increased harnessing of the internet to confront its healthcare challenges. Amazon was the first digital heavy-hitter to enter the telemedicine marketplace, and its competitors there range from the giant Walmart supermarket chain to Facebook, Google, Apple and Microsoft.

Amazon's original 2018 foray was far from successful. A joint venture with several partners named Haven was soon abandoned in favour of AWS – Amazon Web Services. This offers online pharmacies and other clinical services that can be consulted through its digital voicing technology. Walmart's response has been in-store 'clinics' offering laboratory tests, X-rays and other diagnostics. Additionally, there are dental, optical and auditory services.

China's online behemoths aren't far behind. The Alibaba e-commerce empire has launched AliHealth, and its rival Tencent is pushing its WeDoctor service. British and EU regulatory requirements may reshape and reduce telemedicine's spread in Europe, but the likelihood is that digital technologies will be to the fore of efforts to improve the productivity and quality of healthcare.

So far, the emphasis has been on breakthroughs that could be said to compound the ageing problem by extending lifespans. To counterbalance this, more needs to be achieved in areas such as the physical handling of the old and infirm. It can take a team of six to turn a patient over in bed, so a greater availability of lightweight hydraulic devices and robots could revolutionise productivity.

Making hospitals more efficient and less labour intensive should have higher priority than at present, as should the development of care facilities that would keep otherwise healthy older people away from inappropriate hospitalisations. These are comparatively straightforward policy issues where cost–benefit analyses will clearly show governments the way forward. Far less obvious is the plethora of questions about the future nature of welfare and social benefits in ageing societies. Meeting the needs of older people risks depriving other less privileged socio-economic sectors of much-needed benefits. The educational and training improvements that younger people need if they are to add greater value to the economy may be jeopardised by the increased financial demands of the elderly.

At EU level as well as nationally, there has been a growing focus on the 'social contract' and the need to widen the range of policies that help the disadvantaged. So far, it seems fair to say that the requirements of older Europeans have not been made subsidiary to those of younger ones. There must nevertheless be a re-evaluation at some point of the welfare state's priorities and limitations.

What the advocates of a new social contract may have in mind seems to depend on their political standpoint. 'Man is born free, but is everywhere in chains' is how the Swiss-born political philosopher Jean-Jacques Rousseau opened his hugely influential mid-18th-century book *The Social Contract*, credited with igniting the flames of both the American and French revolutions. Contemporary voices demanding a renewed social focus are generally less radical than that, but nevertheless represent growing concerns over the wealth gap in many European countries and the deprivations suffered by the underprivileged.

When assessing the need for more ambitious social policies, it's instructive to look back at the cost of policies already in place. In fiscal terms, there's very little room for manoeuvre. The UK's independent and much-respected Institute for Fiscal Studies (IFS) paints a grim picture of past and future trends in social spending, and the implications of these for taxpayers.

The IFS has drawn on figures published by the government and by the independent Office for Budget Responsibility (OBR). For the sake of clarity, it cut through Whitehall's obfuscating jargon and also excluded Britain's soaring debt interest payments from its calculations. It says that health and pensions, which currently account for a third of government spending, will rise to 45 per cent over the coming 50 years. Back in the 1950s, they made up only one-sixth.

The IFS report reflects the trade-offs that future British governments will have to wrestle with as they try to reconcile competing policy commitments. It points out that if other forms of spending were to be cut, say by a quarter, to free more funding for pensions and healthcare, those two elements will by 2067 absorb 55 per cent of all government spending. If this were to be paid for by higher taxes, then these would have to be raised to 44 per cent of national income, a level not seen since the gloomy 1950s when Britain was struggling to pay off its bankrupting wartime debts.[9]

Add in the share of taxpayers' money already being spent on interest payments for government debt, and the outlook goes from bleak to disastrous. The OBR has said that projected social costs over the coming 50 years will so widen the gap between tax receipts and spending that the country's national debt will rise to

230 per cent of GDP. It's already on an 'unsustainable trajectory' that's forecast to push it past the milestone of 100 per cent of national income at some point in the late 2030s.[10]

Paying for the UK government's state pension commitments will be a major part of this. Although less expensive than welfare benefits that absorb almost a quarter of British taxpayers' contributions to the national budget, or healthcare that accounts for a fifth, the 13 per cent taken up by pensions is also rising fast. Together, these social costs dwarf items such as defence, which gets around 5 per cent, or environmental spending's 1.5 per cent.

The young must pay for lavish pensions they will never enjoy

It's a fact of life that longer lives mean higher pension costs. While we as individuals may rejoice in the idea of 70 being the 'new 60' or even the 'new 50', our lengthening lifespans are wrecking the long-standing balance between our working lives and our non-productive years of retirement.

Throughout the 20th century, pensions were a straightforward deal between the citizen and society – a proportion of income during one's working years is saved, invested and then returned in cast-iron, regular pension payments. Britain introduced these in 1908, following the example set in the late 19th century by Germany's 'Iron Chancellor' Otto von Bismarck.

What those early pension arrangements had in common was that very few workers would receive a pension for long, if at all. Pensions payable upon retirement at 65 when average life expectancy in Europe was around 55 were scarcely a burden for either state or employer. Britain's average male lifespan was 61 years when its post-Second World War pensions kicked in at age 65.

That has, of course, been turned on its head. Half of today's newborn babies are forecast to live until the age of 105, and anyone in a relatively prosperous European country now aged 60 has a fair chance of reaching 90. In pension terms, this means that young people starting out on their working lives won't be able to retire comfortably until they are 85 if their pension savings remain pegged at about a tenth of their gross monthly income.[11]

Governments across Europe have been scratching their heads over forecasts of the huge sums needed to fund state pensions. Some may even contemplate the collapse of systems originally designed as state-run investment funds, whose profits would pay for pensions without recourse to taxpayers. These, needless to say, were raided over past years by finance ministers desperate for the cash that could be obtained without unpopular tax increases.

Much the same pension problems loom in the US. A quarter of all Americans have no retirement savings at all, according to PwC, the financial services consultancy. Another report, by Boston College's Center for Retirement Research, warns that half the US population will suffer sharp falls in their living standards upon retirement because they haven't saved enough for their pensions.[12]

Trouble over pensions has been brewing for decades, but few British or European governments have wanted to confront the problem openly. There have been frequent warnings from independent analysts, but these have either been ignored or swept under the carpet rather than debated as a pressing political challenge. 'Industrialised economies have been caught flat-footed, unprepared for the cost of providing retirement income for so many, for so long,' charged Germany's Max Planck Institute for Demographic Research when setting out the hard facts of the pensions crisis. Analysing data from 1900 onwards, it concluded that '72 is the new 30'.[13]

The seeds of Europe's looming pensions crisis were sown back in the prosperous 1980s when talk of a 'leisure revolution' was paralleled by a trend towards earlier retirement. People began to leave the active workforce when still in their fifties, at first on the grounds of physical exhaustion in heavier industries and later as a quality of life entitlement for all and sundry. Since then, governments have been trying to reverse that trend by using longevity to justify later retirement, but it's proving a hard slog.

The OECD says that getting average pensionable ages back to where they were in 1950 – just under 65 for men and 63 for women – won't be reached before 2030. 'Today's retirees', it commented in a landmark report on pensions, 'are living through what might prove to have been a golden age for pensions and pensioners.'[14]

The picture isn't entirely one of gloom and doom. Experts convened by the European Commission to look at the future of 'Social Europe' were able to report in 2022 that pension costs in the EU are lower than had been feared. A number of factors have combined to reduce member governments' pension pay-outs, so they are about a quarter less than demographic calculations had predicted. A major factor was that more women and older people are being encouraged to work by the rising cost of living. Europe's labour shortages have also been forcing pay rates up and making employment and even part-time jobs more attractive.

If these pressures could somehow be institutionalised and turned into a new pattern of working, then perhaps a full-blown pensions crisis might be averted. Some specialists conjure with the idea of the 'effective' retirement age rising to 72 by mid-century, although that would require female employment rates to match Scandinavian levels with four-fifths of working age women actively engaged in a paid job. The baby boom generation will also have died off by then, thus easing pension pressures.[15]

This sunnier view of the pensions outlook is buttressed by other encouraging developments. Britain's introduction in 2012 of an 'auto-enrolment' system that automatically makes employers extend a pension scheme to their employees has genuinely been a success. The number of workers covered by some form of in-house pension had been slipping, but four-fifths now participate following the UK's decision to join other European countries in insisting that both companies and their employees contribute.

Sadly, the self-employed are not covered, and because of the growth of gig economy jobs and zero-hours contracts, more and more young people are being forced into self-employment. Only 16 per cent of the UK's almost 5 million self-employed contribute to a private pension scheme, down from 48 per cent in 1998.[16]

This is where the pensions question gets nasty. Younger people are being saddled with pension costs that cushion today's older people but will be unaffordable by the time it's their turn to retire. 'Anyone aged 30 today should be planning their life around their age of retirement being 70 or higher,' cautioned Adair Turner, author of a seminal 2006 report on the UK's pension challenges and a former head of the Confederation of British Industry, the employers' organisation. Since then, the situation of younger people has gone from bad to worse.

Sluggish equity markets have reduced the profits that pension funds' financial investments redistribute to retirees. Instead of getting a fixed pension when they are old, it's now young people's liabilities that are fixed. Rather than the defined benefit (DB) schemes their elders enjoy, they have had to sign up to defined contribution (DC) schemes in which their monthly payment is fixed but their future pension will depend on market conditions.

Low interest rates over the decade up to 2022 have squeezed retirement incomes hard. At the beginning of this century, every £100,000 in a DC 'pot' yielded a yearly pension of almost £12,000, but two decades on that had shrunk to only £5,000. To put these figures into perspective, the pensions investment company Royal London reckons the average person must set aside £260,000 during their working life to ensure a comfortable retirement.

The providers of financial services, along with many of the major companies that operated in-house pension schemes, have been forced to progressively abandon DB schemes because they are such huge liabilities. When times were good, DB pensions encouraged employee loyalty and were seen as a way of limiting pay rises. But stagnant economic growth has ended that, and DB schemes still in operation represent billions in debt. Bankers at Citigroup have calculated that unfunded pension liabilities in 20 of the world's richest countries amount to $78 trillion. For the UK alone, the pension funding deficit is around £460 billion, while its Pension Protection Fund is only £23 billion.

Nobody can say when this rapidly deteriorating situation will turn into full-blown crisis, or even what that crisis might look like. The complex web of pension schemes' investments and financial commitments may be ramshackle, but it has also proved to be durable. It remains to be seen whether it's a house of cards that will eventually collapse or a model of flexibility that 'financial engineers' can patch up. If the pensions architecture were to teeter and then fall, that would undoubtedly trigger a global financial crisis on an almost unimaginable scale.

Some experts have been warning for years that many pension arrangements are unsustainable, and that officialdom has been dangerously complacent. 'It is difficult to see how the existing models can be maintained,' wrote Peter Askins, formerly head of the UK government department that oversees defined benefit pensions. In an excoriating article he contributed to *Pensions: An International Journal* back in 2010, Askins listed the many pressures that are condemning retirement schemes to the scrap heap.

'The speed of changing economic and financial factors has left us all gasping,' he said, 'but the necessary corresponding policy change has barely got under way.' Askins added that the EU, too, is failing to address the problem. 'The issue is so big and the time scales so long there is little political will across Europe to deal with these issues.' He criticised the EU's Green Paper on pensions for its 'lack of intellectual rigour, concentrating as it does on outdated dogma-driven issues'.[17]

Peter Askins's article created a stir within the financial services industry, but made little impact on politicians and policy makers. Yet he put his finger on the root problem when he wrote, 'So great is the fear of the electoral power of Europe's older generations … that little or nothing has been done to address the pensions issue.' It's certainly fair to say, therefore, that in the years since his highly critical article appeared, the emphasis of most governments has been on protecting the interests of older people.

Finding a way out of the pensions maze

The obvious solution to the problem of snowballing pensions commitments is to raise the retirement age, and that's what governments have been trying to do. But that's little more than a sticking plaster on a cancer; the pensions malaise is deep-seated and symptomatic of Europe's increasingly toxic intergenerational imbalance.

Cutting the cost of paying pensions to hale and hearty older people is just one facet of the policy prescriptions governments should be looking at. The mismatch between pensioners' financial needs and the capital markets' inability to deliver adequate profits is also crucially important. A third major element is the need to overhaul pensions systems in such a way that within a quarter-century or so they will provide today's middle-aged taxpayers with the same financial security their parents currently enjoy.

Political decision-makers are thus caught in a three-way trap. Exert too much pressures on today's pensioners and they will try to vote you out of office. This was the risk Emmanuel Macron ran in France. His re-election in April 2022 to a second term as president was marred by the loss of his parliamentary majority in the Assemblée Nationale, and pensions have been a prominent element of the issues that have dogged him subsequently. Public protests and trade union opposition to even watered-down versions of his pension reform plan have played a major part in sapping Macron's authority.

Backroom experts within mainstream political parties throughout Europe are increasingly conscious of the need to pander to the 'silver vote'. At the same time, there will in all likelihood come a point when younger taxpayers revolt against governments that levy taxes on an ever-larger proportion of their earnings while delivering fewer benefits than were available to previous generations. Young Europeans are often criticised for failing to vote and for their general lack of political commitment, but it seems inevitable that at some future point the worm will turn. To ignore the unfairness to which many younger Europeans are subjected risks inviting electoral catastrophe.

Pension funds' poor financial yields are the root of the problem. Attention is therefore being focused within the financial services sector on ways to make the investment of pensioners' savings more profitable without becoming dangerously risky. As a global financial services hub, the City of London has produced a number of interesting suggestions.

The UK's Centre for the Study of Financial Innovation (CSFI) put forward a package of ideas in its 2015 report 'The death of retirement', and other experts in the City have proposed a global shake-up that would consolidate smaller pension funds into giant ones able to combine higher yields with greater security. The case for creating risk-sharing collective funds has also been made by specialists in the US, the Netherlands and Canada.

The CSFI's recommendations included pegging the UK's state pension to 60 per cent of the national living wage and abolishing the retirement age by setting eligibility to 20 years before average life expectancy. This, said its report, 'means accelerating the raising of the state pension age to 70'.

More far-reaching still are ideas now under discussion for a radical rethink of the whole concept of pensions. The point of departure here is that retirement savings are a cornerstone of market economies, and were structured to suit the more stable conditions of yesteryear. Martin Wolf, the *Financial Times* economics guru, has argued that the risk aversion of pension funds is largely responsible for the sluggish performance of equity markets. He therefore urges the decoupling of those corporate direct benefit funds that still exist from the companies that operate them, with the assets they manage to be merged into larger and more muscular collectives.[18]

These discussions may sound theoretical, but the need to develop new retirement savings models is urgent. Young people and those in early middle age will require guaranteed pensions once they begin to retire in mid-century. Many already have to cope with insecure, poorly paid jobs and cripplingly high housing costs, and will clearly be hard put to save over two decades the fifth of their disposable income that experts say is necessary.

The difficulties facing millennials and Gen-Zers in Europe and America tend to be eclipsed in the public mind by heart-rending reports of older people whose pensions don't stretch far enough or who must sell family property to part-finance their care in a retirement home. The consensus among researchers, however, is that today's younger generations also need special help to ensure they save enough to finance pensions that will begin to be paid out in 30 or 40 years' time, but may well have to span many more years because of pensioners' longer lifespans.

Pension providers have been among the first to warn of the dangers ahead. Scottish Widows, a pensions arm of Lloyds Bank, issues regular 'Future of retirement' reports and emphasises that 'UK pension contribution rates over the past few decades have been chronically low compared to European countries.' Although welcoming Britain's auto-enrolment scheme, it says 'the joint employee-employer contribution rate of 8 per cent will not be enough to sustain a decent living in retirement'. It has therefore proposed its 'Brit Saver' concept, which would increase contributions while offering limited access to pensions savings to help with a deposit for a first home.[19]

The financial pressures on younger people are also ringing alarm bells in the US. Alicia Munnell, a former US Treasury

Department official who is now a retirement expert at Boston College's management school, believes that 'Millennials' lack of wealth relative to earlier cohorts should be a source of great concern, given that they will live longer than previous cohorts and will face higher healthcare costs.'

Young adults are sometimes characterised as carefree and irresponsible, yet researchers suggest otherwise. Adecco, the giant Swiss-based international employment agency, says that at least a third of Gen-Z jobseekers still in their teens 'expect a pension as standard with their first job', and that it's more important to them than perks such as gym membership. In the UK, that view is echoed by the Ashridge Business School, whose research director says 'yes, they expect a pension from the word go'.[20]

Some demographers suggest that Gen-Zers may be spared the adverse pressures that millennials will suffer. The eventual deaths of the many baby boomers now in retirement will, they argue, lighten the burden on European society towards the end of the 2050s. The Resolution Foundation estimates that while British men currently in their forties will on average get smaller pensions than those of today, those of zoomers will have more or less recovered. It reckons an average weekly pension of £310 in 2020 will fall in real terms to £285 in the mid-2040s, rising back to £300 by the late 2050s. For women, the present £225 a week reaches £235 in the mid-2030s and stays there.[21]

Looked at more broadly in pan-European terms, the gap between people's savings and their future pension needs has widened alarmingly. An extra €2 trillion is needed if Europeans are to continue taking their retirement in much the same circumstances as in most of the post-Second World War years. That's a substantial sum when set against the EU's yearly GDP of €18 trillion or so.

These are among the statistics published every year by Aviva, Britain's largest insurance and pensions company. Its 'Mind the gap' reports take regular snapshots of pensions problems in Europe and around the world, and caution that 'no single policy measure will close the gap alone – even radical measures like increasing the retirement age by five or ten years only reduces the gap by a quarter and a half respectively'.

With 18 million customers to call on, Aviva's attitude surveys cast an interesting light on the level of people's concern over pensions. A sample taken of 300,000 people to measure what Aviva calls its 'Worry-Action Gap' has shown that while 44 per cent of UK respondents are seriously worried, only 35 per cent were actually taking steps to save enough. In other parts of Europe, worry levels were 50 per cent or more, but steps being taken were also at the same 35 per cent level.

A social spending 'crunch' is a very real danger

At risk of labouring the point, all the analyses and statistics drawn upon in this chapter add up to a simple and unavoidable conclusion – the social, healthcare and pension costs of the UK, and of Europe as a whole, are unsustainable.

To avoid a moment of reckoning that would be socially and politically disastrous, Europeans must embark on a long, hard climb back to some form of economic equilibrium. The interests of the electorally powerful older recipients of social benefits must be counterbalanced by an array of new measures favouring the young.

If younger Europeans are to fund their own pensions, healthcare and social costs, the low pay and expensive housing that traps many of them must be radically addressed. To save for the future while funding the present means there must be major shifts in European countries' tax systems. That's always easier said than done, but methods of taxation that serve the interests of society as well as those of the marketplace will be crucial to Europe's future well-being. So, too, will be a far-reaching rethink of wealth creation and debt management in market economies that are being sapped by waning growth and rising debt.

10

The deepening debt quagmire

Older people are getting richer and younger people poorer, with intergenerational unfairness heading to crisis proportions. Debt is snowballing, and in the UK a report to MPs warns that 'future generations will inherit liabilities of just over five times annual GDP'. Hopes for a solution are pinned on greater productivity, but like all magic wands it's elusive, not to say illusory.

'Blessed be the young, for they shall inherit our national debt,' quipped the President of the US almost a hundred years ago. Herbert Hoover was speaking as the tentacles of the Great Depression were spreading out across America, with millions of evicted and bankrupt people seeking shelter in hurriedly built shanty towns known as 'Hoovervilles'.

Robust economic growth will be crucial to resolving Europeans' demographic problems. How that can be achieved when ageing is slowing growth and depressing productivity is becoming the great question of our Age. Hoover's successor in the White House, Franklin Delano Roosevelt, astounded the world with his controversial 'New Deal' of vast public works projects and risky government indebtedness. His century-old playbook has lessons for today.

The vulnerability of market economies to disruption is painfully clear. The COVID-19 global pandemic and then Russia's invasion of Ukraine exacerbated the flaws and weaknesses inherent in liberal democracies' capitalist systems. Coming into plain sight now is the politically explosive question of which sections of society should pay for past neglect and future investment.

In Britain, and elsewhere in Europe, political leaders pin their hopes on productivity boosts they say will produce greater output and more wealth. Technology, argue some, can if properly harnessed streamline manufacturing and service industries and reverse the flatlining and even downward trends that are depressing wealth creation. Theoretically that's possible, of course, but it demands massive investments that often would have to be publicly funded.

That in turn raises the thorny issue of public debt so neatly encapsulated by President Hoover's wry comment. How much can, and should, governments borrow, and how fairly will the burden of servicing and eventually repaying that debt be distributed? Questions around intergenerational fairness are nowadays much debated by economists, but if projections of national debts across Europe and in the US are to be believed, today's youth will stagger in years ahead under the weight of huge interest payments.

On top of the debt question there's the increasingly heated discussion about capitalism itself. Quite simply, it hasn't been delivering the benefits that ordinary citizens are promised. Excessive rewards to bankers and financial wheeler-dealers were tolerated when times were good, but have become politically toxic.

Economic theorists and hard-bitten politicos are faced with the need to overhaul capitalism's rules and mechanisms before it's too late. In the higher reaches of government and corporate governance there's a growing awareness that ageing and demographic change are poised to exert hugely destructive pressures on the system.

Overhauling capitalism is almost too great a challenge to contemplate. The market economy's structures are constantly tinkered with at national levels and internationally to accommodate new developments, but the idea of wholesale reform remains anathema. Changing the global financial architecture would demand an extraordinary degree of international consensus between sovereign states that have very different and often competing national interests. It's nevertheless being urged by the IMF.

The IMF is worried about poorer countries' soaring and probably unrepayable external debts, not only for their own sakes but in the wider global context. Sovereign debt crises reveal that international markets' delicate stability is akin to a house of cards, prompting the IMF to suggest a new global bankruptcy regime. Similar proposals have been made to limit the risks around corporate debt in richer countries, for some major companies have become worryingly over-leveraged and owe their investors and creditors far more than they could ever raise in cash.

The fundamental problem, meanwhile, is that capitalism in its broadest sense isn't producing enough added value to satisfy either investors or employees. Nor are the tax arrangements that should harness companies' financial profits to the wider needs of society delivering adequately. Tax squabbles within individual countries and between national governments have become an unsettling source of friction.

It's easy to blame the declining living standards of a good many Western liberal democracies on competition from low-wage Asian countries, but that's misleadingly simple. A more convincing argument is that their governments have been wrong-headedly overprotective of big companies. The reasons for doing so are to safeguard jobs, to retain dominant market shares and to preserve technological secrets, but these have all backfired. The result has been a defanging of the 'creative destruction' famously championed by the influential mid-20th-century American economist Joseph Schumpeter.

The result, warn some analysts, has been the rise of 'zombie companies', the living dead of the corporate world. They are said to no longer have the energy and know-how needed to survive against their tough international competitors unless they take on more debt, or, when they are state-owned, given transfusions of taxpayers' money.

In contrast to Schumpeter's vision of the survival of the fittest in a rough and tumble marketplace, the growth of zombies is said to promise a 'Day of the Dinosaurs'. There were only a few zombies in the US at the beginning of this century, but by some accounts they are now a fifth of all America's listed companies. In Europe, where the privatisation of state-owned enterprises has been patchy, the proportion is higher still.

Rethinking the way market economies try to balance supply and demand with the needs of producers and consumers won't be accomplished any time soon. It may take a near-catastrophic crisis to get systemic reform onto the global agenda.

Hitting the brakes on the runaway debt train

The whirling rows of numbers on an unusual piece of street furniture in downtown Manhattan tell passers-by how deeply they and their fellow Americans are in hock. Mounted on a wall near Times Square next to a local office of the Federal government's Internal Revenue Service, the US 'Debt Clock' tracks in real time the money America owes to its creditors.

It's maybe a bit kitsch, but an interesting glimpse of how the world's richest and most powerful nation is floundering helplessly in a quagmire of debt. When the clock was installed in 1989 by a civic-minded New York real estate dealer, the US national debt stood at a mere $3 trillion. A decade later, at the turn of the century, that had doubled to almost $6 trillion; by 2016 it was $20 trillion and in 2022 it surged past $30 trillion.

Debt comes in all shapes and sizes. It also makes the world go round because mortgages and consumer credit arrangements are vital to our way of living. Crucial, too, are governments' arrangements for financing social infrastructure, whether healthcare and schools or roads and armed forces. The difference is that personal commitments must be repaid over an agreed period, whereas governments' indebtedness is open-ended.

The most problematic borrowings are those that are used to play the financial markets and are therefore inherently risky – as are those where interest payments grow because, far from being repaid, the debt is piled higher and higher. Governments of richer countries kick the can of their national debt down the road almost indefinitely, even if that means taxpayers yet unborn must pay accumulating interest costs. When corporations, on the other hand, fail to invest their borrowings profitably they may collapse, sometimes triggering global crises.

The US's national debt, experts agree, will keep on growing at a faster rate than the economy, not just over the coming years but forever. And that's not necessarily a bad thing because the deficit in federal expenditure over tax receipts reflects the US government's commitment to social programs that include healthcare and ageing's costs.

America's debt is due to be almost double the nation's annual GDP by mid-century. The raw figures are less important, though, than the cost of servicing the debt. Low interest rates in the aftermath of the 2008 global financial crisis became an incentive to borrow; in 2019, they had dipped so low that America's debt servicing costs were, at 1.8 per cent of GDP, less than when the debt clock was unveiled 30 years earlier.

As debt issuers, both governments and major companies are becoming ruefully aware that this is no longer the case thanks to the double whammy of COVID-19 and Putin's war against Ukraine. Inflation will whittle away the real value of long-standing debts, but since the 2008 crisis many creditors have been loath to lend on other than a short-term basis. As interest rates have risen, so has the expense for taxpayers of servicing the growing debt mountain. Governments that took the easy option of borrowing to cover their deficits are going to be increasingly cash-strapped.

Worldwide, the total indebtedness of big institutional borrowers reached $300 trillion at about the time COVID-19-related problems were beginning to ebb away but Vladimir Putin was launching his Ukraine invasion. To put this figure into perspective, global economic output was then around $85 trillion, so world debt was about three and a half times total annual GDP.

There's much discussion about how worrying this is. Some analysts recall national debts that for a while reached astronomical heights – in Britain and the US after the Second World War – but which in the growth years of the 1960s were nursed back down to manageable levels. Others warn that runaway global debt is inherently unsustainable, and the question must be whether it eventually comes down gently or catastrophically hard.

The chances of it being the latter look to be worsening. Corporate debt has been rising fast, and fastest of all in areas where creditors lack security. The 2008 crisis was triggered at first by the collapse of dodgy subprime mortgages in the US, so there was a subsequent shake-out of questionable banking practices that might have international consequences.

But 'shadow banking' that eludes supervision has stealthily returned and is even more dangerous than before. Profit-hungry investors who were frustrated by low interest rates after 2008 have ploughed $10 trillion into equities that increasingly have been unlisted or are worryingly opaque. Market jitters, say warning voices, may yet tip the world's financial markets into chaos.[1]

Governments are also becoming riskier borrowers. At the dawn of the 21st century, only a small handful of countries were considered risky, but two decades on they have grown fourfold in number. The half-dozen sovereign states in 2000 whose debt stood at more than 300 per cent of their GDP have become two dozen, and climbing. The US is among them, but of course it can always print more dollars when in difficulty. Others cannot, and that's where the threat to global economic stability is greatest.[2]

Although the UK's public sector indebtedness isn't as enormous as America's, debt will be a far greater political headache for future British governments than for US administrations. When Britain's debt hit £2 trillion in 2020, equal to 100 per cent of that year's GDP, some commentators played this milestone down. They pointed out that when the Napoleonic wars ended in 1815 with Wellington's victory at Waterloo, it had been 200 per cent of GDP. The fruits of Britain's expanding empire and careful Victorian debt management tamed it to around 30 per cent, but the costs of the Second World War pushed it back up to 270 per cent, and it took 60 years before it was finally clawed back in 2006 to 35 per cent.

The fact that sky-high debt-to-GDP ratios can be whittled away over time sounds reassuring, but it has had to be achieved through measures that will depress living standards. It therefore requires sound underlying growth in the economy. As matters stand in the UK, half of today's public debt is short term and liable to interest rate hikes that may prove ruinously expensive and could also risk baking in high inflation.[3]

Britain's economy, along with those of continental European countries, is neither as large nor as dynamic as that of the US. Nor, despite the euro, do Europeans have the powers inherent in owning what is by far the world's most widely used international reserve currency – the dollar. The greatest difference of all, though, is that America isn't weighed down by the same demographic problems as Europe. The US, too, is ageing and grappling with the retirement costs of its large baby boomer generation, but its total population is growing. Year on year, however furious are its debates on immigration, America will have a larger workforce to finance its social needs, whereas Europeans will not.

Nobody can say where the world's appetite for debt will take us. Borrowing is essential to productive investment and also fuels consumption, so it is a vital element in any economy, whether free market or state controlled. But rising and increasingly fragile debt seems a discouraging backdrop to economies, in Europe especially, that must find far more money than before to finance the costs of ageing.

The battle lines have long been drawn between advocates of deficit financing, borrowing to invest in growth, and fiscal discipline, meaning governments should balance their spending with their tax revenues. Among Charles Dickens' most memorable characters, the hapless debt-ridden Wilkins Micawber stands out as a piteous advocate of fiscal rectitude. 'Annual income twenty pounds and annual expenditure nineteen pounds, nineteen shillings and sixpence, result happiness. Annual income twenty pounds and annual expenditure twenty pounds and sixpence, result misery,' says Micawber in Dickens' semi-autobiographical 1850 novel *David Copperfield*.

Mr Micawber is believed to have been loosely modelled on Charles Dickens' own improvident father, and many people would agree with his gloomy sentiments in light of their personal experience. But in debates among economists spanning two centuries on how to view debt, the case for balancing the books so scrupulously is far from proven.

From John Maynard Keynes during the doldrum inter-war years of the 1920s and 1930s to a host of present-day experts, strong arguments have been put forward for borrowing more to fund projects that promise higher living standards and a better quality of life for the underprivileged. 'More borrowing today is likely to be better for long-run fiscal sustainability than a stingy response that depresses incomes for years to come,' said the influential weekly *The Economist* when commenting on policies to help pull Britain out of its post-COVID-19 tailspin.[4]

The issues around debt are endlessly complicated, from both ethical and practical standpoints. Nobel laureate Paul Krugman, whose opinion articles in the *New York Times* could spark furious discussion, has remarked of debt that 'talk of leaving a burden to our children is especially nonsensical; what we are leaving behind is promises that some of our children will pay money to other children'. That's true, but it doesn't overcome the moral question of whether it is right for one generation to impose obligations on its successors, nor whether in practical economic and political terms it's OK to pass the buck to one's children and grandchildren.

How poisonous is the legacy being handed down to the young?

Although intergenerational fairness is an increasingly hot question, it's far from new. Among the earliest efforts to fit deficit financing into a theoretical framework, the trail-blazing English economist David Ricardo came up with an idea still known as 'Ricardian equivalence'. He argued that because taxpayers know that the government's borrowings will eventually have to be financed by tax increases, they will put more money aside against that day.

As well as being ranked with Adam Smith as a hugely influential thinker on economics. Ricardo was a dazzling ornament to Regency England. His stately home, Gatcombe Park, is today occupied by Princess Anne, and having invested in what was in effect the purchase of a House of Commons seat, he promoted his laissez-faire ideas on economic issues to a wide public.

Reputed to have made his fortune by betting presciently on the outcome of the Battle of Waterloo, Ricardo is best known for his theory of countries' comparative advantage in international trade. He also influenced thinking on questions ranging from wages and profits to inflation and monetarism. On long-term debt, however, he admitted to being something of an agnostic because he reckoned that whether a government taxes immediately or later, in the long term demand and output will not be greatly changed.

In Ricardo's day there were far fewer taxpayers, and some of them were more concerned with bricking up windows to avoid window tax than the rights and wrongs of passing debt on to their heirs. Now, with fiscal pressures of a very different dimension, the moral rectitude of driving future generations ever-deeper into debt is fiercely debated.

In the US, Larry Kotlikoff became a standard-bearer of 'intergenerational accounting' with his book *The Coming*

Generational Storm, published in 2004 by MIT. Kotlikoff and co-author Scott Burns made the case for an approach 'that would directly measure the fiscal burden we are leaving our kids'. They explained that the concept of generational accounting 'may sound new, but it's been around for about 15 years and has been applied in roughly 30 countries. The IMF, World Bank, Bank of England, Bundesbank, the EU and official institutions in Japan, Norway and New Zealand have sponsored generational accounting studies.'

Kotlikoff is no stranger to disputed ideas. When, in the 1980s, President Ronald Reagan was fashioning his controversial 'Reaganomics' policies, Kotlikoff was asked by the Council of Economic Advisors to discuss 'ideas for a rosy economic forecast in defence of huge tax cuts'. To encourage discussion, the council's chairman enquired, 'In what course at graduate school do they teach this?' Larry Kotlikoff answered, 'Creative writing.'

'A six-decade long generational Ponzi scheme' was how Kotlikoff described the system that since the 1950s has seen younger Americans transferring money to their elders on the implicit promise that they themselves will benefit when their turn comes. The result has been America's runaway national debt, which he calculates could only be tackled by a permanent increase in all major taxes of 64 per cent or a 40 per cent cut in all federal spending. 'There is just no way we can double the tax rates of future Americans,' says Kotlikoff in his book. 'They'll stop working, stop reporting their income, or leave the country. So we need to make some immediate and very painful sacrifices to protect our descendants and save the nation.'[5]

For 40 years, Kotlikoff and a few other like-minded economists have been voices crying in the wilderness, their warnings either ignored or drowned out by those who say public debt shouldn't be such a bogeyman. Some of these naysayers subscribe to a beguiling new doctrine called modern monetary theory (MMT), which is music to the ears of politicians who shy away from electorally unpopular tax increases.

Critics of MMT say it's more a cult than a genuine economic theory. If so, its high priestess is Stephanie Kelton, a former chief economist for the US Senate's budget committee. She is the author of a book called *The Deficit Myth*, which advocates 'shaking free from orthodox thinking about fiscal deficits rooted in a bygone era.' Kelton believes the US dollar offers the means to ignore budget constraints. In crude terms, MMT says governments that issue their own currency can stimulate economic activity by creating more money. The idea is popular among left-leaning American politicians such as US Senator Bernie Sanders, but its opponents warn that printing more banknotes always leads to hyper-inflation.[6]

It's certainly true that governments and private borrowers should shy away from running up debt in a currency other than their own. The degree of flexibility that MMT offers the US cannot disguise the overall problem of debt being racked up so rapidly at a time when slow growth makes its repayment improbable, if not impossible.

There must be times when Europe's finance ministers and their Treasury officials look wistfully at the powers wielded by the Federal Reserve in Washington DC and dream of a time the European Central Bank in Frankfurt might experiment with MMT and issue tens of billions of euros. Sadly, the eurozone's sovereign debt crises of 2009–10 showed how vulnerable a currency can be when shared by richer and poorer countries.

How bad a deal are young people getting?

Cambridge University in the aftermath of the 1914–18 First World War was a ferment of new and exciting ideas about how to build a better, fairer future. Safeguarding, and indeed improving, the interests of younger people was among the priorities of the rising generation of European intellectuals who flocked to Cambridge in the 1920s.

These stars included John Maynard Keynes, arguably the most influential economist of his time, and the Austrian-born philosopher Ludwig Wittgenstein. Less famous because he died so prematurely was Frank Ramsey, a precociously brilliant young thinker who advanced the then-controversial view that future generations' well-being was as important to the shaping of policies as present needs. 'It is ethically indefensible', he wrote, 'to discount the interests of future people, and to do so arises merely from the weakness of the imagination.'

Ramsey died suddenly in 1930 while still in his twenties, probably from an infection picked up after a swim in the River Cam, so he didn't live to see his brother Michael enthroned as Archbishop of Canterbury or his own work hailed as truly remarkable. Keynes readily acknowledged Ramsey's impact on tax and other theories, and almost a century later Nobel economics laureate Joseph Stiglitz paid homage to the way Ramsey had launched a 'major moral debate' on intergenerational fairness.[7]

Reconciling the interests of younger people with those of retirees came to the fore two decades after Ramsey's death with the growth of the welfare state in post-Second World War Britain and in much of continental Europe. More social spending meant finding an equitable balance between taxes and benefits, especially pensions. The upshots included a formula, known as the Musgrave Rule after the late American economist Richard Musgrave, for fixing a fair ratio between retirees' benefits and the average earnings of taxpaying workers.

Arrangements of this sort worked pretty well until demographic change began to upset humanity's fixed patterns of life. Although infant mortality had mercifully been reduced to very little, the balance between generations had remained fairly constant until the closing quarter of the 20th century. At that point, longer lives and dramatically falling birth rates torpedoed it.

The focus has therefore moved to the financial handicaps that younger people in Europe and America must contend with in relation to the benefits that previous generations earned through their contributions when working. Europeans and Americans born in the immediate post-Second World War years have enjoyed conditions that today's young can only envy. Much is written about the financial hardships suffered by the retired and the frail – and individual cases are often heart-rending – but in overall 'macro' terms the baby boomers are the generation that never had it so good.

Tax policies and the benefits they finance are like the proverbial supertanker – they take a long time to turn around. Legions of distinguished economists began to analyse intergenerational imbalances as soon as increased longevity and diminishing fertility became apparent, but over the last 30 years or so the fairness gap has continued to widen. Older people are better off, and that improvement has come at the expense of younger ones.

Researchers at the Bruegel think tank in Brussels have reported that the intergenerational income and wealth divide is widening, with younger people 'significantly poorer, while poverty among pensioners has been reduced'. Its 2015 study of the divide between old and young also emphasised that as well as 'material deprivation', Europe's youth suffer surges of unemployment that have the effect of hitting everyone by braking the EU's productivity growth.[8]

The difference between what Gen-Zers and millennials can expect when they retire and the 'deal' given to baby boomers has been neatly summed-up by *Wall Street Journal* reporter Joseph Sternberg. The numbers he has crunched are for the US, but they are broadly in line with the trend in many parts of Europe, including the UK.

In his book *The Theft of a Decade: How the Baby Boomers Stole the Millennials' Economic Future*, Sternberg compares the average tax payments and post-retirement benefits of an American married couple born in 1950 with those of couples born later. On the basis of constant 2017 dollars, he reckons a typical baby boomer couple will have paid about $700,000 in taxes over their working lives, but stand to receive social security and healthcare benefits worth just over a million dollars after they have retired.

That means there's a $350,000 deficit to be borne by the system, and it grows to an average deficit of more than half a million dollars per couple for people born in 1965 as a result of their longer lifespans. With America's retirement community due to grow from 50 million people in 2017 to 85 million by 2035, the likelihood of millennials and Gen-Zers getting a similar deal is slim. The most probable solution is that their tax contributions will have to rise. On top of high mortgage costs, and for many Americans the burden of student loans that now total $1.5 trillion, this sounds like a recipe for trouble.[9]

Increasing taxes to pay for rising retirement costs is for most governments the obvious reflex, but the scale of the tax hikes needed is eye-watering. Calculations by Oxford University's Institute of Population Ageing suggested back in 2004 that income tax in the UK would have to rise by at least 5.7 per cent to restore 'generational balance'. When various other factors are taken into account, that would mean an income tax hike of almost 10 per cent.[10]

Those figures have since been overtaken by much more dramatic estimates from the UK's Office for Budget Responsibility and from the Institute for Fiscal Studies think tank. On the basis of their calculations, a UK House of Commons report in 2017 put the nation's intergenerational budget imbalance at an astounding aggregated sum of £7.6 trillion. 'Future generations', said the parliamentary reporters, 'will in effect inherit net liabilities of just over five times annual GDP. The rise in tax revenue (or reduction in expenditure) needed to plug the gap would be around six per cent of GDP.'[11]

The amounts under discussion are so huge it's tempting for elected politicians to downplay or even ignore them as sectoral problems that don't immediately affect the bulk of society. That would be a big mistake future decision-makers would greatly regret.

The dispiriting outlook for young people is bad news for everyone. Europe's market economies aren't paying their way, so the growing gaps between what Europeans take out of the system and what they contribute can only be bridged by borrowing. Snowballing debts have to be serviced, and interest payments that since 2008 or so had taken a comparatively modest slice of GDPs are becoming a significant strain on national resources.

The tensions between the 20-member eurozone's richer north and poorer south are intensifying, raising once again the risk of a sovereign debt crisis like that which engulfed Greece in 2010 and then affected other 'Club Med' countries of the EU like Spain, Portugal and Italy. As well as weighing heavily on governments' national budgets, the debt problem is destabilising Europe's efforts to forge stronger economic partnerships.

Is capitalism the culprit?

The obvious answer to the problem of national debts whose sheer size is braking economic growth is to reduce these borrowings to more manageable proportions. But to do so would require a revolutionary improvement in the performance of Europe's economies. Capitalism is quite simply failing to create enough wealth to pay for Europeans' increasingly expensive social welfare 'safety nets'.

Capitalism's worth in both moral and economic terms has been hotly debated ever since Karl Marx emerged in 1867 from the Reading Room of London's British Museum to publish *Das Kapital*, and some would say well before then. The tenor of debates is quite different if the topic is the value of a market economy rather than the more loaded term capitalism. Among the more recent contributions have been books by UK-based scholars Sir Paul Collier and Mariana Mazzucato. Both take a long, hard look at capitalism and conclude that it's overdue for an overhaul.

Collier, an Oxford University economics professor whose earlier book *The Bottom Billion* shone a harsh light on development aid policies, is sceptical in his book *The Future of Capitalism* about its efficiency and about the worth to society of 'stakeholder' capitalism. Mazzucato, who specialises at University College London in innovation policies, poses equally searching questions about the international financial system in her book *The Value of Everything: Making and Taking in the Global Economy*.[12]

Capitalism's critics can be found, too, in corporate boardrooms. Microsoft's billionaire founder Bill Gates remarked of Paul Collier's book, 'I agree with him that capitalism "needs to be managed, not defeated". We should do more to curb its excesses and minimise its negative aspects.'[13]

For their part, politicians tend to invoke competing ideologies when urging their solutions to the problem. The contributions they make to the discussion are usually more a dialogue of the deaf than constructive proposals. The reality is that there are two fundamental reasons why Europe's economic growth is faltering: the demographic deficit and stagnant productivity. If these can be addressed, the situation will improve, but both are major constraints that defy easy answers.

A study by German researchers assesses the impact of demographic change in no uncertain terms. 'It is leading to massive income losses,' reported the Bertelsmann Stiftung in 2019. After looking at ageing and the shrinkage of active workforces, in five European countries together with Japan and the US, it forecast alarming reductions in real wages and spending power across the board. It warned the effects will be serious for all by 2050, although worst for Japan and the least harmful in the US.

The best solution, says the think tank, which is owned by one of Germany's largest publishing empires, is to invest hugely in advanced labour-saving technologies. It suggests that spending on research and innovation in information and communications technology should be five to six times higher than at present in Japan, Italy and Spain, and two to three times more in France, Germany and Austria. Only enormous investment drives of these dimensions, it argues, can compensate for working populations that will be smaller and older. The Bertelsmann report also emphasises that individuals' productivity starts to fall after the age of 50.[14]

Productivity is the magic wand that almost everyone wants to wave over sluggish economies. Like all magic, it's an illusion. Productivity has more or less flatlined in most Western European countries – not least in Britain – since the 21st century got into its stride. Experts warn that the prospects of substantial improvements in output per person, and thus wealth, are negligible.

It isn't necessarily a lost cause. McKinsey Global Institute researchers have found that the COVID-19 pandemic had an extraordinary impact on companies' digitisation. A survey in October 2020 found that firms were introducing digital systems up to 25 times faster 'than they had previously thought possible'. The lesson seems to be that shock therapy works better and faster than sermons by governments and academics.

The backdrop to this remarkable improvement is nevertheless gloomy. Although the US maintains a lead over Europe in the productivity stakes, neither has been achieving much productivity growth, if any. The McKinsey experts say that fewer than a fifth of American companies are using the new technologies as much as they should, and in Europe it's barely a tenth.[15]

Suggestions abound on both sides of the Atlantic for how to kick-start productivity, although few seem likely to yield dramatic results. Diane Coyle at Cambridge University reckons that a shake-up of the UK's public sector and a much stronger focus on infrastructure projects outside London and south-east England would help, as would more high-tech start-ups. More controversially, she points out that Britain's overall productivity would be improved if economic recession were to cull weak companies that have avoided bankruptcy but are a drag on the UK's economic dynamism.[16]

Discussion of productivity and the complex reasons that its growth has tailed off inevitably raises wider questions about the efficiency and worth of market economies. The wealth gaps between the top and bottom echelons of society in Europe and America are widening into chasms, and although present day society has tolerated this so far, it's far from certain that younger generations will continue to do so.

The seeds of political unrest may already have been sown. The richest 10 per cent of people in the OECD's 38 member countries earn ten times more than the bottom tenth. Forty years ago that multiple was seven, and the change has since accelerated, spurred by economic recessions that have seen the wages of many stagnate and their purchasing power wane. It's scarcely surprising, then, that political support across Europe for mainstream Social Democrat politicians who advocate mildly progressive solutions has shifted into votes for radical populist movements.

The shortcomings of capitalism go far beyond its failure to reconcile the interests of investors, employers and employees. The pressure to deliver profits in the short term is also militating against longer term goals such as environmental sustainability. There's much talk of 'stakeholder capitalism' and 'employee ownership', but the widespread public perception is of a boss class that's increasingly self-serving. Its wealth contrasts with the rise of the 'precariat' of poorly paid workers who have no real job security.

Many of the business leaders who rub shoulders with government ministers and the like at the annual meeting of the World Economic Forum in Davos pay lip service to calls for the upgrading of the 'social contract' and a fairer deal for the working poor. The reality, however, is that too often corporate executives are complicit in the practices that load the dice against wage earners.

Corporations lobby powerfully against redistributive taxes and in favour of special dispensations for their own industry. They resist efforts to stamp out tax havens and race-to-the-bottom tax breaks offered by competing national governments. Some have even been accused of involvement in the criminal laundering of dirty money. Employers' organisations preach social responsibility, but polls show that in the public mind confidence is dwindling.

Capitalism's failure to respond satisfactorily to the combination of accelerating climate change and deepening economic hardships may yet bring about political turmoil on a scale that radical change makes unavoidable. So far, though, the simplistic ideas advanced by populist politicians, while attracting votes, are unconvincing as policy solutions. How long this deadlock will persist depends on whether younger voters lose patience with the prevailing economic conditions in much of Europe, and instead turn their attention to the deepening crises that most certainly lie ahead.

It's looking increasingly difficult to haul market economies out of their 'secular [entrenched] stagnation'. Many national economies seem threatened with decades in the doldrums instead of prospering in the newly dynamic Digital Age we have been promised. The likely response in the UK and most European economies to the many negative pressures will be a bigger role for governments. Big government is the bogeyman of tax-cutting politicians who promise to reduce the powers of the state, but the reality is that governments have been getting steadily bigger and will continue to do so.

The state's share of the economy varies considerably from country to country: it's between 40 and 60 per cent of GDP. The common denominator is that it keeps rising: in Victorian England it was 10 per cent, in the 1920s it reached 20 per cent and now in the UK it's nudging 50 per cent. The more that society demands stronger social safety nets and state benefits, the higher it rises. A private sector that fails to create enough wealth to fund ageing's growing demands will inevitably mean that people turn to the state, however loudly the political mood music may demand the slimming down of government.

Opponents of big government trot out a familiar litany of arguments. 'It infringes upon the rights of individual citizens because of its extensive bureaucracy and intrusive regulations,' complained a prominent American conservative 100 years ago. Since then the responsibilities of the state in the US and around the world have greatly increased, responding to a growing faith in the benefits of the 'common good'.

The key question isn't so much the ship of state's size but who's at the helm. It's the course being set that matters, and in Britain and most EU countries government policies to promote intergenerational fairness have been few and far between. Bigger government is inevitable, but better government is all too often elusive.

A strategy for ageing and for rebalancing the interests of the millennials and Gen-Zers who must pay for it is badly needed, both for Britain and at a European level, Brexit notwithstanding. Ageing is an international phenomenon that risks straining relations in sectors such as education, research and development, and freedom of movement, so a collective approach will be essential.

The area where a Europe-wide approach is most important of all is tax. Who pays for the costs of ageing, and how, will boil down to taxation. Substantial shifts in long-standing tax policies are needed at a national level, to avoid fruitless intergovernmental tax competition at a European level and globally. Properly handled, tax reforms could do much to fine-tune markets and cure capitalism's malaise while increasing the tax take that Europe's ageing requires. If mishandled, the tax needs of cash-strapped governments could easily become the catalyst for civil catastrophe.

11

'Soaking the rich' isn't that easy

Tax the super-rich, insist reformers who believe that's the way to bridge or at least narrow the 'wealth gap'. Tax cheats are reckoned to cost both the EU and the US a yearly trillion dollars or euros. Yet all efforts to 'soak the rich' have failed, partly because investment-hungry governments create tax loopholes and havens. Will ageing's soaring costs eventually force governments into tax reforms to benefit millennials and Gen-Zers?

A discreet, almost secretive, country club get-together in rural California must rank among the stranger events of our times: some of America's richest people had gathered in the nation's wealthiest township to discuss new ways to give away their money and, crucially, pay more tax.

The venue was Los Altos, an exclusive wooded community about 35 miles south of San Francisco. Inhabited by Silicon Valley billionaires like Google's CEO Sundar Pichai, it has been designated by the US Census as the most expensive neighbourhood anywhere in the US. Homes must by law be set in at least an acre of garden.

The meeting at the local golf course's clubhouse created the California Chapter of Patriotic Millionaires, an organisation whose leading light is Abigail Disney, heir to the Walt Disney fortune. It aims to channel at least half of its members' riches into underfunded social projects, and more broadly seeks to correct the glaring unfairness of the US tax system. Half a million Americans now earn more than $1 million a year, yet they pay tax at the lowest rates. 'Instead of saying multi-millionaires, why not say mega-millionaires?', reportedly volunteered one of the Los Altos invitees when discussion turned to tax thresholds.[1]

Needless to say, the eagerness of the 200 or so members of
Patriotic Millionaires to share their wealth isn't a common feature
of the super-rich, but nor is it entirely unknown. America's
wealthiest people nevertheless have a strong philanthropic culture
that helps compensate for its uncompromising rule of the market.
Giving money away is far less evident in Europe, although one
or two cases are noteworthy.

Marlene Engelhorn made headlines when she announced she'll
be passing on a substantial chunk of the billions she had just
inherited to 21 deserving causes. The young literature student at
the University of Vienna is the great-great-granddaughter of the
founder of Germany's BASF chemicals giant, and she set out the
reasons for donating so much in her newly published book *Geld*.[2]

Another development, this time in Geneva, points towards
a similarly progressive mood among Europe's money-makers.
Michel Jabré, son of a prominent hedge fund operator, has
launched a new venture within the family firm that he intends
will counter 'greed in the financial system'.

'Our over-arching philosophy', he told a *Financial Times*
reporter, 'is based on "conscious capitalism", whereby businesses
should serve all stakeholders, including employees, humanity, the
environment.' His very laudable project is a remarkable example of
a poacher turning gamekeeper: in 2006 Michel's father, Philippe,
had been fined the then record sum of £750,000 by the UK's
financial regulator for insider trading.[3]

The Engelhorn and Jabré initiatives may be significant straws in
the wind, for Europeans too are beginning to think hard about
ways to bridge the wealth gap. Overhauling taxation around
Europe and worldwide is the only practical solution, and society's
willingness to seize this prickly nettle will depend on the degree
to which public attitudes to unfairness continue to harden.

That's possibly why the European Commission has thrown its
usual caution to the winds in a hard-hitting note entitled 'Wealth
concentration'. Its litany of unfair practices and conditions
included the astounding claim that just eight individuals own
assets worth as much as those of the 3.6 billion people who
constitute the poorest half of the global population.

That's a mere eight people, while the thousands more who
make up the world's wealthiest 1 per cent, adds the EU report,

own more than the remaining 99 per cent. Over the last 30 years, the super-rich have enjoyed a 300 per cent increase in their incomes, whereas the poorest half have seen zero improvement. By 2050, forecast the EU's executive body, the top 0.1 per cent 'will own more wealth than the total global middle class'.

The EU paper concluded with an ambitious wish-list of tax reforms that it would like member governments to introduce. 'Higher inequality is associated with greater demand for redistribution of income, and ultimately with redistributive policy outcomes,' the report says, adding that 'European countries have a stronger demand for redistribution than the rest of the world.'[4]

How enthusiastic European governments are to undertake controversial tax reforms is debatable. That tax revolutions are the only practicable way to fund ageing's spiralling costs is beyond dispute, but how feasible are they politically? All national tax codes are grotesquely complicated – successive layers of reform and fine-tuning have ensured that – and those of European countries when taken together are a Gordian knot. In any case, it's useless to speak of 'taking them together' because European governments jealously guard their fiscal sovereignty and independence from the EU.

Daunting though the challenges of tax reform may be, governments will at some point have no alternative but to accept greater collaboration. Ageing is increasing social security and healthcare costs at such a rate that their searches for more revenue are becoming more desperate than ever. Welfare and health costs are exacerbated by post-COVID-19 spending and the consequences of the Ukraine war, snuffing out hopes in most European countries of economic recovery that could rescue their public finances.

Something's got to give, and soaking the rich would certainly be the most popular solution. Imposing much higher taxes on the wealthiest corporations and individuals is, though, fraught with difficulty. Efforts in a number of countries to extract more revenues from the owners of valuable assets suggest that even a determined clampdown is unlikely to yield the levels of cash demanded by demographic decline.

At the same time, higher taxes look unavoidable. So what sort of taxes, and to be paid by whom? The difficulties of taxing the super-rich are illustrated by Warren Buffett, the celebrated US 'investment genius' whose Berkshire Hathaway company almost unerringly selects winners and avoids losers in the casino of American capitalism. In 2012, the mild-mannered 'Sage of Omaha' denounced as ridiculously unfair the fact that his secretary pays tax on her modest salary at a higher rate than he does on all his billions. He declared there should be a 30 per cent levy on the wealth of all millionaires, including himself.

Ten years later, a watchdog website in the US called ProPublica revealed that from 2014 to 2018 Buffett's fortune grew by $23 billion, yet his tax bill for the period was only a thousandth of that – $23.7 million. America's capital-friendly tax laws and his company's ingenious tax lawyers had frustrated Buffett's own desire to pay more tax. ProPublica also reported that in some years Amazon's Jeff Bezos, Tesla's Elon Musk, Michael Bloomberg and the philanthropist financier George Soros paid no tax at all to the US federal government. In others, when they did pay tax, their tax bills were absurdly low in relation to their profits and capital gains.

Taxing rich people and large corporations is far from just an American problem. The efforts of left-of-centre governments in France to wring more revenue from the rich stand as a cautionary tale for all of Europe. Two determined attempts have proved sadly disappointing, not only because they produced less money than hoped for, but also because they sparked capital outflows that saw investors moving their money outside France.

Thomas Piketty, the French economist whose magisterial book *Capital in the Twenty-First Century* caused a considerable stir in 2014 with its analysis of rising unfairness, reckons that the top tenth in France own well over half the country's wealth. Thirty years earlier, François Mitterrand had reached a similar conclusion, when as the nation's powerful president he introduced swingeing tax measures in 1982 to level the fiscal playing field.

Mitterrand's 'Impôt sur la Fortune' (ISF), targeted people whose net worth was the then-equivalent of €1.3 million or more and who had assets of at least €10 million. But the ISF's contribution to tax receipts is reckoned never to have exceeded a meagre 2 per cent, while triggering an exodus of thousands of millionaire investors.[5]

French tax specialist Eric Pichet estimated in a 2008 paper that the ISF cost the country almost twice as much as it generated. He put the yearly gap between its revenues and losses of income it caused at €7 billion. He believed that, thanks to the ISF, France's annual GDP growth rate was consistently 0.2 per cent less than it should have been.

The French wealth tax's chequered history reflects these doubts. It was abolished in 1986 after right-winger Jacques Chirac ousted Mitterrand from the presidency. Then in 2012, a new socialist president, François Hollande, introduced a successor to the ISF called the 'Super-Tax' that imposed a 75 per cent levy on yearly earnings above €1 million. This made headlines when movie stars such as Gérard Depardieu and business mogul Bernard Arnault moved to tax-friendlier Belgium. It was successfully challenged in the courts, and in 2014 it, too, was rescinded.[6]

Could new taxes be earmarked to pay the costs of ageing?

Strange to say, the immediate problem on the tax front isn't how to raise more money, or from whom, vitally important though both questions are. The first challenge is to earmark more spending for neglected areas now being turned into priorities by the impact of ageing.

Much-needed investments in infrastructure and services to tackle ageing's pressures have long been crowded out by more immediate problems. The expansion and modernisation of healthcare, public transport and social housing has been widely neglected for decades. On both sides of the Atlantic, most so-called rich countries have inherited a legacy of unresolved problems that urgently need more funding.

Post-COVID-19 and Ukraine-related costs have shifted attention away from the looming demographic disaster the impact of which will be inescapable by 2030, if not before. The economic damage to European countries of Russian's reduced oil and gas supplies could, say some analysts, be a yearly €1 trillion. Add to that the 'stagflationary' recession triggered by the COVID-19 lockdowns, and it's easy to see why proposed new financial instruments to soften ageing's impact are being pushed aside.[7]

It will be hard for cash-strapped governments to justify extra spending on problems that are not yet visible to the public eye. Hard, but not impossible. The focus must therefore be on taxes that can specifically address the issues people most readily identify with, and that speak to their sense of community and social justice.

The turning point in the debate over taxation was arguably the summer of 2020, when COVID-19 lockdowns were freezing so much economic and social activity. Attention turned in a number of countries to future tax policies. How, people began to ask, could the pandemic's damage to lifestyles and livelihoods be paid for? In the UK, an organisation called Tax Justice organised virtual focus groups to take the pulse of public opinion on possible policy shifts.

Attitudes divided broadly between those who saw taxation as an instrument of wealth redistribution and those who insisted that the 'fairness' of taxes is measured by what contributors receive back from the state. The *realpolitik* is that governments of whatever political colour must strive to satisfy both camps as much as they can.

The issues discussed in a number of online public meetings included the £38 billion a year in tax relief the British government has allowed as a way to encourage pension savings. It isn't as fair a concession as it sounds. The system favours high earners so much that half of that tax relief goes to the top 10 per cent. It's a glaring example of the way benefits accruing to richer, older people come at the expense of the young and the poor.

The gap between the interests of the old and the young is so clear that it has begun to transcend traditional Left–Right political affiliations. 'According to our research,' says Tax Justice's director Robert Palmer, 'seventy-four per cent want to see the wealthy taxed more, including sixty-four per cent of Conservative voters.' He added that 46 per cent of Tory supporters surveyed were prepared to pay more tax themselves, and that three-quarters of them favoured a hike in the UK's corporation tax.[8]

Attitudes to taxation are shifting. The Ukraine invasion and the ensuing energy crisis have heightened the importance of public services, and would seem to have increased people's tolerance of tax hikes. Whether that short-term effect will favour a narrowing of the intergenerational gap remains to be seen. In wider societal terms, the view from the high ground must be that taxes to ensure social stability over the coming decades are more important than 'tactical' taxes that address immediate challenges, pressing though these may be.

It would help if major political parties were to temper their more outdated Left–Right fixations by sharpening their focus on the Young–Old balance. Adjusting the way younger generations are presently taxed to fund benefits for wealthier older people is an important key to resolving Europe's demographic difficulties.

How taxes are unfairly skewed against younger wage earners

'Lower taxes spark greater growth' has been the mantra of many populist politicians, not least within the UK's Conservative party. The case is hotly argued with regard to taxes on businesses, but it makes no sense at all in the area of personal taxation.

Older people hold the bulk of assets and wealth, and lighter taxes on them would do little to stimulate business. Most people who are of pensionable age no longer work, and as their savings tend to be invested safely rather than speculatively they can't be said to spearhead high-tech ventures. Because older people are less likely to back technologically advanced start-ups, it's unlikely that reducing taxes on their wealth would stimulate innovation.

For the young, though, there would be enormous dividends from lightening their tax burden. They pay proportionately more in income tax and are also overtaxed through a host of indirect costs and levies on consumption. Lower taxes on housing, employment and services that relate to child-rearing would give them an invaluable fillip. If today's millennials and Gen-Zers are to pay for tomorrow's pensioners, their living standards and future prospects must rapidly be improved. Tax is the best, some would say the only, instrument capable of achieving that.

Across Europe, taxes are skewed in favour of the owners of wealth and against its producers. Analyses of EU governments' tax policy sources have shown that by far the largest share of states' revenues comes from taxing labour and the various aspects of employment. And while taxes on employers and employees average half of all receipts into state coffers, revenues from taxing consumption contribute about a third and taxes on capital only a fifth.

A shake-up is long overdue, and a rebalancing of the interests of different generations would be the best way to achieve it. Inadequate funding of education is common to almost all European countries, and seems particularly disappointing in the UK. Raising wealthier older people's tax thresholds could funnel more cash into the education sector – from kindergartens to universities. Rather than doing so under the heading of 'general taxation', it would be more acceptable if it were labelled as a separate intergenerational fund.

Tax experts suggest an array of measures to help younger people and relieve them of some of their fiscal burdens. Exempting the under-thirties in Britain from National Insurance contributions could be accompanied by increased child benefits and tax credits for children. Subsidising mortgages to get younger people onto the first rungs of the property ladder would benefit them, and thus society as a whole.

Taxation of property values and transactions is an area where substantial advantages could be transferred to younger people. Ideas for taxing the value of the land a building sits on rather than the building itself have for many years been fiercely resisted by corporations and owner-occupiers, yet governments are being deprived of huge revenues by glaring undervaluations of property in city centres and in exclusive residential districts. Reforming land valuation, perhaps on a progressive and rolling basis, would release major revenue streams that could fund tax benefits for young people.

Taxing the ground beneath buildings so as to increase state revenues looks an attractive political proposition. Public opinion strongly supports higher taxes on expensive property. When Tax Justice UK polled attitudes to property taxes, it found 70 per cent in favour of a 'mansion tax' on homes worth £2 million or more. And 67 per cent back the idea of assessing local levies such as council tax in the UK on the basis of property values.

Fifty years or more of soaring property values in the UK, and to a slightly lesser degree in continental Europe, have greatly exacerbated the wealth gap between younger and older people.

Property taxation is therefore an obvious candidate for extensive reform. Tax can be used as a lever to address the under-use and under-occupation of buildings. It can also transform these buildings into social housing for the less-privileged, including young people who may be hesitating to start a family because of housing difficulties. In Belgium, the regional government of Flanders has shown the way with a tax on households with more rooms than occupants.

There's a widespread but wrong view that the taxman's appetite is insatiable, and that taxes bite increasingly into ordinary people's hard-earned incomes. It's simply untrue, yet if a common denominator could be found in the election debates that flared across Europe in 2024 it's that people are increasingly overtaxed. Political rivals in the European Parliament elections and in the British and French midsummer general elections bandied about statistics and promises, but didn't challenge the idea that taxes are too high and should somehow be forced down.

It's more accurate to say that too many Europeans are underpaid. So far as taxes are concerned, most people's earnings have in fact more or less kept pace with tax increases. It's the growing number of the truly poor whose purchasing power has been squeezed that's the greater problem. Establishing a clearer picture of tax burdens is therefore essential if long-overdue reviews of tax policies are to take place.

In the UK and most developed market economies, personal taxes have been falling. In some countries they are a lesser burden on people than they were half a century ago. The Paris-based OECD, which does much of the heavy lifting on the collection of tax statistics around the world, and above all from its 38 richer member countries, has been very clear on the trend. In a detailed analysis of the first two decades of the 21st century, it reported that the weight of taxes on wage earners and on households of various shapes and sizes has declined. On the other hand, consumption taxes such as VAT have risen steadily.

The way different countries levy their taxes of course varies considerably. In the UK, thanks in part to the 'low tax' Conservative governments in office from 2010 to 2024, taxes on labour take an average 30 per cent of an employee's income. Just across the English Channel in Belgium, it's over 50 per cent. The overall trend throughout the OECD has been downwards since the start of this century, with reductions of up to 2 per cent in income taxes, and in Britain of as much as 5 per cent.[9]

There won't be enough tax revenues to fund ageing

Tax revenues in most of the OECD's comparatively wealthy member countries have been rising in relation to GDP since 1965. At first glance, this suggests that taxpayers may be able to keep on shelling out enough to keep pace with the rising costs of ageing. A closer look reveals a more worrying picture.

The good news is that figures prepared by His Majesty's Revenue and Customs (HMRC) for the UK, and for the EU by Eurostat, look reassuring. Both show steady year-on-year increases in governments' tax incomes, with rising graphs that point towards a continuing ability to fund social welfare benefits and health systems that are envied by many countries elsewhere. Britain's tax collectors were able to report receipts for the 2021–2022 financial year of almost £720 billion, substantially up on the £400 billion collected at the turn of the century. Economic growth over the last 20 years, although disappointingly slow, has yielded a progressively larger tax income that has spared the UK's taxpayers from stumping up greater slices of their earnings or assets.

The EU as a whole – which included the UK up to 31 January 2020 – recorded a similarly impressive rise in tax incomes. Its member governments' revenues for 2020 were just over €5.5 trillion, a hefty increase on the €2.5 trillion they had collected in 1995, when almost half of them had yet to formally join the EU. But the overall pattern changes little: nine-tenths of all European governments' revenues are derived from taxation.

The burning question is whether finance ministers across Europe can look forward to tax revenues that will keep up with the snowballing costs of ageing. Among their options they may be contemplating increased taxation of their wealthier citizens, even though experience so far in the 21st century isn't encouraging. Wealth tax receipts, says Eurostat, actually dropped in the years leading up to 2010, then enjoyed a brief increase from 2011 to 2013 and have more or less stagnated ever since.[10]

In Britain, where the tax authorities tend to have big business and major corporations in their sights rather than wealthy individuals, the picture is blurred by Brexit. Leaving the EU has devastated the country's tax income from offshore sources, raising doubts about future yields from corporation tax in general. Only 100th of the UK's post-Brexit 2020–22 corporation tax revenues came from offshore sources – £500 million out of £50 billion. Before Brexit it had been close to a quarter – £9 billion from offshore and £33 billion onshore – at a time when EU membership was still being debated in advance of the referendum that was widely expected to be won by the 'Remainers'.

If forecasts of European governments' future financial requirements are even remotely accurate, the pressures for much higher taxes will be irresistible. Over the 25 years to mid-century, Europeans are set to be trapped between declining real wages and mounting tax bills. Once the full force of Brexit falls on its economy, Britain will be among the chief sufferers from rising costs and stagnating revenues.

A House of Commons report has estimated the UK will need increased tax revenues equivalent to 6 per cent of GDP. This paralleled an earlier study by Oxford University researchers who, long before Brexit, reckoned a 10 per cent income tax boost is needed if the UK's intergenerational balance is to be restored.[11]

Some experts maintain that more efficient forms of taxation and improved methods of tax collection are needed, rather than ingenious new taxes or swingeing increases in personal taxes. They chiefly have in mind the multinational corporations that play off competing national tax regimes against each other, and even domestic companies or the super-wealthy who employ batteries of lawyers familiar with tax loopholes and offshore havens.

Tax avoidance that's perfectly legal but morally questionable diverts tens if not hundreds of billions every year away from the coffers of national governments. There's also tax evasion, of course, which is said to be flourishing because many governments have reduced the budgets for policing their own tax rules. A concerted effort by European tax authorities, including those of the UK, federal agencies in the US and governments around the world could net huge sums and go a long way towards bridging yawning tax gaps.

The staggering scale of global tax dodging

The sheer scale of tax dodging – both avoidance and evasion – is mind-blowing. Some $650 billion is reckoned to be lost every year to tax authorities because of perfectly legal loopholes. As to criminal tax evasion, in the US the Internal Revenue Service (IRS) believes it's robbed annually of a trillion dollars by people who illegally hide or under-report their wealth. The EU puts yearly tax losses at a trillion euros.

Tax dodging around the world has become a major contributor to the budgetary difficulties of financially struggling governments. And it greatly increases the burden on ordinary wage earners and smaller companies whose transparent incomes make them easily taxed. Tax authorities are fighting back with tighter rules and better cross-border coordination, but it's proving an uphill struggle. At stake is the sustainability of social benefits in welfare states that risk buckling beneath the weight of ageing populations.

Cut-throat competition between national governments to attract investment is at the root of much tax avoidance, and plays a big part in the growth of illicit financial activities. After decades of lobbying, the OECD has put together a global tax framework that aims to clip the wings of multinational corporations. Because companies can play governments off against each other, they often pay next to nothing in taxes on their far-flung activities.

The Paris-based OECD triumphantly announced in mid-2021 that it had secured agreement with 130 governments that they will all charge corporation tax at a minimum rate of 15 per cent. The aim is to put a stop to governments' 'race to the bottom' tax incentives, although it's far from sure that enough of them will stand by the pledges they've signed up to.

The crackdown is also meant to spell the end to the tax havens operated by some Caribbean islands and in Europe by mini-states such as Liechtenstein and Andorra, or the UK's Channel Islands and Isle of Man. Of the nine countries that refused to sign-up, Ireland, Hungary and Estonia stood out as EU members in a line-up that included Nigeria, Kenya, Peru and Sri Lanka.

If the OECD initiative could be firmly pursued – despite US president Donald Trump's opposition – its crackdown on tax-avoiding big business is calculated to yield at least $150 billion a year once it starts to bite, and more after 2030 when the threshold on the corporations in its cross-hairs will fall from yearly sales of $20 billion to $10 billion. The most obvious targets are internet giants such as Facebook, Amazon, Netflix, Google and Apple – nicknamed the Fangs – but they are just the tip of the corporate tax avoidance iceberg.

In 2018, the US-based Institute on Taxation and Economic Policy calculated that 90 of the leading Fortune 500 companies, including Chevron, IBM and Amazon, had paid zero federal taxes in America. Two years on, in 2020, Nike and FedEx were among the 55 major US corporations revealed as having paid no tax at all on combined profits amounting to $40 billion.

America's business-friendly political culture has in recent years led to a loosening rather than tightening of tax controls. In Europe, national governments' dogged defence of their sovereign fiscal powers has stymied efforts to introduce a more concerted EU approach to taxation. In 2021, US president Joe Biden moved to boost the budget of the IRS by an additional tenth in the hopes of improving its waning tax collecting powers. Thanks to earlier cutbacks, the IRS no longer automatically audits all major US corporations but only about half, and as a result loses hundreds of billions in uncollected tax dollars.

In Brussels, the European Commission announced in the autumn of that same year its own plan to stem the flows of illicit 'black' money at the heart of tax evasion. A new EU body called the Anti-Money Laundering Authority became operational in 2024 as the coordinator of EU member states' financial policing operations and as the supervisor of banks' efforts to stamp out illicit money transfers.

Where banks stand on the collection of taxes is an interesting question. Some are seen as poachers who must be pressured into turning gamekeeper. Although many banks appear to be trying hard to detect customer transactions that launder dirty money, they themselves stand accused of avoiding taxes as a standard banking practice. A study by the European Tax Observatory has charged the largest banks in the EU with reporting their profits in such a way that 25 per cent of that money avoids corporation tax by apparently emanating from low-tax countries.

Most of the tactics used to avoid paying tax involve specialist lawyers and accountants who are able to thread their way through the mazes of tax legislation. The US tax code, for instance, runs to 4 million words, and enables skilled consultants to dodge and delay IRS demands almost perpetually.

Occasionally, a bizarre new approach to tax avoiding makes headlines. Such was the case when Thailand's navy towed ashore a floating home that billionaire bitcoin investor Peter Thiel had claimed was an independent 'nation state'. He and co-investor Patri Friedman, grandson of the late Nobel prize-winning economist Milton Friedman, champion the idea of tax-free sea homes that can be anchored in international waters.

Their project has to all intents and purposes foundered. Far less sinkable are the multitudes of schemes and subterfuges that ingeniously combine tax avoidance and evasion. These are the practices laid bare by investigative journalists who have published such momentous scoops as the Panama, Pandora and Paradise Papers and the LuxLeaks revelations. They have shone light onto the dark world of secretive tax deals and outright criminality that continues to hide taxable wealth and divert money away from much-needed government spending.

The lid began to be lifted on the scale of global tax avoidance in 2012, when it was revealed that a nondescript modern office building in Luxembourg was the improbable headquarters of 1,600 multinational corporations. The Grand Duchy's crafty tax rules were the magnet, so it was no surprise that the tax dodging companies went unscathed while the two whistleblowers responsible for the LuxLeaks revelations ended up in court.

In 2016, a far greater scandal broke with the worldwide publication of the Panama Papers. Computerised records mysteriously obtained from an offshore law firm in tax-friendly Panama detailed 40 years of shady arrangements by 214,000 companies and individuals. High up on the long list of people named were the Emir of Qatar, several Ukrainian presidents and Italy's Silvio Berlusconi. Of the 21 tax havens, the British Virgin Islands featured prominently.

The following year saw the Paradise Papers featured in the Munich-based newspaper *Süddeutsche Zeitung*, with highlights from a treasure trove of 13 million different documents that had been handed to two of its journalists. The headlines this provoked were subsequently eclipsed in October 2021 by the Pandora Papers, which named 35 heads of state and prime ministers along with 100 billionaires. A network of almost 400 reporters connected with the Washington DC-based International Consortium of Investigative Journalists (ICIJ) is still doggedly following up on the leads from all these papers, with more embarrassing revelations certain to come.

It's impossible to say how much money may have been nefariously hidden from national tax authorities, but the ICIJ cautiously estimates it at a minimum of $5.6 trillion and possibly as much as $32 trillion. The true amount will never be known, but the signs are that massive tax evasion has become the norm. On the other hand, it's getting harder for tax cheats to avoid scrutiny, so governments will increasingly find it impossible to turn a blind eye to systematic tax evasion.

In Britain and throughout most of Europe, the less egregious forms of tax avoidance nevertheless continue to sap the tax base and shift the burden onto small fry, whether waged employees or modest little companies and shops. HMRC estimated in November 2020 that the use by some 2,000 large UK companies of 'profit diversion' techniques meant they owed the Exchequer £34.8 billion more in tax than they had paid. The introduction in 2015 of a Diverted Profits Tax has gone some way towards reducing scope for dodges, but not far enough. 'Thin capitalisation', in which debt is shifted around inside a corporate group's subsidiaries, can in some years cost the British taxman £10 billion.

Rethinking taxation is tough, yet it's the easiest option

The problem of unpaid taxes can be resolved, or at least greatly reduced, if governments choose to do so. Persuading them to dismantle and then streamline their tax codes wouldn't be easy, but it's doable. Much harder is the political challenge of devising more equitable forms of taxation that would be seen by taxpayers as fair, collectable and sufficient.

To begin with, governments should start by recovering missing tax revenues. Almost ten years ago, when he was president of the European Parliament, German socialist politician Martin Schulz suggested to his fellow MEPs that EU countries' teetering levels of sovereign debt could be wiped away inside a decade if the €1 trillion denied them every year through tax dodging could be brought to an end.

Schulz's point was that it's up to governments to clamp down on the avoidance and evasion of the taxes on their statute books. That means scrapping the host of competing tax incentives introduced to attract 'mobile' investment funds and cash deposits. The dog-eat-dog competition between national governments – many of them fellow EU member states – is at the root of tax avoidance.

A tentative step towards this was taken within Europe in mid-2021, when EU governments and members of the European Parliament ended years of stalled talks with a deal that forces multinational corporations to disclose where they book their profits and pay taxes. As well as obliging transparency on operations within the EU, the new rules mean that any company with annual sales of €750 million or more must report its financial dealings in tax jurisdictions that Brussels has labelled 'non-cooperative'; that means 19 blacklisted tax havens such as Guam or the US Virgin Islands and greylisted ones that include Panama, Fiji and Samoa.

Many EU member governments had been resisting this move since it was first proposed in 2013, but even the strongest opponents among them finally gave in under pressure. Critics of the deal point out that because it's limited in large part to within the EU, it leaves out 'notorious' tax havens such as Switzerland, the Bahamas and the Cayman Islands. The fact is, they say, that the EU corporate tax pact doesn't cover four-fifths of the countries around the world where companies continue to hide the true extent of their taxable income.

But thanks to these EU measures and the OECD-backed international deal on the 15 per cent minimum corporation tax, the avoidance of tax is getting harder, although is still far from impossible. Some governments in Europe are even kicking back against tougher tax rules. Their response has been to counter international anti-avoidance measures by offering new tax holidays and loopholes. Italy and Greece, for instance, have introduced personal flat tax schemes designed to attract wealthy foreigners to their shores, and to their banks.

Germany is deeply dissatisfied with the incentives employed by its neighbours. A German analyst complained in late 2021 that the Netherlands and Belgium have defended their model of 'informal capital taxation' for almost two decades because the model gives Dutch or Belgian subsidiaries of multinational corporations the right to include in their tax returns deductions for cross-border payments that do not appear in their official annual reports. Using this ploy, corporations can sometimes cut their tax bill in the country in which they are headquartered by up to 90 per cent.

The German complaint added that the Netherlands has become such a popular location for holding, or 'shell', companies that a third of global foreign investments now flow through the 15,000 of them that are based there. 'In the end, multi-billion euro corporations pay hardly any taxes at all – and the EU does virtually nothing to stop that.'[12]

That jibe directed at the European Commission is not wholly fair. Despite the obdurate refusals of the EU's 27 governments to loosen their grip on fiscal policies, the Eurocrats in Brussels have been striving to persuade member states that common measures are the only lasting solution to their tax problems. In the summer of 2020, they proposed a policy package entitled 'Fair and Simple Taxation' that set out a 25-point action plan and suggestions for reforming the rules on tax competition.

'We need to make life easier for honest citizens and businesses when it comes to paying their taxes, and harder for fraudsters and tax cheats,' said the EU's then economic affairs commissioner, the former Italian prime minister Paolo Gentiloni. How successful his plan will be remains to be seen. Intended as the first stage of a long-term tax strategy, its proposals are prey to the lengthy nature of EU decision-making, during which dissenting governments can all too easily block them.

It may require a political miracle for there to be an EU-wide rethink of tax fairness, but that doesn't mean individual governments should not pursue national reforms to adapt their taxation to the pressures of ageing and intergenerational tensions.

Younger people are overtaxed in relation to their incomes and overall living standards. That's a generalisation, but across Europe it's nonetheless clear that their prospects are not as bright as were those of their parents. Cost projections of ageing show, meanwhile, that today's youngsters will need to be far more prosperous if they are to sustain that burden. *Ipso facto*, tax changes are needed that will put more money into the pockets of millennials and Gen-Zers.

A pot-pourri of tax changes to help fund ageing

The ingredients for a rich stew of fiscal ideas have been put forward by a number of experts and interest groups, but many of them look politically indigestible even if economically sound. Here are some, in no particular order, and served up with the caveat that a number are in operation in some countries but not in others. Moreover, some of these ideas are contradictory and pull in opposite directions.

- Exempt under-thirties from health and social payments.
- Means test pensioners' contributions to a social care levy.
- Increase child benefits and improve child-based tax benefits.
- Means test pensioners' tax relief.
- Overhaul property taxation to benefit first-time buyers.
- Reform capital gains taxation to reduce burdens on wage earners.
- Shift labour taxes (e.g. UK's National Insurance) to income and capital.
- Tax the value of land beneath buildings.
- Shake up and increase (re)training tax breaks for employers.
- Tax incentives for employment of women, elderly, immigrants, etc.
- Shift business taxes away from small or medium-sized enterprises and retailers to larger companies.
- Link income tax thresholds to property costs and rent levels.
- Increase tax benefits that encourage pension savings.
- Introduce 'sumptuary taxes' on conspicuously costly items.
- Review elderly care tax/financing (inheritances, 'viager' deals, etc.).

This is a more or less random selection of proposals current in Britain and continental Europe. They are, of course, not nearly as straightforward as their advocates tend to suggest. Changes to complicated national tax codes upset fiscal equilibriums and usually have international ramifications too. The 15 areas listed here nevertheless have the merit of addressing key unfairnesses while also holding out the promise of increased revenues.

More horizontally, there are far-reaching ideas for a European wealth tax and for a system of universal basic income (UBI). They are gaining ground amongst decision-makers, but their cross-border characteristics make them unlikely to flourish in the foreseeable future. Their advantages are intellectually attractive, even if in practical political terms they may be unattainable.

Cutting through the confusions and contradictions that typify most social benefit systems with a UBI for everyone has been dismissed by most decision-makers as an impractical and Utopian idea. That was until the COVID-19 pandemic struck. The furlough schemes introduced to protect jobs, along with other bail-outs for poorer people hit by inflation and energy prices rises, have triggered tentative rethinks of UBI. A number of its long-standing advocates argue that UBI might be introduced initially to give all under-40 year olds a much-needed financial safety net.

A similar approach has been proposed by Thomas Piketty, the French economist who is a standard bearer of radical reformist thinking. He has put forward a UBI-style scheme that would award a lump sum of €120,000 to young French people when they reach 25 years of age. This would aim to give them a substantial start in life to compensate for all the handicaps younger people face. Piketty suggests it could be largely funded by a wealth tax aimed most of all at large inheritances.

Disappointing though wealth taxes have proved to be, calls for a Europe-wide scheme are getting louder. Intensified by the COVID-19 pandemic and the economic fallout from the war in Ukraine, there are suggestions that a progressive EU wealth tax on Europe's richest individuals could yield 1.05 per cent of the EU's GDP.

The plan would target 330 billionaires who are said to possess combined taxable wealth of €1 trillion. Its advocates argue that by increasing the marginal tax rate on these billionaires by 3 per cent, and by 1–2 per cent on merely wealthy millionaires, much could be done to redress the difficulties of the European economy.

The scheme's advocates acknowledge there's no legal basis for a European tax, but say 'treaties can and will be changed to allow for debt mutualisation'. They add that 'should an EU-wide agreement fail to materialise, a smaller group of countries could choose to create a common wealth tax'.[13]

The spectre haunting many governments is cross-border capital flight if they clamp down too hard on tax avoidance or introduce major tax increases. This risk would be greatly reduced by a pan-European wealth tax, but it is far from certain that EU governments have sufficient appetite for so momentous a move. That said, it's all too clear that 20th-century tax arrangements no longer match the needs of the 21st century.

National debt levels cannot rise indefinitely, but nor can spending commitments related to ageing be contained. The tax spotlight is therefore shifting to wealthy individuals and to corporations and their shareholders; the pressures on them to share more with the disadvantaged is intensifying. Much as undertaxed sources of revenue may resist these, they may also come to realise that paying more tax is in their own longer-term interests. In the words of the Prince of Salina, the main character in Giuseppe di Lampedusa's Risorgimento-era novel *The Leopard*, 'Everything must change for everything to remain the same.'

12

Ten ways to defuse the timebomb

No single policy can resolve the problems of demographic change. But a clear strategy could soften ageing's impact and make it more manageable. National measures also have far-reaching tax and trade implications that require intra-European cooperation. Whatever the UK's post-Brexit relationship is with Europe, it will need much closer cooperation with the EU if it's to counter demographic pressures.

The thread running through this book has been 'we can't go on like this – something's got to give', and this concluding chapter looks at ten areas where appropriate policy responses could do much to blunt the impact of ageing and defuse its most damaging aspects.

These suggestions are elements for national strategies, and not for a pan-European 'master plan'. Ageing reaches deep into national cultures and practices, so a 'one size fits all' approach has no future. What Europeans *can* do, though, is to confront their common difficulties and share ideas on what works and what doesn't.

Ageing isn't the only shared challenge. The transfer of wealth from the young to the old is equally problematic. Unless we stem this flow, it will be impossible for tomorrow's private citizens to fund the enlarged public services ageing demands.

The last 30 years have seen the disposable incomes of Europe's 18–25 year olds shrink so fast that they now earn less than the average for the population as a whole. This is unprecedented and truly alarming because young people starting out have far fewer fixed responsibilities than their elders, and so always enjoyed greater discretionary spending power.

Older people, meanwhile, have been getting richer. Heart-rending cases of poverty-stricken elderly people frequently make harrowing headlines, but in statistical terms the overall picture for Europe tells a different story. Back in the mid-1990s, a fifth of the over-65s lived in poverty, and now that's down to just over 14 per cent. Today, it's the young not the old who most risk falling into poverty.[1]

This is the core of the ageing crisis. While it's commendable that social policies should favour pensioners, particularly those with health problems, this has created a daunting policy challenge. How, without impoverishing the elderly, can governments restore brighter opportunities for the young?

This isn't just a moral question but a vitally important practical one: unless Gen-Z, the millennials who preceded them and Gen-Alpha now in education can be presented with more welcoming and lucrative career paths, they won't be able to fund the runaway costs of Europe's ageing. Low salaries, insecure jobs, unaffordable housing and expensive childcare are major handicaps for today's under-forties.

What's to be done? By the 2050s, the imbalance between dwindling tax receipts because of shrinking workforces and the growing needs of more pensioners will reach crisis point. Before then, by the late 2030s and early 2040s, Europeans will already be grappling with a host of new social and political tensions as fiscal strains intensify. And just as a week can be a long time in politics, two decades is a short time in policy making. To conceive new policies and then implement them is a laborious process that European governments should have embarked on at the dawn of this century, when the demographic signposts were plainly visible.

Most policy areas relating to ageing are purely national, so an EU-level approach is unlikely to find much favour. But the EU's national governments also know that ageing's impact disproportionately affects poorer, weaker member states, raising the spectre of the EU's eventual disintegration. The 2009–12 eurozone sovereign debt crisis is a grim reminder of the EU's vulnerability once its cohesion is threatened.

The European Commission regularly publishes reports that track the deteriorating demographic position. While Brussels might be reproached for failing to stimulate concern early enough, it has since woken to the enormity of the problem. It created a new portfolio to handle demography issues, but stopped short of equipping it with either an adequate budget or staffing resources.

From 2019 to 2024, veteran Croatian politician Dubravka Suica enjoyed the title of Vice-President for Democracy and Demography, but had all too few powers to wield. She remains Croatia's member of Ursula von der Leyen's second commission and retains responsibility for demographic questions. However, her vice-presidential title has been downgraded to simple commissioner, and demography is just a part of her overall portfolio for the Mediterranean. The mission statement she's been given includes a newly invented 'Demography Toolbox' to help EU member states address their demographic problems, but there's little clarity on the tools it may contain.

Precisely what role the EU might play is in any case far from clear. The incoming Commission for 2025–30 has yet to detail its thinking on the challenges of ageing. Its links with transnational civil society organisations nevertheless give it an important platform for addressing social policy issues. EU institutions provide many of the frameworks open to NGOs, trade unions and other political players that will be important once policies to confront ageing take shape.

Ten 'strategy points' that fit broadly into three groups

At risk of stating the obvious, extended families are now a rarity in Europe. Swedish sociologist Livia Oláh drew attention to the passing in the 1960s of what she called 'the Golden Age of the Family'. Until then, for centuries immemorial, three generations or more lived beneath one roof and took care of each other from cradle to grave.[2]

Since then, 'the state' has had to take over. Governments have created national and even regional rules and structures to cope with the responsibilities formerly borne by family members. Now these same governments are quailing before the growing weight of their ageing populations, with the only solutions open to them being more intelligent and imaginative policies than those in place.

This concluding chapter sets out the ten areas that Europe's ageing nation states should recognise as overdue for reform, if not radical surgery. For the sake of clarity, they should be seen as three separate groups. Because political cultures and existing policies differ so much from country to country, no attempt is made here to detail proposed health and social benefits or tax ceilings and thresholds. The aim is, rather, to marshal in general terms the areas ripe for a far-reaching rethink.

Group one is 'Care' – (1) care for the elderly, (2) healthcare to maximise workforce participation and (3) better childcare arrangements to encourage larger families.

Group two is 'Equality' – in (4) housing, (5) jobs, (6) incomes, (7) taxation and (8) pensions.

Group three is 'Manpower' – (9) immigration and (10) the European dimension.

(1) Improving care arrangements for the elderly

Spending on social services and healthcare is set to bankrupt all but the richest European countries. It isn't possible to brake these costs abruptly, but they can be brought under tighter control. A first step could be to hive off care services for the elderly from day-to-day healthcare.

Hospitals are often overwhelmed by the needs of older patients who could be treated more effectively and cheaply in clinics and retirement homes specially designed for their needs. The cost in the UK of occupancy of a hospital bed for a week averages £2,500, while a place in a care home runs at £1,000 weekly. Yet a quarter of hospital beds in Britain are at times made over to older people who might be better cared for in a retirement home or in a hospice for the dying.[3]

This pattern holds true throughout Europe. National healthcare models vary, and are generally less centralised than Britain's NHS. But all face the new reality of lengthening lifespans and a growing proportion of older people. Europeans over 60 years old make up a quarter of the population and have an average life expectancy of 80-plus. By mid-century, the proportion of over-65s will rise to a third.

Caring for the elderly is a booming business sector as well as a fiscal challenge. The UK has Europe's largest private care homes industry, but along with the continent as a whole suffers from the uncoordinated growth of both public and private care homes, and chaotic care arrangements for the elderly in their own homes. It's also a confused mosaic of different subsidy arrangements.

Introducing a more coherent approach to care services wouldn't do much to reduce costs in the short term, but it could ensure that in the longer run these costs are more disciplined and predictable. On average, just over a tenth of national health budgets is spent on long-term residential care, and that's set to rise sharply. In the Netherlands it has reached 27 per cent of all healthcare spending.[4]

To establish care as a regulated sector in its own right, rather than leaving it as an underprivileged but expensive offshoot of clinical healthcare, would make it easier to strengthen quality standards. It would also improve recruitment through more attractive minimum pay and working conditions. There's an accelerating shortage throughout Europe of carers, with the numbers of unfilled vacancies increasing at more or less the same rate as the population of older people in need of care.

The answer so far in most countries has been to encourage older people into care homes even when they'd prefer to remain living independently. Efforts have been made in most parts of Europe to improve the recruitment and training of carers, but to little avail. Unrealistically low wages in both private and public sectors, together with an absence of structure and planning, has turned care from a problem sector into a disaster.[5]

Bold policy initiatives are needed at national level to create autonomous bodies separate from medical and healthcare administrations. These would shape arrangements at regional and local levels while dealing directly with central government. The aim should be to unshackle hospitals and general practitioners from the care sector, while also bringing greater clarity to the financial commitments that ageing demands.

For decades, warnings of the need for a far more structured approach to care for the elderly have gathered dust in European governments' health and social affairs ministries. The European Investment Bank has a modest funding instrument to help finance more care homes, but this is often a jealously guarded area of national competence. Other than by providing information and giving backing to NGOs such as the Brussels-based Age Platform Europe, the EU has been a bystander and not an actor.[6]

(2) Healthcare is key to an active workforce

There's no room for doubt: penny-pinching on healthcare is a false economy. Chronic ill-health has driven more and more people out of the active workforce and transformed them from taxpayers into welfare recipients.

This isn't a new and sudden revelation: experts have long been warning that social deprivation determines health and longevity, and that communities where health standards are poor can be trapped in a vicious circle of low wages and high unemployment. In the UK, the independent OBR has warned of the way that adverse developments in the economy can be traced back to health-related issues.

COVID-19 hasn't helped matters. In Britain and elsewhere, it led to massive waiting lists for hospital appointments and contributed to the 'Great Resignation' that saw millions of employees staying away from work long after the virus had subsided. The pandemic's after-effects now appear to be symptoms of a much deeper malaise. In February 2020, just as epidemiologists were pondering the new coronavirus strain in the Chinese city of Wuhan, a UK report made it clear that ill-health in less-privileged regions has become a persistent economic burden.

In a review ten years after his milestone 2010 report on health inequality, Sir Michael Marmot of University College London warned that the UK's health problems have deteriorated further, with mortality rates rising and life expectancy shortening in the most deprived regions. He presented a gloomy picture of health policy failures that contribute to child poverty and inadequate housing, and that compare badly with much of continental Europe.[7]

Britain is not alone in seeing its healthcare needs outstrip its resources. Shortages of nurses and doctors are widespread across Europe, caused by self-imposed limits on recruitment and training. In some countries, short-sighted tax policies have forced well-paid senior doctors into early retirement. The upshot is a surge in the recruitment of medical staff from poorer developing countries, even though these can ill afford to lose them.

Britain's NHS performs well in value-for-money league tables, but its critics say this partly reflects a decade of cheese-paring budgetary cutbacks and a refusal by central government to invest more in modern hospitals. Advocates of an NHS modernisation drive claim that for each £1 invested, the UK economy would get a £4 boost. As it is, the annual cost of the NHS is rocketing upwards: it stood at £150 billion in 2019 and rose to £180 billion in 2022 without there being any major investments during that period. The NHS now consumes four-tenths of all spending on public services.

Even these runaway figures pale in comparison with those of Germany and France. Different statistical bases confuse things, but Germany reports a healthcare workforce of 5.7 million people and an annual budget of €411 billion, and France a more modest 2.7 million health workers at a cost of €210 billion. The NHS employs about 1.5 million, with a further 1.6 million in the social care sector. Berlin and Paris are collaborating on digital e-health technologies and on setting standards for medical applications of AI, but that gives no clue to how they plan to contain their massive health costs.

The answer, needless to say, is tax. There's a welter of ideas about how to wring out more funding to pay for growing numbers of patients, but because different countries in Europe – and indeed within the UK – have different healthcare structures, there's no universal formula.

Suggestions in the UK include an 'NHS levy' that would chiefly target richer pensioners. It's among the proposals of the Resolution Foundation, which has played a prominent part in raising the profile of demographic change. Its president, David Willetts, served as Universities Minister from 2010 to 2014 and is the author of *The Pinch*, a trailblazing book on Britain's intergenerational inequalities.[8]

Taxes always sound like attractive solutions, yet on closer examination present daunting political obstacles. If these could be overcome, that would release funds to reach into and perhaps resolve almost all the problems of ageing. Tax solutions are looked at in Section (7) of this chapter.

Reconciling the irresistible growth of an ageing population's healthcare needs with Britain's 'low tax' mentality will take more than tweaks and new levies to raise a few billion pounds here and there. What's needed is a more far-reaching and honest debate between political parties on the fiscal landscape to mid-century and beyond.

The decline of the extended family has ineluctably led to a new era of 'big government', and that inevitably means much higher taxation. Northern Europe and Scandinavia are already there; Britain and southern Europe are still in denial.

(3) Better childcare would encourage larger families

It's no secret that costly and complicated childcare arrangements are the bane of a working mother's life. The patchwork of contradictory bureaucratic rules by local authorities seems deliberately at odds with the needs of most employers, leaving the hapless mothers of preschool toddlers at the mercy of conflicting pressures.

Today's women need nerves of steel to cope with the demands of rearing small children while leading a working life of their own. This helps to explain an intriguing statistic first announced at the beginning of 2022: Only half of the women born in England and Wales in 1990 had yet had children, said the Office for National Statistics (ONS). Never before had so many young women remained childless when reaching their thirties.

There are many reasons for plummeting birth rates in Britain and across Europe. Changing social patterns reflect a variety of pressures: insecure jobs, low wages and housing difficulties are clearly contributing to infertility. A sidelight on the ONS findings of childless 30 year olds was that 51.3 per cent of births in 2021 were to single mothers who were unmarried or without a partner.

These are not particularly British trends, of course. They reflect upheavals and uncertainties that have become the hallmark of the 21st century and are the legacy of slow-burning social changes over the last 50 years or so. The point is, however, that this abrupt interruption of long-standing childbearing patterns bodes ill, and must be ended as quickly as possible. It isn't too late to revive long-standing fertility rates, but that would require determined action by policy makers.

The continental European situation is no less dire. Of those EU households where there are children, only 12 per cent are home to three or more, and half are one-child households. It's no wonder demographic projections point so relentlessly downwards.

Improved childcare facilities are among the solutions in comparatively easy reach. Day care for preschool children has been given little priority, and even Germany's vaunted KITA system of subsidised '*Kindertagesstätte*' is showing signs of neglect. These are operated regionally, so the cost and the availability of places can differ. KITA's administrators have revealed that they lack over 340,000 kindergarten places, and that was before the influx of refugee Ukrainian families.

The UK, meanwhile, languishes at the bottom of UNICEF's league table of childcare arrangements. It occupies 35th place out of 40 and shares its ranking with the US and Slovakia. Britain's complex formula offering 30 hours of free childcare over 38 weeks harks back to bygone days when nuclear families lived in ordered communities with reliable public transport and had a male breadwinner with regular work. For today's lifestyles and conditions it's lamentably insufficient.

Much the same can be said of childcare throughout the world's richer countries. The OECD reckons that at least a quarter of a working mother's earnings will be absorbed by day care if she has two preschool children.

For a single mother on a low wage in an EU country, it calculates that more than two-thirds of her gross earnings is mopped up by taxes and childcare costs along with lost social benefits. In Denmark, Austria, Cyprus and Slovenia that can rise to 90 per cent, leading the OECD to conclude that some mothers in those countries are financially better off if they don't work.[9]

There are countries that have tackled the childcare problem far more effectively. Finland offers universal childcare free of charge, and Estonia's system places a ceiling of €70 on the monthly cost charged to parents. In the UK, a new and much more affordable system has been devised by a partnership of Save the Children and the Left-leaning Institute for Public Policy Research think tank, although its chances of being adopted are anyone's guess.

There's no saying where reform proposals of this sort will end up, but the need for improved arrangements enticing more mothers into work is plain to see. The relevant statistics are the usual jumble of different bases and assumptions, but the bottom line is that European women are far more likely than men to find work only on a part-time basis and at a significantly lower pay rate. Faced by high day care costs for preschool children, it's unsurprising that many mothers opt to stay at home.

The labour shortages already afflicting Europe will tighten further, so perhaps employers will begin to woo female workers with more attractive conditions. The low wages and irregular hours that are such a feature of women's jobs are both a discouragement and a drag on economic growth. If the pay gap between men and women were to be eliminated, it's reckoned that Europe's workforces would swell in numbers by 15 per cent. The OECD says that if that gender gap could be closed over, say, 15 years, the EU's GDP could be boosted by as much as 12 per cent.

(4) Housing shortages at the root of many problems

There's no magic wand to fix housing crises across Europe, but nor is it rocket science. A plethora of viable solutions have for years been largely ignored. Short-sightedness and the self-interest of older people has done much to condemn younger generations to the prohibitively expensive housing costs that discourage larger families.

Tackling housing shortages across Europe could do much to defuse the demographic crisis. If average birth rates of 1.5 children per couple could be nursed back by better housing towards the 2.1 replacement level, or even a magical 2.5, then the costs of ageing could from 2040 onwards be absorbed by a steadily growing workforce. But that would require a crash programme of home-building to be launched immediately.

Nowhere in Europe is the housing crisis more acute than in the UK, where new homes have for more than three decades been built at half the rate at which the workforce has grown. It's a scandal that taints both of the main political parties for their sins of commission and omission.

Booming house prices are partly explained by the fact that property is generally seen as a more reliable investment than stocks and shares. The underlying reason is that the growing shortage of affordable housing is driving up property values, and pushing prices way beyond the reach of young people and workers on low wages. As well as being a moral issue in which younger generations are unjustly discriminated against, it's also a policy blunder that's holding back economic growth.

The lengthy list of progressive new policies that should be adopted in Britain and much of Europe consists both of mega-measures and more targeted ideas. Top of the agenda should be the World Bank's three recommendations: earmark public land for housing, it said in a 2018 report on Europe's affordable homes crisis; improve transport around major cities; and make prices much more transparent through public registries of property sales.

Releasing land certainly looks to be an easy first step for public authorities that hold swathes of buildable land for military or civil use. Development in the UK of some of the thousands of acres of army training areas held by the Ministry of Defence in prime areas of southern England such as Salisbury Plain would make squabbles about the sanctity of green belts around cities seem much less relevant. There are also reckoned by Action for Empty Homes, an NGO, to be a quarter of a million unused homes in the UK that are owned by the government, plus a further quarter of a million furnished but empty homes that should be released onto the market.

Advocates of many more 'new towns' include some of the most authoritative voices in Britain's debate on housing. Dame Kate Barker, who 20 years ago chaired an official report that sadly fell on deaf ears in Westminster, has urged ambitious construction drives that would loosen the strangleholds of the big private corporations that cynically 'freeze' their landholdings so as to boost future profits.

Other European countries need, like the UK, to cut through layers of accumulated privilege if housing is to be given the importance it deserves. How to do this will differ, but the appointment of national 'housing czars' with powers to question and abolish restrictive practices would seem essential. The conversion of old or unsuitable premises to meet the demand for smaller households is an obvious priority. Unused industrial buildings and offices made unviable by the trend towards WFH are clearly candidates for government support, and even compulsory purchase.

So, too, is the encouragement through tax and other incentives of a huge increase in factory-built housing. A striking feature of Europe's housing shortage is the inefficiency of traditional construction methods when skilled building trades are being squeezed by manpower shortages.

Instead of allowing house construction to be slowed by the problems of smaller building companies – and the rapacity of larger ones – governments should be promoting the on-site assembly of factory-made units. Modern prefabrication methods could make a big difference in Britain, given that a pioneering Russian company called PIK reportedly manufactures 40,000 homes a year at its factory near Moscow.[10]

At present, the UK adds a meagre 100,000 new homes a year to its housing stock, although, as a House of Commons research briefing has pointed out, when the Conservative government was elected in 2010 it had pledged to deliver 300,000 yearly. During the Conservatives' 14-year tenure, Britain in fact built at a rate that was proportionately only a third of Switzerland's, where more flexible rules at local authority level pay off well.[11]

Finding land and placing buildings on it is arguably a lesser problem than enabling young people to get a foot on expensive housing ladders. It's reckoned by Housing Europe Observatory, a Brussels NGO, that more than a third of European households are 'overburdened' by housing costs, and that as much as two-thirds of younger couples' disposable incomes can be absorbed by keeping a roof over their heads.[12]

One answer, of course, is to make mortgages cheaper and more accessible. Thirty years ago, nine out of ten first-time mortgage applications in the UK were successful, but that has shrunk to six in ten nationally and in Greater London just one in three. Yet it's a problem that governments can quite easily solve if they want to.

Greece has shown the way with an imaginative €1.75 billion affordable housing scheme that brings 1 per cent mortgage interest rates within the reach of young people. It's a pilot rather than a universal scheme, and is aimed chiefly at those in the Athens region who find it impossible to either rent or buy. Almost half of the country's 18–44 year olds say they struggle to afford housing or even cannot pay their rent.[13]

Interfering in home loans and mortgages is a sensitive area for governments, but they can wield the very flexible instrument of tax. How to approach the question of bringing housing costs down is clearly a vast topic, but it comes into perspective when placed beside the scale of Europe's other shortages. Unless younger people – and above all women of child-bearing age – can afford homes large enough for bigger families, the demographic noose strangling economic growth will continue to tighten.

The European Commission has been trying to prime the pump of an EU-wide housing investment drive, but the strains of faltering national economies in the wake of COVID-19 and the ripple effects of the Ukraine war started to hinder this before it could show results. The influx of Ukrainian refugees has exacerbated housing difficulties that in some countries were already at crisis point, but this has yet to translate into a consensus on emergency housebuilding.

(5) Dice are loaded against the neediest jobseekers

The return of the 'working poor' after more than 75 years of socio-economic progress is a disaster, and stands ominously in the way of efforts to alleviate ageing's impact.

Nobody can say what labour markets may look like in a few years' time. New technologies, post-COVID-19 shake-outs and the buffeting of stormy economic cross-winds are clouding the picture as never before. What we *do* know, however, is that everyone in Europe will suffer if the divide between 'good' and 'bad' jobs continues to widen.

It will be impossible to finance the social services and pensions that ageing demands if the working poor are still so underprivileged that their tax contributions are minimal. The need is for a radical improvement of low-pay jobs and a rethink of gig economy employment conditions.

In a market economy, a government's power to influence job creation is relatively constrained. But that shouldn't mean the polarisation of labour markets must continue. Labour shortages that are braking economic growth must be addressed with an array of more inventive policy measures. In the UK, this means intervening in work practices and pay rates in ways that have been anathema to right-wingers and are of dubious value to many on the Left.

First up for reform should be zero-hours contracts and the gig economy's conditions of casual labour. The OECD has pointed to Sweden's insistence on 'umbrella companies' acting as employers of gig workers. These are the legal entities that gig workers must register with, and they are paid a fee to administer a gig worker's payroll tax and social security payments. There's therefore no room for the legal contortions and squabbles that in many other countries surround gig workers in, say, the transport and food delivery sectors.[14]

It's vital that the free-for-all jobs market created around the internet should be made more transparent and less open to abuse. Gig jobs have become a sizeable part of European countries' labour markets, and along with healthcare and care for the elderly are characterised by low wages and a callous insecurity of employment.

Well before the COVID-19 lockdowns and jobs shakeouts, employment experts in the UK were warning that at least a quarter of the British workforce is no longer in a traditional full-time or permanent job, and this is especially true for younger people. Diane Coyle at the University of Cambridge explains: 'Although it has been clear for more than twenty years that the social means of giving enough economic security needs to change, what we have had instead is states and businesses trying to pass the responsibility to each other – with individual workers caught in the middle.'[15]

Any discussion of how to streamline European labour markets inevitably provokes a rejoinder that unemployment has never been so low. This is a dangerous misunderstanding of the situation, but one that governments are eager to promote. Few if any EU member governments have resisted the temptation to claim credit for reducing joblessness so that it's now at a 50-year low. They often reject suggestions that labour shortages have become a major threat to economic growth.

But it's plainly the case. At the top end of the scale, engineering companies and the high-tech sector as a whole are crying out for qualified people without whom they cannot develop new technologies and enter world markets. In the early years of the 21st century, the call went out in Britain and throughout Europe for desperately needed computer programmers. Demand has greatly outstripped supply, so there are now around 2 million unfilled posts in Europe's information and telecommunications sectors, and many more downstream.

That's at the high-tech end of the spectrum, and sadly shows that pledges to overhaul technical training and education methods have yet to bear fruit. The lower levels of the labour market are in their different ways just as alarming. The EU identifies 28 occupations in which manpower shortages are widespread, and lists the first of these in this order of gravity: plumbers, nurses, systems analysts, welders, truck drivers, civil engineers, software developers, carpenters, most specialist construction jobs, doctors and cooks.[16]

The UK's labour shortages have arguably been made worse by the self-inflicted wounds of Brexit. The drying up of young and often well-educated jobseekers from EU countries – and especially from Central Europe and the Baltic republics, has hit a number of business sectors very hard. Employers in the hospitality, agriculture and construction sectors have repeatedly protested. The Confederation of British Industry urged the government in October 2022 to relax its immigration policies, pointing to a survey showing that three-quarters of businesses around the country had recruitment difficulties.

Brexit is only part of the problem. The UK's pool of labour is shrinking because of decades of declining birth rates, and in addition there has been the refusal of many people to return to work in the wake of COVID-19. The phenomenon of the 'Great Resignation' is especially pronounced in Britain for reasons that are unclear. A year and a half after lockdowns ended, half a million employees stayed at home, leaving the overall labour force short of almost a million workers once the chronically sick were counted in.

What *is* clear is that labour markets throughout Europe no longer function as they once did. Demographics are upsetting the pattern by limiting the supply of people who can be found jobs through tried and tested policies. From education through to retirement, governments and companies haven't been nimble enough to adapt to rapidly changing conditions.

The nature of the jobs to be done has changed far faster than policy makers and administrators seem to have grasped. According to a 2018 study by MIT's Work of the Future Task Force, getting on for two-thirds of America's jobs were yet to be invented in 1940. It reported that although 'a robot-driven jobs apocalypse is not on the immediate horizon ... at issue is how to improve the quality of jobs, particularly for middle- and lower-wage workers'.[17]

The answer on both sides of the Atlantic should be to unleash a massive skills strategy. The OECD believes that Europe's economy is going to be seriously disadvantaged by the high proportion of young people who are 'disconnected from both employment and learning'. In 2016, it found that to be the case for 17 per cent of 15–29 year olds in the EU, who thus 'risk being permanently left behind in the labour market'. Its report also noted that the children of immigrants were almost 50 per cent more likely to be unemployed.[18]

There has long been talk of a more determined drive on skills training in Europe. But although the model of Germany's famous 'dual system' for training apprentices in skilled occupations is much admired, it's little copied. The combination of on-the-job training with three years at a vocational education school is expensive and hard to replicate. The result is that skills training remains a neglected and underperforming area in most parts of Europe, despite heady talk of the fourth industrial revolution.

Raising wages, improving training and adapting far faster to technological change are all ways in which the UK and others can start to overcome their labour difficulties. Another important measure that demands much closer attention is that of rethinking job mobility. High priority should be given to the age-old question of whether governments should take the jobs to the people or the people to the jobs. There are pressing reasons for looking at ways in which regional employment hubs could be developed.

Researchers at the McKinsey Global Institute (MGI) found worrying trends when they looked at the likely ways European labour markets will evolve up to 2030. They calculated that something like 21 million people out of a total European workforce of 235 million will find their job has effectively disappeared. That would be fairly straightforward were it a question of finding them alternative employment in labour markets crying out for people, but the McKinsey analysts believe this is not the case.

They reckon that by 2030 something like four Europeans in ten will find themselves living in areas where there are fewer jobs. Employment will be so unevenly spread that the populations of major cities will be able to fill only half of the growing number of jobs. 'These dynamic growth hubs', says MGI, 'will require millions more migrants – equivalent to 4.4 per cent of the current population.' Their study also suggests that more than 90 million Europeans will need to develop new skills, but that only 40 per cent have a degree, whereas 60 per cent of new jobs are going to demand some sort of tertiary education.[19]

(6) Tackling the widening wealth gap

Back in 1960s Britain, a popular children's hymn dating back to Victorian times had to be discreetly doctored. 'All things bright and beautiful' contained an offending stanza:

> The rich man in his castle,
> The poor man at his gate,
> God made them, high or lowly,
> And ordered their estate.

The Church of England was in no doubt that the hymn's endorsement of class differences had to go. Hymn books were recalled in their tens of thousands and replaced with a more acceptable version.

When they took their decision, those Anglican bishops could not have known that the narrowing of the wealth and privilege gap that was such a feature of post-war Britain's 'New Elizabethan Age' was to falter within 50 years and go into reverse. In the UK and much of continental Europe, the most visible socio-economic trend in the 21st century has been a widening of that wealth gap.

Tax structures designed to stimulate investment benefit older people at the expense of younger ones. And the accumulation of property and other assets by well-to-do baby boomers has seen the return of inheritances as a major feature of societies that once proclaimed themselves egalitarian.

The UK is Europe's most unequal country in terms of disposable income, says the OECD, and indeed the most unequal among all its English-speaking members except the US. Incomes are only the tip of the iceberg. When a noted French expert on economic inequalities looked at the UK position, he concluded that it wasn't so much wage and salary differences that divided Britain's rich from the poor, but rather their assets.

Nicholas Sowels of Pantheon-Sorbonne University in Paris observed in a blog for the LSE that beneath the official figures provided by government he could see significant gaps between social groups. Pensioners and even older workers were doing quite well despite the austerity policies that followed the 2009–10 global financial crisis. Under-thirties workers, on the other hand, suffered the most, with incomes still well below pre-crisis levels.

Turning to asset wealth, Sowels scathingly reported that Britain's 'wealth-holders are reticent about declaring their assets. Wealth inequality is, however, a burning issue as it is far greater than income inequality.' The poorest 1 per cent of UK households, he noted, had net negative wealth (in other words, they owed), £12,000 on average, while the top 1 per cent owned £1.4 million.[20]

The root causes, says Princeton University's British-born Nobel laureate economist Sir Angus Deaton, are disparities in education, ethnicity and regional conditions. As chair of an ongoing review of social inequality in Britain by the IFS, Deaton observed that graduates in the UK usually earn 60 per cent more than non-graduates, with the effects of COVID-19 exacerbating the problem. Looking at intergenerational inequalities, Sir Angus stressed that pensioners with savings have generally prospered while the young have struggled.[21]

Europe's wealth gap is in fact much the same as the UK's. 'Europeans are more unequal today than four decades ago,' warned the World Inequality Database (WID) in 2019. Using what they claim to be a novel methodology, WID analysts at the Paris School of Economics calculated that from 1980 to 2017 inequalities were growing both within and between European countries. Although taxes and transfers are more progressive in Europe than in the US, they have not been enough to curb rising pre-tax inequalities.

Wealth inequalities are measured around the world using a ready-reckoner called the Gini coefficient, created just before the First World War by Italian sociologist Corrado Gini. An impossible score of zero would denote a perfectly equal society. Britain appears in the upper reaches of the global league table with a coefficient of about 35 per cent, comparing poorly with Sweden's 23 per cent.

Using Gini figures to illustrate the widening of the wealth gap in the UK, one of Britain's leading advocates of social justice neatly summed up the challenge of returning to more equitable times. The late Sir Tony Atkinson emphasised shortly before his death in 2017 that there's a very long way to go to recover the lost ground of the past half-century.

In his book *Inequality: What Can Be Done?* he wrote of 'a stark story for the UK, from the early 1960s through to 1980 when the coefficient was around 25 per cent'. He went on to say that inequality in the second decade of the 21st century was ten percentage points higher than a generation ago, so 'to get back to where we were when The Beatles were playing is a big challenge' that would require a 16 per cent income tax rate increase.

Atkinson argued that the UK's poverty rate had risen to such an extent that it was above that of the 1960s and 1970s, 'a level that was regarded at the time as profoundly shocking'. His intellectual legacy has been a set of recommendations for reversing inequalities. Some, such as encouraging innovation and more progressive taxes, are widely backed. Others would demand near-revolutionary changes to the mindsets of most political parties.

He believed that the government should guarantee public employment at a statutory minimum wage to anyone who sought it. There should also be a guaranteed rate of interest on savings, with everyone on reaching adulthood receiving a 'capital sum' equivalent to $15,000 to be financed by a 65 per cent death tax. In addition, there should be a child benefit or child basic income as a stepping stone towards the basic income for all that he first proposed in the mid-1990s as a replacement for means-tested social benefits.

Radical as these proposals may sound, Tony Atkinson's thinking has been influential in the debate on a universal basic income, widely referred to as UBI, that's now winning increasing support around Europe. As he himself put it in the introduction to what would be his last book, Atkinson wrote: 'I am not seeking to go from dystopia to utopia. Rather I am concerned with a *reduction* in inequality below its current level.'[22]

Although often dismissed by sceptics as impracticable and unacceptable to public opinion, UBI has been gaining ground. Rising concern over the ostentatious wealth of a cosseted few that contrasts with Europe's sluggish economic performance has caused some politicians to revise their attitude to UBI's 'free handouts for all', as its critics sometimes brand it.

The outlook for UBI is nevertheless uncertain, and of late has been further clouded by policies introduced during the COVID-19 pandemic. Yet the idea of a 'state salary' for all has been around for centuries. It is sometimes ascribed to the 16th-century English philosopher Thomas More in his famous treatise *Utopia*, and also to Thomas Paine, one of the 18th-century architects of American independence. Its modern-day version became the focus of heated debate in the 1920s when another celebrated English philosopher, Bertrand Russell, was among its champions.

The furlough schemes that arguably saved many smaller businesses from bankruptcy during the COVID-19 lockdowns have focused renewed attention on variants of UBI in a number of European countries. Pilot schemes have had mixed receptions: one was defeated in a Swiss referendum because it would allegedly have doubled social welfare spending, and another in Finland suffered a similar fate.

UBI's advocates have nevertheless been drawing attention to the way it would greatly simplify the labyrinthine bureaucracies common to all social benefits systems. They also argue that UBI would do much to counter rural 'desertification' and the impoverishment of rust-bowl post-industrial regions. Above all, they say, it could dramatically improve the career prospects and lifestyles of younger people.

Addressing intergenerational unfairness could, if convincingly presented to voters, do much to give UBI a new lease of life. In contrast to Europeans' lukewarm reception of UBI-style schemes, Americans have begun to experiment with them despite warnings that they would be branded as 'socialist'. In Stockton, California, a two-year guaranteed income scheme that awarded $500 a month to 125 randomly selected residents with no strings attached has been hailed by the town's mayor as a massive success. Jobs and productivity were up, well-being and stress levels improved, and recipients were able to pay off debts. Far from discouraging jobseekers, it triggered a 12 per cent rise in employment.[23]

Similar pilot schemes have been launched in 32 other cities across the US, including Chicago and Los Angeles. Interest in the concept was spurred when in 2020 Jack Dorsey, the founder of Twitter, gave $5 million to Andrew Yang, a former Democratic presidential hopeful, to research the case for UBI. The answer was that if applied nationally as a $12,000 yearly payment to all adults, it would cost $2.8 trillion. That's more or less the combined annual cost to the federal government of pensions together with healthcare for the old and the poor.[24]

Versions of UBI come in all shapes and sizes, but their common denominator is that market economies are malfunctioning even in the world's richest countries. An ambitious pan-European survey of 12,000 people of all ages has shown that more than 70 per cent favour the introduction of UBI. The question yet to be answered, though, is what *sort* of UBI?[25]

Some UBI models are quite modest, others so expensive they seem doomed to failure. Similar to Sir Tony Atkinson's suggestion for a lump sum for everyone in Britain on reaching adulthood, David Willetts at the Resolution Foundation has proposed a £10,000 capital endowment at the age of 30 to boost property ownership.

On a very different scale, Thomas Piketty, the French economist and tireless activist for radical change, has proposed UBI in the form of a universal €120,000 gift from the state at the age of 25. Piketty's version is complicated but interesting, as he suggests that those with educational and income advantages will progressively pay into the scheme to support the less privileged. Calling it 'Inheritance for All', he highlights the way recent decades have seen a sharp retrograde shift away from social equality and back to the divisions of class and privilege. Piketty's message is that inheritances have been turning the wealth gap into a gulf, but can also be used to close it.

The golden years of the Edwardian era before the 1914 outbreak of the First World War were the peak period for inherited wealth. The fortunes and vast estates accumulated in Victorian times and handed down to inheritors made up a fifth of the British economy. Fifty years later, by the 1970s and 1980s, the flow of family money to younger generations had shrunk to barely 5 per cent. Now, inheritances are heading back up towards 15 per cent, with the value of estates being passed on more than doubling since the 21st century began.[26]

Britain's exploding property prices have been partly responsible, but the overall pattern is that richer families are consolidating their wealth at an accelerating rate. It's a feature not only of the UK housing market but also of the hard-pressed farm sector as it struggles to adjust to Brexit and the drying up of EU subsidies. Loopholes in taxes on inheritances and capital gains are said to benefit large landowners, and thus are pricing agricultural land well beyond the reach of would-be younger farmers.[27]

Taxation is, of course, the key instrument available to governments concerned by the way the pendulum of inherited wealth is swinging back towards the 19th century. It remains to be seen whether the frictions and political unrest threatened by growing wealth divergences will push governments into wielding their tax powers. The extent to which they do so will greatly determine the mid-century scale of Europe's demographic crisis.

(7) Taxation: what liabilities for tomorrow's taxpayers?

If governing is, as political scientists like to say, about making difficult choices, politics is quite simply about taxes. The most striking aspect of tax debates around Europe is their narrow focus on the here and now. Governments' pressing need to balance short-term spending requirements against the political dangers of raising taxes to pay for them far outweighs longer-term considerations. Yet it's the tax revenues they'll need in a decade or two that really matter.

The question is how much money will European governments need to raise from taxpayers to pay for ageing. The amounts are so daunting that far-sighted new tax strategies are required, not simply a recognition by today's politicians that their successors in office may have to confront some tricky policy problems.

Governments already have most of the data on how ageing will weigh in future on their economies. Because the columns in future national accounts that will be printed in red make such depressing reading, today's ministers prefer to avert their gaze. That way they don't have to venture into the political minefield of discussing which sections of society will have to pay more into the national tax pot, and which should benefit.

Tax systems vary from country to country, but their common characteristic is that they are based on generations of taxpaying citizens succeeding each other at an even rhythm. That no longer applies. The demographic disruption at the root of Europe's ageing crisis is so fundamental that policy makers must reassess taxes to confront the problems of future generations. That means telling voters they must pay higher tax rates now to fund their children and grandchildren.

It also means admitting that they have been dodging their responsibilities by accumulating debts that future generations must eventually pay for. 'A six-generation Ponzi scheme' is how one prominent American critic labelled the soaring US national debt, and Europeans have been doing much the same by borrowing on international financial markets to avoid raising tax rates.

What elements of taxation therefore need to be changed? How can they be made fairer and more efficient, and how much more should governments collect? The most obvious targets are major corporations and rich individuals, but does that risk killing the geese that lay golden eggs, or at any rate frightening them away to laxer tax regimes elsewhere?

Few would deny that in the UK and the EU income tax is most easily levied from wage earners at source, whereas top executives and professionals can deploy consultants' expertise to diminish or even dodge it. Taxes on business are hard for smaller companies to sidestep, but multinationals are famous for avoiding them by shifting their profits from country to country.

Before saying that tax crackdowns are easier said than done, it's worth recalling how deep national debts are at present, and how much deeper they will be. Pensions are technically bankrupt, and the healthcare costs associated with ageing are cripplingly expensive. Together, these two non-productive sectors are on course to consist of a quarter of the European economy by 2050. The gap between Europeans' savings and their pension needs is reckoned at €2 trillion and widening, while Europe's stressed healthcare systems are still only in the foothills of the ageing curve.

In the UK, the Institute for Fiscal Studies says the one-third of government spending that currently goes on health and pensions will rise to 45 per cent over the coming 50 years. A number of other estimates discussed in earlier chapters put the tax increases needed to balance the books and chip away at the debts being imposed on younger generations at an income tax hike of around 10 per cent, or a rise in overall tax revenues amounting to 6 per cent of Britain's GDP.

Tackling unpaid taxes is an obvious priority: in both the EU and the US, taxes avoided or criminally evaded stand at an estimated yearly trillion euros or dollars. Major investments in tax policing and collection are essential, and should be the focus of far greater public attention and media coverage. Whether or not that happens, the still greater issue is how new thinking on taxes could reverse the decades-long trend favouring older and more prosperous people at the expense of the young and less privileged. Tax can be used to give the needy a leg up as well as forcing the overly well endowed to contribute more to society.

Fifteen ideas for tinkering with taxes and also radically overhauling them are listed at the end of Chapter 11. Among the keys to reform are measures that would speed homeownership by the young, raise wage levels and improve career prospects so that the shrinkage of the active, tax-paying workforce can be slowed. These goals are probably best achieved through reductions of, and even exemptions from, taxes on first-time property buyers, easier mortgages, tax benefits for private pension contributions and tax thresholds that increase take-home pay levels for younger people and the self-employed.

Raising more revenue from the over-fifties is trickier because it could easily amount to a retrospective tax imposed on individuals who have already contributed as much as the laws of the land demanded. But the fact remains that taxes on labour are far higher in European countries and the US than on capital. The EU reckons that on average half of national tax receipts come from employees and employers, a third from taxing consumption and less than a fifth from taxes on capital and financial transactions.

The way forward on tax reforms that can bridge European wealth gaps and pay for ageing will be difficult, but the preferable direction of travel is clear. Unpalatable though the choice is, governments must either raise taxes to levels that will be electorally unpopular, or leave them where they are in the knowledge that ageing can never be paid for.

(8) Pensions: the retirement dreams becoming nightmares

'A golden age for pensions and pensioners' was how the OECD described the retirement conditions enjoyed by the baby boomers born in the wake of the Second World War. In the relatively buoyant post-war years, many of them received 'defined benefit' pensions guaranteeing their retirement income, whereas nowadays only 'defined contribution' schemes are on offer. Savers know what their monthly pension payments will cost, but not how much they can expect when they retire.

The hard fact is that the combination of ageing and sluggish economic growth is turning retirement dreams into pension nightmares. So what can be done to rescue pensions schemes that have been torpedoed by ageing and are holed below the waterline? Some experts calculate that unfunded pension liabilities in the 20 richest countries amount to almost $80 trillion – approaching the present yearly value of the world economy. In the UK alone that hole is reckoned at almost £0.5 trillion.

Pensions, say some analysts, are little more than a Ponzi scheme because they rely on contributors paying in their savings faster than pensioners make withdrawals. In times past, state-backed as well as private pensions had been based on the idea that the financial yields from pension funds' capital investments would largely suffice. But governments, like some unscrupulously criminal corporate boss, have raided their state pensions to fund immediate short-term needs. They have since turned increasingly to paying state pensions out of current tax revenues.

For state pensions, the only viable solution will be later retirement, and even then longer lifespans are aggravating the problem faster than people can be persuaded to delay drawing their pension. Pensionable age varies across Europe, but averages around 65 with many governments trying to raise it to 67, which the UK targets for 2028. The average cost to EU countries of their pension systems is almost 13 per cent of GDP now that nearly 27 per cent of the population are pensioners. That total of 90 million pensioners will rise to 130 million by 2050, in other words to a third of the EU's population.[28]

The way ahead is for older people to remain in work so they can continue to pay taxes rather than draw pensions. Almost half of men aged more than 65 in the EU have some sort of part-time job or are self-employed, and 60 per cent of women. The number of 65–74 year olds who need to earn more to bolster their eventual pension is rising, but too little is being done to encourage employers to extend the careers of older employees.

The UN's ILO emphasises that by 2030 the share of older workers in the European labour force will have risen to 55 per cent, yet often employers are reluctant to retrain them and update their skills. The ILO warns that keeping more women and older people in work is key to limiting labour shortages, yet governments are doing little to combat 'ageism'. There's a clear case for tax breaks and subsidies to encourage today's youthful septuagenarians to remain in harness and resist being sidelined into retirement.

(9) Immigration: taboo perhaps, but a vital solution to ageing

On the eve of the Brexit referendum in 2016, the UK stood on the threshold of an enviably bright future. In Berlin and Paris, they were scratching their heads over projections that Britain would become the largest and richest of all the EU countries. By 2047, it would overtake Germany in sheer numbers thanks to a population increase of around 10 million people over 30 years to 76 million. Other forecasts suggested the UK economy would be larger than Germany's by the late 2030s.

Today, the picture is woefully different, with Britain's GDP reckoned to be shrinking by four to five percentage points as a result of leaving the EU. Less discussed in all the post-Brexit point-scoring is the impact of greatly reduced immigration from

EU countries. Brexit quickly choked off the flow of economic migrants from elsewhere in the EU who had been fuelling growth and expanding the UK's active workforce.

Instead, runaway immigration from beyond Europe is increasingly controversial in Britain and has clouded discussion of the need for more manpower. The reputational damage has been almost as serious, with the ending of free movement for usually well-educated young people from northern and eastern Europe transforming the UK's image in the eyes of the world. No longer a haven for youthful jobseekers, Britain's treatment of desperate asylum applicants has taken it in a few years from hero to zero.

It's not just some British voters' misguided views on EU membership that's at issue. Far more important is the crucial importance to an ageing Europe of overcoming racial and cultural prejudices and accepting that large-scale immigration is an essential solution to the ageing crisis. Not just as workers to fill holes in labour markets that increasingly resemble a Gruyère cheese, but also as the mothers and fathers of new generations of multi-ethnic, multicultural Europeans.

When one of Europe's most respected statesmen warned in 2010 that the ageing continent would need 100 million immigrants, his report was discreetly shelved. Felipe González, who as prime minister turned post-Franco Spain into a poster boy for progressive liberal democracy, had tried to ring loud demographic alarm bells, but was ignored. Europe's politicians – and not just the more unscrupulous populists – shied away from electorates' prejudices against economic migrants and even asylum-seeking refugees.

Anti-immigrant sentiments are a powerful political force, yet they amount to the signing by European society of its own death warrant. The intense financial and economic pressures detailed in this book threaten to throttle the life out of Europe's most valuable achievements. European industries that were once world-beaters are being overtaken by their Asian competitors. Lower birthrates mean there are fewer young Europeans to enter higher education, so innovation is beginning to be stifled. The best and brightest of Europe's young scientists and thinkers now head towards opportunities in America and Asia. Europe urgently needs a transfusion of new blood.

This isn't to deny the huge difficulties of opening Europe's doors to mass immigration. The gun-toting gangs of young migrants that are becoming the scourge of Swedish cities symbolise the inability of even Europe's most progressive societies to integrate newcomers. The solutions are far from clear; opinions differ sharply on the practical policy measures needed to integrate immigrants and adapt them culturally to a more 'European' ethos.

The most practical approach is arguably to view these considerations as secondary to the housing, education and employment that migrants need if they are to contribute more to their host country. First-generation newcomers are often so handicapped by their lack of skills and language proficiency that they are forced into jobs rejected by native Europeans. Just as important, they can also substantially raise birthrate averages. Second-generation newcomers, if accorded equal treatment, can offer a solid economic bonus.

It's hard to put figures on the value of immigration, whereas immediate costs are easily come by. Most of the numbers crunched are confusing, with relatively expensive economic migrants and refugees from Africa and the Arab world, whose value is likely to be long term, lumped in with more immediately productive newcomers from Asia or elsewhere in Europe. The picture is further blurred by the surge of some 5 million Ukrainian refugees, generally women and children, who by the end of 2022 had cost host countries in Europe about €27 billion, but who intend eventually to return home.[29]

In the UK, when the OBR looked at immigration during the first decade of this century, it calculated it had yielded a substantial profit. Roughly £20 billion had been paid out in benefits, but immigrants' fiscal contributions amounted to £25 billion. Germany made a similar analysis of its 2015–16 refugee crisis, and found the short-term cost of well over a million mainly Syrian refugees to be €10 billion, but concluded that would be paid off through the newcomers' activities over five to ten years, with longer-term benefits amounting to a further €11 billion.[30]

These are guesstimates, but they underline the value of admitting more people. Europe's active workforce will by mid-century have shrunk by almost 50 million people, which will represent an enormous reduction in economic output and tax revenues. Yet the EU, like the UK, has no immigration policy worth the name. There's a failure within the Brussels institutions and in European capitals to ignore economic arguments in favour of immigration and instead heed political pressures for erecting higher walls. The result is an EU that's akin to a rabbit frozen in the glare of demographic headlights.

The elements of a progressive strategy are set out in my 2021 book *People Power: Why We Need More Migrants*, and are worth briefly summarising here. A more strategic EU approach should consist of three phases: First, a five-year streamlining plan for immediate implementation by member governments. Second, the simultaneous adoption of ten-year targets for more complex EU-wide policy shifts. Third, the introduction of a 25-year phased restructuring of policies ranging from taxes to trade and an acceleration of the economic development of countries whose population explosions are going to exert even more powerful migratory pressures.

Phase one is fairly straightforward – scrap unnecessary and obstructive red tape, especially any that prevents newcomers from earning a living; also review the outdated and cumbersome distinction between refugees and economic migrants. Phase two would end member states' national immigration rules, possibly by adopting the same structured approach that created the EU's single market. Phase three would reduce the political downside by creating a shared public debate on Europe's manpower shortages and the need for increased immigration. EU governments should warn collectively that Europe is otherwise condemned to economic decline, and its political project of 'ever closer integration' risks death by a thousand cuts.[31]

(10) The European dimension

The EU is powerless to prevent the ageing of Europe, but it can do a great deal to soften the impact. It's high time the European Commission took the bull by the horns and set out a strategy for intra-EU cooperation on key ageing policies.

There's a simple reason it has so far been timid in identifying ageing's threats. For all the talk of a 'European super-state' with Brussels supposedly the hub of systematic power grabs by unelected bureaucrats, the reality is that the EU has little or no clout in most of the problem areas discussed in this book.

So where's the European dimension? If it's up to nation states to address the demographic dangers crowding in on them, what can the EU do? A great deal if it were to play its cards more skilfully. Its 'nuclear weapon' is that the EU is itself at risk of unravelling if its member states don't deal collectively with the pressures of ageing and demographic change. The European Commission has warned that ageing is a growing threat, but has done so half-heartedly when compared with the vigour with which it championed green policies to combat climate change, and before that the EU's single market in the face of opposition from some member governments. Because it has so little competence on tax and social spending, the EU limits itself to reports identifying the scale of demographic decline without advancing much in the way of common policies to handle it.

That has to change, and there's a straightforward way to go about that. The energy performance colour charts that must be displayed before property in Europe can change hands is a good example of the way national governments could present their levels of preparation for demographic change: green, let's say, for increased workforce participation, yellow turning to brown for falling fertility rates and red for lacklustre housing conditions. The notion of colour coding might seem fanciful, but ranking problem areas deserves serious attention.

Governments will want to reject this idea out of hand because there's nothing they like less than transparency. And although the European Commission is well set up to institute a scheme to monitor the sectors most vulnerable to ageing, it doesn't have the political muscle to do so. The years since the 2009–10 global financial crisis have seen the EU becoming more an interministerial mechanism than the semi-autonomous executive it was in the 1980s and 1990s. The commission retains its powers in areas such as trade and competition policy, and is the watchdog that guards the EU treaties against abuses, but increasingly it's the secretariat of its member governments.

The commission has one important instrument, if it cares to use it. It has the means to shape public opinion. Not overnight, because it is itself saddled with perception problems, some deserved and others not. The Brussels executive would nonetheless be able to mount a sustained and sophisticated information campaign without clashing with EU capitals.

It could, if it summoned the political will, focus on the problem areas that would make up the colour-coded charts outlined here and present them to the media as an ongoing analysis of the EU's socio-economic strengths and weaknesses. Beset as the commission always is by pressing immediate problems, it's easy to forget that an important part of its role is to look far ahead and identify the opportunities and the dangers that lie over the horizon.

The purpose wouldn't be to reprove or embarrass EU governments, but to alert European opinion to the realities of demographic change, and to marshal seemingly unconnected areas such as housing and pensions, or hospitals and tax havens, into a coherent narrative. If it chooses to use them, the EU has an array of communications tools and social media at its fingertips to create awareness of ageing's societal consequences.

It also has a duty to warn that ageing's impact on its weakest economies risks shattering the EU's unity. Monitoring member states' vulnerability to demographic disruption could be a basis for reinforcing the EU's economic cohesion mechanisms. The richer northern members have been increasingly reluctant to bail out the poorer countries of southern and eastern Europe. It's essential that politicians of all hues should be persuaded of the need to 'save the EU' from the disintegration that ageing threatens.

The next quarter-century to 2050 will see ageing biting hard into living standards. At the same time, pressures on the EU will intensify. The EU seems certain to grow bigger – perhaps to 35 member states – and hopefully will have steeled itself to be more unified politically; there's little doubt among political scientists that the EU risks falling apart unless its member governments relinquish more powers to muscular new central bodies.

A stronger EU could soften the impact of ageing. A more collective approach to tax reforms and social benefits, including pensions, would pay handsome dividends. These need not be rigidly contained within the EU but opened to all European nations, including Britain. Just as the 21st century's tectonic geopolitical shifts underscore Europe's need for 'ever-closer union', so too do the internal pressures of ageing. Without consensus on ways to deal with demographic disruption, Europeans will find themselves its victims.

Notes

Chapter 1

1   Bill Gates (2017) 'The robot that takes your job should pay taxes, says Bill Gates', *Quartz*, 17 February, Available from: https://qz.com/911968/bill-gates-the-robot-that-takes-your-job-should-pay-taxes.

2   Eurostat (2023) 'Europop report', 30 March, Available from: https://ec.europa.eu/eurostat/statistics-explained/index.php?oldid=497115#:~:text=EUROPOP2023,%20the%20latest%20population%20projectionsreleased.

3   OECD (2023) *Health at a Glance 2023, OECD Indicators*, Paris: OECD Publishing, https://doi.org/10.1787/7a7afb35-en.

4   Tingyun Chen, Jean-Jacques Hallaert, Alexander Pitt, Haonan Qu, Maximilien Queyranne, Alaina P. Rhee, et al (2018) 'Inequality and poverty across generations in the European Union', IMF, Staff Discussion Notes, 24 January, Available from: https://www.imf.org/en/Publications/Staff-Discussion-Notes/Issues/2018/01/23/Inequality-and-Poverty-across-Generations-in-the-European-Union-45137.

5   Alice Pittini (2019) 'The state of housing in the EU 2019: decoding the new housing reality', Housing Europe, 1 October, Available from: https://pmay-urban.gov.in/material/component4/The%20State%20of%20Housing%20in%20the%20EU_2019.pdf.

6   European Commission (2018) '2018 ageing report: policy challenges for ageing societies', European Commission, 25 May, Available from: https://economy-finance.ec.europa.eu/news/2018-ageing-report-policy-challenges-ageing-societies-2018-05-25_en#:~:text=Population%20ageing%20to%20put%20pressure%20on%20public%20spending&text=Long%2Dterm%20care%20and%20health,to%20current%20levels%20by%202070.

Chapter 2

1   Andy Haldane (2022) 'Worsening health is an economic headwind', *Financial Times*, 25 November, Available from https://www.ft.com/content/46119e99-cc7c-4058-b76c-3117e3b376ae.

2   Tommy Stubbington (2022), '"Who is going to buy?" UK set to unleash historic debt deluge', *Financial Times*, 6 December, Available from: https://www.ft.com/content/6446220c-41e8-4937-9860-8d075d297aa8.

3   Martin Wolf (2021) 'It is time to lop off the dead hand of the Treasury', *Financial Times*, 3 October, Available from: https://www.ft.com/content/7890885b-89e8-45e8-bc70-5fa09ba35aea.

[4] Resolution Foundation (2018) 'A new generational contract: the final report of the Intergenerational Commission', 19 May, Available from: https://www.resolutionfoundation.org/app/uploads/2018/05/A-New-Generational-Contract-Full-PDF.pdf.

[5] International Labour Organization (2022) 'Global wage report 2022–23', 30 November, Available from: https://webapps.ilo.org/digitalguides/en-gb/story/globalwagereport2022-23#home.

[6] World Economic Forum (2016) 'An ageing population is about to have a big impact on Europe's economy', World Economic Forum, in collaboration with Business Insider, 25 August, Available from: https://www.weforum.org/stories/2016/08/an-ageing-population-is-about-to-have-a-big-impact-on-europes-economy/.

[7] Resolution Foundation & LSE Economic Performance Centre (2021) 'Ending stagnation: shaping a decade of change', the final report of the Economy 2030 Inquiry, May, Available from: https://economy2030.resolutionfoundation.org/.

[8] European Commission (2018) '2018 ageing report: policy challenges for ageing societies', 25 May, Available from: https://economy-finance.ec.europa.eu/news/2018-ageing-report-policy-challenges-ageing-societies-2018-05-25_en#:~:text=The%202018%20Ageing%20Report%20shows,population%20continues%20to%20age%20significantly.

[9] IMF (2016) 'The impact of workforce ageing on European productivity', IMF Working Papers, 8 December, Available from: https://www.imf.org/en/Publications/WP/Issues/2016/12/31/The-Impact-of-Workforce-Aging-on-European-Productivity-44450#:~:text=We%20find%20that%20workforce%20aging,policies%20could%20ameliorate%20this%20effect.

[10] Kate Alexander Shaw (2018) 'Baby boomers versus millennials: rhetorical conflicts and interest-construction in the new politics of intergenerational fairness', Foundation for European Progressive Studies and Sheffield Political Economy Research Institute, 19 January, Available from: https://feps-europe.eu/wp-content/uploads/2018/02/Baby-Boomers-versus-Milennials-Kate-Alexander-Shaw.pdf.

[11] Equality Trust (2018) 'The scale of economic inequality in the UK', Equality Trust, Available from: https://equalitytrust.org.uk/scale-economic-inequality-uk/#:~:text=The%20UK%20has%20a%20wealth%20GINI%20coefficient%20of%2074.6%25.&text=Over%2050%25%20of%20UK's%20adult,97%2C169%20wealth%2C%20as%20of%202018.

[12] Daron Acemoglu and Pascual Restrepo (2020) 'Unpacking skill bias: automation and new tasks', *AEA Papers and Proceedings*, 110: 356–61, https://doi.org/10.1257/pandp.20201063.

[13] MGI (2017) 'Jobs lost, jobs gained: workforce transitions in a time of automation', 6 December, Available from: https://www.mckinsey.com/~/media/mckinsey/industries/public%20and%20social%20sector/our%20insights/what%20the%20future%20of%20work%20will%20mean%20for%20jobs%20skills%20and%20wages/mgi-jobs-lost-jobs-gained-executive-summary-december-6-2017.PDF.

[14] MGI (2016) 'Europe's new refugees: a road map for better integration outcomes', 1 December, Available from: https://www.mckinsey.com/~/media/mckinsey/featured%20insights/employment%20and%20growth/a%20road%20map%20for%20integrating%20europes%20refugees/a-road-map-for-integrating-europes-refugees.pdf.

[15] PwC (2017) 'The world in 2050: how will the global economic order change?', February, Available from: https://www.pwc.com/gx/en/world-2050/assets/pwc-world-in-2050-slide-pack-feb-2017.pdf.

Chapter 3

[1] Tingyun Chen, Jean-Jacques Hallaert, Alexander Pitt, Haonan Qu, Maximilien Queyranne, Alaina P. Rhee, et al (2017) 'Inequality and poverty across generations in the EU', IMF, Staff Discussion Notes, 24 January, Available from: https://www.imf.org/en/Publications/Staff-Discussion-Notes/Issues/2018/01/23/Inequality-and-Poverty-across-Generations-in-the-European-Union-45137.

[2] OECD and COPE (2017) 'Understanding the socio-economic divide in Europe', 26 January, Available from: https://mronline.org/wp-content/uploads/2019/04/cope-divide-europe-2017-background-report.pdf.

[3] David Willetts (2019) *The Pinch*, London: Atlantic Books.

[4] Jean-Michel Bezat (2021) 'Tensions en série autour du plan d'investissement', *Le Monde*, 7 September.

[5] European Food Banks Federation (2023) 'State of food security and nutrition in the World Report 2023', 13 July, Available from: https://www.eurofoodbank.org/state-of-food-security-and-nutrition-in-the-world-report-2023/#:~:text=735%20million%20people%20face%20undernourishment,suffer%20from%20wasting%20or%20stunting.

[6] Joseph Stiglitz, Jayati Ghosh and 230 others (2023) 'Setting serious goals to combat inequality: open letter to the United Nations Secretary-General and President of the World Bank', 17 July, Available from: https://www.oxfamfrance.org/communiques-de-presse/setting-serious-goals-to-combat-inequality-open-letter-to-the-united-nations-secretary-general-and-president-of-the-world-bank/.

[7] James Manyika and Michael Spence (2023) 'The coming AI economic revolution: can Artificial Intelligence reverse the productivity slowdown?' *Foreign Affairs*, November/December, Available from: https://www.foreignaffairs.com/world/coming-ai-economic-revolution.

[8] Richard Wilkinson and Kate Pickett (2009) *The Spirit Level: Why More Equal Societies Almost Always Do Better*, London: Penguin Books; Thomas Piketty (2014) *Capital in the Twenty-First Century*, Cambridge, MA: Harvard University Press; Polly Toynbee and David Walker (2009) *Unjust Rewards: Exposing Greed and Inequality in Britain Today*, London: Granta; Joseph Stiglitz (2012) *The Price of Inequality*, New York: W.W. Norton; Ferdinand Mount (2012) *The New Few, or a Very British Oligarchy*, London: Simon & Schuster; Danny Dorling (2014) *Inequality and the 1%*, London: Verso Books; Stewart Lansley (2012) *The Cost of Inequality*, London: Gibson Square Books; Will

Hutton (2010) *Them and Us: Changing Britain – Why We Need a Fair Society*, London: Little Brown; Andrew Sayer (2014) *Why We Can't Afford the Rich*, Bristol: Policy Press; Ben Phillips (2020) *How to Fight Inequality (and Why That Fight Needs You)*, London: Polity Press.

Chapter 4

[1] Vasilis Margaras (2019) 'Demographic trends in EU regions', European Parliamentary Research Service, Briefing, 29 January, Available from: https://ec.europa.eu/futurium/en/system/files/ged/eprs-briefing-633160-demographic-trends-eu-regions-final.pdf.

[2] Giles Merritt (2021) *People Power: Why We Need More Migrants*, London: I.B. Tauris.

[3] Stein Emil Vollset, Emily Goren, Chun-Wei Yuan, Jackie Cao, Amanda E. Smith, Thomas Hsiao, et al (2020) 'Fertility, mortality, migration, and population scenarios for 195 countries and territories from 2017 to 2100: a forecasting analysis for the Global Burden of Disease Study', *The Lancet*, 396 (10258), 1285–1306. Available from: https://www.thelancet.com/journals/lancet/article/PIIS0140-6736(20)30677-2/fulltext.

[4] European Commission: Joint Research Centre, M. Stonawski, P. Sabourin, A. Bélanger, E. Loichinger, et al (2019) *Demographic Scenarios for the EU – Migration, Population and Education*, W. Lutz (ed.), Publications Office, Luxembourg, https://doi.org/10.2760/590301.

[5] Margaras, 'Demographic trends'.

[6] European Commission: Joint Research Centre et al, *Demographic Scenarios for the EU*.

[7] Destatis (Statistische Bundesamt) (2008) 'Germany's population by 2050 – results of 11th coordinated population projection', 15 April, Available from: https://www.destatis.de/EN/Themes/Society-Environment/Population/Population-Projection/Publications/Downloads-Population-Projection/germany-population-2050.html.

[8] Alfonso Giordano with Giuseppe Terranova (2012) 'Europe 2050: L'exception démographique française', *Outre-Terre, Revue Européenne de Géopolitique*, 33–34, European Centre for International Affairs, Available from: https://www.european-centre.org/2017/09/23/europe-2050-lexception-demographique-francaise/.

[9] Le Monde (2019) *Le Monde*, 13 June.

[10] The Economist (2020) 'The Balkans are getting short of people', *The Economist*, 22 August, Available from: https://www.economist.com/europe/2020/08/20/the-balkans-are-getting-short-of-people.

[11] Uliana Pavlova (2021) '5 million Russian citizens left Russia under Putin: young, well-educated Russians are seeking a better life abroad', *The Moscow Times*, 13 October, Available from: https://www.themoscowtimes.com/2021/10/13/5-million-russian-citizens-left-russia-under-putin-a75246.

[12] Financial Times (2022) *Financial Times*, 30 November.

13 Vollset et al, 'Fertility, mortality, migration, and population scenarios'.

14 Adrien Auclert, Hannes Malmberg, Fréderic Martenet and Matthew Rognlie (2021) 'Demographics, wealth, and global imbalances in the twenty-first century', *National Bureau of Economic Research Working Paper Series*, No. 29161, https://doi.org/10.3386/w29161.

15 OECD (2006) 'Projecting OECD health and long-term care expenditures: What are the main drivers?', *OECD Economics Department Working Papers*, No. 477, Paris: OECD Publishing, https://doi.org/10.1787/736341548748.

16 Andrew Mason and Ronald Lee (2022) 'Six ways population change will affect the global economy', *Population & Development Review*, February, https://doi.org/10.1111/padr.12469.

17 Julia Kollewe (2019) 'Some parts of UK ageing twice as fast as others, new research finds', *The Guardian,* 28 October, Available from: https://www.theguardian.com/science/2019/oct/28/some-parts-of-uk-ageing-twice-as-fast-as-others-new-research-finds.

Chapter 5

1 Vision Critical (2016) *The Everything Guide to Generation Z*, Toronto: Vision Critical, Available from: https://cdn2.hubspot.net/hubfs/4976390/E-books/English%20e-books/The%20everything%20guide%20to%20gen%20z/the-everything-guide-to-gen-z.pdf.

2 Bobby Duffy, Hannah Shrimpton, Michael Clemence, Ffion Thomas, Hannah Whyte-Smith and Tara Abboud (2018) 'Beyond binary – the lives and choices of Generation Z', London: Ipsos-MORI, Available from: https://www.ipsos.com/sites/default/files/2018-08/ipsos_-_beyond_binary_-_the_lives_and_choices_of_gen_z.pdf.

3 Marc Loriol (2022) 'La notion de "génération Z" entrave l'intégration des jeunes sur le marché du travail', *La Tribune*, 25 October, Available from: https://www.latribune.fr/opinions/tribunes/la-notion-de-generation-z-entrave-l-integration-des-jeunes-sur-le-marche-du-travail-937863.html.

4 Kim Parker and Ruth Igielnik (2020) 'On the cusp of adulthood and facing an uncertain future: what we know about Gen Z so far', Pew Research Center, 14 May, Available from: https://www.pewresearch.org/social-trends/2020/05/14/on-the-cusp-of-adulthood-and-facing-an-uncertain-future-what-we-know-about-gen-z-so-far/.

5 Tom Koulopoulos and Dan Keldsen (2014) 'Will Gen Z be the startup generation that never retires?', bizjournals.com, 13 November, Available from: https://www.bizjournals.com/bizjournals/news/2014/11/13/will-gen-z-be-the-startup-generation-that-never.html.

6 Oval Money (2019) 'Ten shocking statistics about Millennials and money', March, Available from: ovalmoney.com.

7 Morgan Stanley (2019) 'How a "youth boom" could shake up spending trends', 16 August, Available from: https://www.morganstanley.com/ideas/gen-z-millennials-set-for-consumer-spending-increases.

8   Emma Broadbent, John Gougoulis, Nicole Lui, Vikas Pota and Jonathan Simons (2017) 'What the world's young people think and feel', London: Varkey Foundation, Available from: https://legale.savethechildren.it/wp-content/uploads/wpallimport/files/attachments/_0RodDGqxwU_P_G5pbj9Jjtg==.pdf.

9   James Kynge (2021) 'China's young "lie flat" instead of accepting stress', *Financial Times*, 3 August, Available from: https://www.ft.com/content/ea13fed5-5994-4b82-9001-980d1f1ecc48.

10 Matthieu Limongi (2021) 'La jeunesse chinoise réclame un droit à la paresse', *Le Monde*, 16 June, Available from: https://www.lemonde.fr/international/article/2021/06/16/la-jeunesse-chinoise-reclame-un-droit-a-la-paresse_6084398_3210.html.

Chapter 6

1   European Commission (2017) 'Employment and social developments in Europe, 2017', 17 July, Available from: https://ec.europa.eu/social/main.jsp?catId=738&langId=en&pubId=8030&furtherPubs=yes.

2   Frances O'Grady (2021) 'Letter: Paying workers more will resolve labour shortages', *Financial Times*, 31 August, Available from: https://www.ft.com/content/b698a3eb-0b61-4ece-9a07-027bf4c7bde8.

3   Sven Smit, Tilman Tacke, Susan Lund, James Manyika and Lea Thiel (2020) 'The future of work in Europe', McKinsey Global Institute, 10 June, Available from: https://www.mckinsey.com/featured-insights/future-ofwork/the-future-of-work-in-europe.

4   Diane Coyle (2019) 'Something is seriously awry in the world of work', *Financial Times*, 19 September, Available from: https://www.ft.com/content/eca406c4-d880-11e9-9c26-419d783e10e8.

5   Lord Skidelsky (2019) *How to Achieve Shorter Working Hours*, Progressive Economy Forum, August, Available from: https://progressiveeconomyforum.com/wp-content/uploads/2019/08/PEF_Skidelsky_How_to_achieve_shorter_working_hours.pdf.

6   Yukio Ishizuka (2021) *Nikkei Asia*, 6 January.

7   Sam Smith (2020) 'Letter: Closing the gender pay gap would aid recovery', *Financial Times*, 22 June, Available from: https://www.ft.com/content/622b5f61-79d8-4538-a740-028ab6bbab18.

8   Klaus Regling (2006) 'How ageing will torpedo Europe's growth potential', *Europe's World*, 2, Spring, Available from: https://www.europeansources.info/record/how-ageing-will-torpedo-europes-growth-potential/.

9   David Autor, David Mindell and Elisabeth Reynolds (2020) 'The Work of the Future: Building Better Jobs in an Age of Intelligent Machines', MIT Work of the Future Task Force, July, Available from: https://workofthefuture-taskforce.mit.edu/wp-content/uploads/2021/01/2020-Final-Report4.pdf.

10 David Chinn, Solveigh Hieronimus, Julian Kirchherr and Julia Klier (2020) 'The future is now: closing the skills gap in Europe's public sector',

McKinsey & Company, 27 April, Available from: https://www.mckinsey.com/industries/public-sector/our-insights/the-future-is-now-closing-the-skills-gap-in-europes-public-sector.

Chapter 7

1   Office for National Statistics, https://www.ons.gov.uk/.
2   High-Level Task Force (HLTF) in association with the European Commission (DG ECFIN) and the European Long- Term Investors Association (ELTI), 2018. 'Boosting Investment in Social Infrastructure in Europe', January, Available from: https://economy-finance.ec.europa.eu/publications/boosting-investment-social-infrastructure-europe_en.
3   Housing Europe (2019) *The State of Housing in the EU, 2019*, Housing Europe Observatory, 1 October, Available from: https://www.housingeurope.eu/file/860/download.
4   Paul Cheshire (2019) 'Housing: "no shortage" – is it nonsense?', Centre for Economic Performance, CEP Urban and Spatial Programme Blog, 17 December, Available from: https://spatial-economics.blogspot.com/2019/12/housing-no-shortage-is-it-nonsense.html.
5   Martin Arnold (2021) 'Netherlands grapples with social consequences of soaring house prices', *Financial Times*, 8 August, Available from: https://www.ft.com/content/04dc1e93-2e1e-4e5a-9c5c-b472b406bd42.
6   Jonathan Cribb and Polly Simpson (2018) 'Barriers to homeownership for young adults', IFS, 8 October, Available from: https://ifs.org.uk/books/barriers-homeownership-young-adults.
7   The Economist (2019) 'Wobbles in Britain's housing market may augur something worse', *The Economist*, 20 July, Available from: https://www.economist.com/britain/2019/07/20/wobbles-in-britains-housing-market-may-augur-something-worse.
8   Martin Wolf (2021) 'It's time to lop off the dead hand of the Treasury', *Financial Times*, 4 October, Available from: https://www.ft.com/content/7890885b-89e8-45e8-bc70-5fa09ba35aea.
9   The Guardian (2021) *The Guardian*, 1 April.
10 Le Monde (2021) 'Loin des urnes, le ras-le-bol très politique de la jeunesse', *Le Monde*, 11 September, Available from: https://www.lemonde.fr/idees/article/2021/09/10/loin-des-urnes-le-ras-le-bol-tres-politique-des-jeunes_6094123_3232.html.
11 Liam Geraghty (2021) *The Big Issue*, 22 January.
12 Rebecca McDonald, Lahari Ramuni and Lizzy Tan (2019) 'What's in Store? How and Why Cities Differ for Consumers', London: Centre for Cities, Available from: https://www.centreforcities.org/wp-content/uploads/2019/09/Whats-in-store.pdf.
13 Le Monde (2021) 'Urbanisme: Les villes édictent leurs régles', *Le Monde*, 17 July.
14 David Adler and Ben Ansell (2020) 'Housing and Populism', *West European Politics*, 43(2): 344–65, https://doi.org/10.1080/01402382.2019.1615322.

15 The Economist (2020) 'Home ownership is the West's biggest economic-policy mistake', *The Economist*, 16 January, Available from: https://www.economist.com/leaders/2020/01/16/home-ownership-is-the-wests-biggest-economic-policy-mistake.

16 Elena Lutz (2021) 'The housing crisis as a problem of intergenerational justice: the case of Germany', Discussion Paper for the Foundation for the Rights of Future Generations, Available from: https://igjr.org/ojs/index.php/igjr/article/view/796/701.

17 Jack Airey and Chris Doughty (2020) 'Rethinking the Planning System for the 21st Century', London: Policy Exchange, Available from: https://policyexchange.org.uk/wp-content/uploads/Rethinking-the-Planning-System-for-the-21st-Century.pdf.

18 World Bank Group (2018) 'Joint press release of the third "1+6" roundtable', 8 November, Available from: https://www.worldbank.org/en/news/press-release/2018/11/08/joint-press-release-of-the-third-16-roundtable.

Chapter 8

1   Council of Europe (2008) '8th Conference of Ministers responsible for Youth, 10–11 October 2008, Kyiv, Ukraine'. Available from: https://www.coe.int/t/dc/files/ministerial_conferences/2008_youth/default_EN.asp.

2   Frédéric Lerais and Antoine Math (2013) 'Jeunes européens en temps de crises', *Informations sociales*, 6(180): 32–40.

3   Deutscher Bundestag (2019) 'EU-Wahl 2019: Ältere Wähler einflussreicher als jüngere', *Deutscher Bundestag*, Available from: https://www.bundestag.de/dokumente/textarchiv/2019/kw40-bundeswahlleiter-pressekonferenz-660662.

4   Joseph de Weck and Niall Ferguson (2019) 'European millennials are not like their American counterparts', *The Atlantic*, 30 September, Available from: https://www.theatlantic.com/ideas/archive/2019/09/europes-young-not-so-woke/598783/.

5   Emily Ashton (2016), 'Young people are being "outvoted" by soaring numbers of old people, warns report', *BuzzFeedNews*, 3 February, Available from: https://www.buzzfeed.com/emilyashton/young-people-outvoted.

6   Jennie Bristow (2019) *Stop Mugging Grandma: The 'Generation Wars' and Why Boomer Blaming Won't Solve Anything*, New Haven, CT: Yale University Press, https://doi.org/10.2307/j.ctvhrcxvg.

7   Ruchir Sharma (2021) 'The idea the state has been shrinking for 40 years is a myth', *Financial Times*, 26 April, Available from: https://www.ft.com/content/e4b2b28d-5697-4579-88cf-31f6228278e8.

8   R.S. Foa, A. Klassen, M. Slade, A. Rand and R. Collins (2020) *The Global Satisfaction with Democracy Report 2020*, Cambridge: Centre for the Future of Democracy/Bennett Institute for Public Policy, Available from: https://www.cam.ac.uk/system/files/report2020_003.pdf.

9   Nicholas Charron, Víctor Lapuente, Monika Bauhr and Paola Annoni (2022) 'Cambio y Continuidad en la Calidad de Gobierno: Tendencias en la

calidad de gobierno subnacional en los estados miembros de la UE (Change and continuity in quality of government: trends in subnational quality of government in EU member states)', *Investigaciones Regionales-Journal of Regional Research*, 53: 5–23, https://doi.org/10.38191/iirr-jorr.22.008.

10 Harald Wilkoszewski, Elke Loichinger and Patrick I. Dick (2016) 'Turning the tables: policy and politics in an age of ageing', Population-Europe, Berlin, Available from: https://population-europe.eu/research/policy-insights/turning-tables-policy-and-politics-age-ageing.

Chapter 9

1 Giuseppe Carone and Declan Costello (2006) 'Can Europe afford to grow old?', *Finance & Development*, 43(3), Available from: https://www.imf.org/external/pubs/ft/fandd/2006/09/carone.htm.

2 France Stratégie (2021) 'Protection sociale: qui paie le coût du vieillissement de la population?' *France Stratégie*, 103, December, Available from: https://www.strategie.gouv.fr/publications/protection-sociale-paie-cout-vieillissement-de-population.

3 Mirko Licchetta and Michal Stelmach (2016), 'Fiscal sustainability analytical paper: Fiscal sustainability and public spending on health', Office for Budget Responsibility, September, Available from: https://obr.uk/docs/dlm_uploads/Health-FSAP.pdf.

4 Luca Lorenzoni, Alberto Marino, David Morgan and Chris James (2019) 'Health spending projections to 2030: New results based on a revised OECD methodology', *OECD Health Working Papers*, No. 110, https://doi.org/10.1787/5667f23d-en.

5 Catherine Vincent (2020) 'Quand le Covid-19 sera derrière nous, je crains qu'on oublie de nouveau les vieux', *Le Monde*, 2 August, Available from: https://www.lemonde.fr/idees/article/2020/08/02/le-covid-19-nous-renvoie-avec-violence-a-la-maniere-dont-on-tente-de-rendre-nos-vieux-invisibles_6047957_3232.html.

6 Sarah O'Connor (2022) 'Exploitation of migrants is rising as care homes struggle to fill jobs', *Financial Times*, 26 July, Available from: https://www.ft.com/content/2165c833-2886-4aa0-94a0-b6b7d80fbd25.

7 The Economist (2020) 'Europe's public finances: The fiscal question', *The Economist*, 25 July.

8 Rana Foroohar (2022) 'Pursuit of profit bodes ill for US healthcare', *Financial Times*, 10 April, Available from: https://www.ft.com/content/4aed2bc5-6bcb-4938-b565-d69031311f8a.

9 Rowena Crawford and Carl Emmerson (2017) 'Inevitable trade-offs ahead: long-run public spending pressures', Institute for Fiscal Studies Briefing Note, 12 May, Available from: https://ifs.org.uk/publications/inevitable-trade-offs-ahead-long-run-public-spending-pressures.

10 Office for Budget Responsibility (2017) 'Fiscal sustainability report – January 2017', Available from: https://obr.uk/frs/fiscal-sustainability-report-january-2017/.

11 Lynda Gratton and Andrew J. Scott (2017) *The 100-Year Life: Living and Working in an Age of Longevity*, London: Bloomsbury.

12 Alan Beattie (2022) 'The euro's drama is not an existential crisis', *Financial Times*, 27 July, Available from: https://www.ft.com/content/725f3ac4-77ea-4d7c-a8ff-5947b9d04231.

13 Max Planck Institute (2019) 'Lower pension, shorter life', 11 April, Available from: https://www.mpg.de/13326414/lower-pension-shorter-life.

14 OECD (2017) *Pensions at a glance 2017: OECD and G20 indicators*, Paris: OECD Publishing, https://doi.org/10.1787/pension_glance-2017-en.

15 Anton Hemelrijk, European University Institute, author interview, 26 April 2022.

16 The editorial board (2021) 'A new deal for the young: how to fix the housing crisis', *Financial Times*, 28 April, Available from: https://www.ft.com/content/c58f5522-e58f-4f3d-b4b9-9a4ea62a74a1.

17 Peter Askins (2010) 'The future of pensions policy in Europe', *Pensions: An International Journal*, 15: 245–48, https://doi.org/10.1057/pm.2010.24.

18 Martin Wolf (2021) 'Radical reform of British pension provision is urgent', *Financial Times*, 13 June, Available from: https://www.ft.com/content/791876ae-7ce2-4c0b-9f7a-c12b4f39f6d5.

19 Scottish Widows (2022) *2022 Retirement Report*, Scottish Widows, 29 June, Available from: https://adviser.scottishwidows.co.uk/assets/literature/docs/60677.pdf.

20 Robert Crawford (2015) 'Pensions for Generation Z', *HR Magazine*, 21 September, Available from: https://www.hrmagazine.co.uk/content/features/pensions-for-generation-z/.

21 David Finch and Laura Gardiner (2017) 'As good as it gets? The adequacy of retirement income for current and future generations of pensioners', Resolution Foundation: Intergenerational Commission Report: Wealth Series, November, Available from: https://www.resolutionfoundation.org/app/uploads/2017/11/Pensions.pdf.

Chapter 10

1 Satyajit Das (2022) 'Next financial crisis likely to centre on private markets', *Financial Times*, 12 August, Available from: https://www.ft.com/content/6de0250b-bd46-45e7-ba0e-0b798a6c3471.

2 Ruchir Sharma (2022) 'Here's how to solve the productivity paradox', *Financial Times*, 18 July, Available from: https://www.ft.com/content/1c7bba9f-4e01-4e54-921b-198369f25950.

3 Barry Eichengreen, 'A world awash with debt: can governments learn to rule while drowning in the red?', *Prospect*, October 2, Available from: https://www.prospectmagazine.co.uk/ideas/economics/40625/a-world-awash-with-debt-can-governments-learn-to-rule-while-drowning-in-the-red.

4 The Economist (2020) 'What GDP can and cannot tell you about the post-pandemic economy: Third-quarter figures are dramatic, but need careful interpretation', *The Economist*, 29 October, Available from: https://www.

economist.com/finance-and-economics/2020/10/29/what-gdp-can-and-cannot-tell-you-about-the-post-pandemic-economy.

5   Laurence J. Kotlikoff and Scott Burns (2004) *The Coming Generational Storm*, Cambridge, MA: MIT Press.

6   Stephanie Kelton (2020) *The Deficit Myth: Modern Monetary Theory and the Birth of the People's Economy*, New York: Public Affairs and Hachette Book Group.

7   Joseph E. Stiglitz (2015) 'In praise of Frank Ramsey's contribution to the theory of taxation', *The Economic Journal*, 125(583): 235–68, https://doi.org/10.1111/ecoj.12187.

8   Guntram B. Wolff, Karen Wilson and Pia Hüttl (2015) 'The growing intergenerational divide in Europe', *Bruegel Policy Brief*, 10 November, Available from: https://www.bruegel.org/policy-brief/growing-intergenerational-divide-europe.

9   Joseph C. Sternberg (2019) *The Theft of a Decade*, New York: Public Affairs and Hachette Book Group.

10 David Collard (2004) 'Generational accounting and generational transfers', *Ageing Horizons*, 1, The Oxford Institute of Population Ageing, Available from: https://www.ageing.ox.ac.uk/download/11.

11 UK Parliament (2016/17) 'The inter-generational contract under strain', UK Parliament, Available from: https://publications.parliament.uk/pa/cm201617/cmselect/cmworpen/59/5905.htm.

12 Paul Collier (2018) *The Future of Capitalism*, New York: HarperCollins; Mariana Mazzucato (2022) *Mission Economy: A Moonshot Guide to Changing Capitalism*, New York: Harper Business.

13 Bill Gates (2019) 'I always bring this one thing with me on vacation', Gates Notes, 20 May, Available from: https://www.gatesnotes.com/media/GN_Newsletter_Archive/TGN-Newsletter-Online-V05202019.html.

14 Martina Lizarazo López and Thieß Petersen (2019) 'Demographic change is leading to massive income losses in developed countries', Bertelsmann Stiftung, 12 December, Available from: https://www.bertelsmann-stiftung.de/en/topics/latest-news/2019/december/demographic-change-is-leading-to-massive-income-losses-in-developed-countries.

15 James Manyika and Michael Spence (2021) 'A better boom: how to capture the pandemic's productivity potential', *Foreign Affairs*, July/August, Available from: https://www.foreignaffairs.com/articles/united-states/2021-06-22/better-boom.

16 Diane Coyle (2022) 'Tax cut vows are a distraction from the UK's woeful productivity', *Financial Times*, 3 August, Available from: https://www.ft.com/content/3c482227-8c5a-4ccc-9cf4-e7af09d60640.

Chapter 11

1   Sheelah Kolhatkar (2019) 'The ultra-wealthy who argue that they should be paying higher taxes', *The New Yorker*, 30 December, Available from: https://www.newyorker.com/magazine/2020/01/06/the-ultra-wealthy-who-argue-that-they-should-be-paying-higher-taxes.

2   Marlene Engelhorn (2022) *Geld*, Vienna: Kremayr und Scheriau.
3   Sam Jones (2021) 'Rich remain skeptical about changing the world with their money', *Financial Times*, 13 May.
4   Competence Centre on Foresight (2020) 'Wealth concentration', European Commission, Knowledge for Policy, 26 March, Available from: https://knowledge4policy.ec.europa.eu/foresight/topic/diversifying-inequalities/rich-poor-gap_en.
5   Thomas Piketty (2021) *Le Monde*, 15 May.
6   Mary McDougall (2021) 'Lessons from history: France's wealth tax did more harm than good', *Investors Chronicle*, 11 February, Available from: https://www.investorschronicle.co.uk/content/c2a0a5ab-11a8-50a3-a098-240f320fc795.
7   Chris Mulder (2022) 'Letter to the Editor', *Financial Times*, 31 August.
8   The Guardian (2020) 'Tax Justice UK's "Talking Tax" report', *The Guardian*, 14 September.
9   OECD (2021) '2020 tax burdens', in *Taxing Wages 2021*, Paris: OECD Publishing, https://doi.org/10.1787/bce7b97b-en.
10 Eurostat (2021) 'Tax revenue statistics', October, Available from: https://ec.europa.eu/eurostat/statistics-explained/index.php?title=Tax_revenue_statistics.
11 UK Parliament (2016/17) 'The Inter-generational contract under strain'; (2004) *Ageing Horizons*, 1, Available from: https://www.ageing.ox.ac.uk/publications/view/8.
12 Der Spiegel (2021) *Der Spiegel*, 12 November.
13 Vox CEPR (2020) Vox CEPR Policy Portal, 3 April.

Chapter 12

1   Javier García Arenas (2018) 'The challenges of ageing: a new society, a new economy', Caixa Bank Research, 14 November, Available from: https://www.caixabankresearch.com/en/economics-markets/labour-market-demographics/challenges-ageing-new-society-new-economy.
2   Livia Sz. Oláh (2015) 'Changing Families in the European Union: trends and policy implications', *Families and Societies, Working Paper Series*, 44, Available from: http://www.familiesandsocieties.eu/wp-content/uploads/2015/09/WP44Olah2015.pdf.
3   Public Health England (2020) 'Older people's hospital admissions in the last year of life', 25 February, Available from: https://www.gov.uk/government/publications/older-peoples-hospital-admissions-in-the-last-year-of-life/older-peoples-hospital-admissions-in-the-last-year-of-life.
4   Frédéric Michas (2021) 'Residential care in Europe – statistics & facts', statista.com, 8 June.
5   Daniel Molinuevo and Robert Anderson (2017) 'Care homes for older Europeans: public, for-profit and non-profit providers', Eurofound, 28 November, Available from: https://www.eurofound.europa.eu/en/publications/2017/care-homes-older-europeans-public-profit-and-non-profit-providers.

[6] Daniel Molinuevo (2008) 'Services for Older People in Europe: Facts and Figures about Long Term Care Services in Europe', European Social Network, October, Available from: https://health.ec.europa.eu/system/files/2016-11/services_older_0.pdf.

[7] Michael Marmot, Jessica Allen, Tammy Boyce, Peter Goldblatt and Joana Morrison (2020) 'Marmot Review 10 years on', Institute of Health Equity, February, Available from: https://www.instituteofhealthequity.org/resources-reports/marmot-review-10-years-on.

[8] Resolution Foundation (2018) 'A new generational contract: the final report of the Intergenerational Commission', The Resolution Foundation, 8 May, Available from: https://www.resolutionfoundation.org/app/uploads/2018/05/A-New-Generational-Contract-Full-PDF.pdf.

[9] 'Net Childcare Costs', OECD, Available from: https://www.oecd.org/en/data/indicators/net-childcare-costs.html.

[10] Financial Times (2021) *Financial Times*, 4 October.

[11] House of Commons (2021) 'House of Commons research briefing', 1 April.

[12] Housing Europe Observatory (2019) 'The state of housing in Europe, 2019: decoding the new housing reality', Housing Europe, 1 October, Available from: https://www.housingeurope.eu/resource-1323/the-state-of-housing-in-the-eu-2019.

[13] Eleni Varvitsioti (2022), 'Cheap loans set to give young Greeks a shot at a home of their own', *Financial Times*, 5 December, Available from: https://www.ft.com/content/a098a165-2c33-4e13-abe0-12c26ba39901.

[14] Anna Vindics (2020) 'Inclusive social insurance for the 21st century, OECD shaping Covid recovery'.

[15] Diane Coyle (2019) 'Something is seriously awry in the world of work', *Financial Times*, 19 September, Available from: https://www.ft.com/content/eca406c4-d880-11e9-9c26-419d783e10e8.

[16] John McGrath (2021) *Report on Labour Shortages and Surpluses*, Bratislava: European Labour Authority, November, Available from: https://www.ela.europa.eu/sites/default/files/2023-12/2021_Labour_shortages_surpluses_report.pdf.

[17] MIT (2020) 'MIT work of the future', Available from: https://ipc.mit.edu/research/work-of-the-future/.

[18] OECD (2016) *Society at a glance 2016: OECD social indicators*, Paris: OECD Publishing, https://doi.org/10.1787/9789264261488-en.

[19] Sven Smit, Tilman Tacke, Susan Lund, James Manyika and Lea Thiel (2020) 'The future of work in Europe', McKinsey Global Institute, 10 June, Available from: https://www.mckinsey.com/featured-insights/future-of-work/the-future-of-work-in-europe.

[20] Nicholas Sowels (2018) 'Economic inequalities in Britain – from the 2008 financial crisis to Brexit', LSE blog, 16 January, Available from: https://blogs.lse.ac.uk/brexit/2018/01/16/an-up-to-date-account-of-economic-inequalities-in-britain-since-2008/.

[21] Angus Deaton (2021) 'Covid shows how the state can address social inequality', *Financial Times*, 5 January, Available from: https://www.ft.com/content/caa37763-9c71-4f8d-9c29-b16ccf53d780.

[22] A.B. Atkinson (2015) *Inequality: What Can Be Done?*, Cambridge, MA: Harvard University Press.

[23] NPR National Public Radio (2021) *NPR National Public Radio*, 4 March.

[24] The Economist (2020), 'Universal basic income gains momentum in America', *The Economist*, 8 August, Available from: https://www.economist.com/united-states/2020/08/08/universal-basic-income-gains-momentum-in-america.

[25] EU Opinions (2025) 'St Antony's, Oxford, and Bertelsmann Stiftung', *EU Opinions,* 5–25 March.

[26] The Economist (2019) 'Inherited wealth is making a comeback. What does it mean for Britain?', 27 April, Available from: https://www.economist.com/britain/2019/04/27/inherited-wealth-is-making-a-comeback-what-does-it-mean-for-britain.

[27] Aidan Harrison (2021) 'Letter: Sustainable farming needs reform and new blood', *Financial Times*, 12 April, Available from: https://www.ft.com/content/a937fb64-e4f5-4f82-9d99-17710af72102.

[28] Eurostat (2020) *Ageing Europe: Looking at the Lives of Older People in the EU*, Luxembourg: Publications Office of the European Union, Available from: https://ec.europa.eu/eurostat/documents/3217494/11478057/KS-02-20-655-EN-N.pdf/9b09606c-d4e8-4c33-63d2-3b20d5c19c91?t=1604055531000.

[29] OECD International Migration Outlook, October 2022 Available from: https://www.oecd-ilibrary.org/social-issues-migration-health/international-migration-outlook-2022_30fe16d2-en.

[30] DIW Institute (2017) 'Seven questions for Stefan Bach: "Education is the driving force for labor market integration"', *DIW Economic Bulletin*, 3–4, Available from: https://www.diw.de/documents/publikationen/73/diw_01.c.551765.de/diw_econ_bull_2017-03-2.pdf.

[31] Giles Merritt (2021) *People Power: Why We Need More Migrants*, London: I.B. Tauris.

Index

Index